THE LIVING WORD

in 3D

50 AMAZING WORDS

This is written for those who have come to put their faith, trust and hope in the finished work of the risen Yeshua Ha-Mashiach (Jesus the Christ) and to those who may yet!

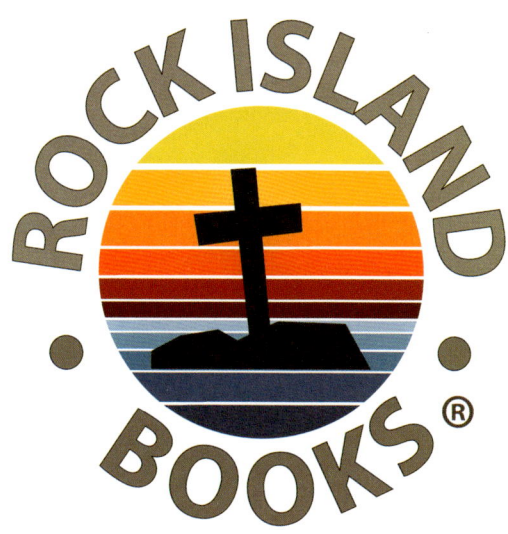

www.rockislandbooks.com

Visit our website to purchase books
and preview upcoming titles.

Contact us at:
feedback@rockislandbooks.com

Contents

Contents

Matthew 11:25,26

At that time Jesus answered and said,

I thank thee, O Father, Lord of heaven and

earth, because thou hast hid these things from

the wise and prudent, and hast revealed them

unto babes. Even so, Father: for so it seemed

good in thy sight.

To my dear friends Jeff and June Speichinger, whose faithful service to the Lord Jesus Christ has been a constant encouragement to my wife and me.

The Scarlet Thread

THE

Y BIBL

CONTAINING THE

D NEW TES

OF THE ORIGINAL TON

LATIONS DILIGENTLY CO

HIS MAJESTY'S S

Psalms 119:97-105 KJV

O how love I thy law! it is my meditation all the day.

Thou through thy commandments hast made me wiser than mine enemies: for they are ever with me.

I have more understanding than all my teachers: for thy testimonies are my meditation.

I understand more than the ancients, because I keep thy precepts.

I have refrained my feet from every evil way, that I might keep thy word.

I have not departed from thy judgments: for thou hast taught me.

How sweet are thy words unto my taste! yea, sweeter than honey to my mouth!

Through thy precepts I get understanding: therefore I hate every false way.

Thy word is a lamp unto my feet, and a light unto my path.

Finding the Jewels Beneath the Surface

DID you know that the first language God used to communicate His revelation to Man is actually three languages?

You most certainly know about one of the languages of the Old Testament. It is the language of words used to communicate His truth. That language of course is Hebrew. But did you know that there are two other languages God used to communicate His Truth?

The Living Word In 3D series examines the other two languages that were embedded in Hebrew Scriptures from its very beginning.

The Hebrew language has three overlapping layers of communication, which make it unique among all other languages. Chinese has two layers: conventional usage and pictographic. Greek has two layers: conventional and numeric.

Only Hebrew has, and always has had, all three-communication layers.

God designed His revelation to be understood at the primary conventional level, the level that uses words to communicate ideas and concepts.

Most people are surprised to find out that the Words of Scriptures are based on pictures or what we call pictographic images. This is the second language that God uses to communicate His revelation.

The third level of communication is numbers. And what do the numbers mean? You must read the Scriptures and only the Scriptures to discover their hidden meanings.

The Hebrew language combines these three layers to create a unified message of revelation. Each layer of communication contains either confirmation of the primary conventional Hebrew meaning or in many cases it shines a light on a larger underlying truth that God wants repeated and magnified.

The key to understanding each layer of meaning in the Hebrew aleph-beyt is to explore all three layers. This exploration of the three layers needs to be done in a way that pays special attention to the contextual boundaries of each word in the conventional text.

It is also important to carefully try to understand the clear historical meaning of the surrounding conventional text. And finally, it is imperative to keep the primary message of the conventional text in focus.

So the question must be asked. If all three layers of communications reveal the same thing, then why do we need three languages when just one will do nicely?

The answer is stunning.

The conventional language – the one that has been translated into English – is plainly there in order that you understand clearly what God is revealing.

The pictographic language found when you examine every letter of the Hebrew text supports the meaning of the conventional text, which is one of its purposes. But it has another purpose. I have discovered, after examining the picture meaning of each letter that makes up hundreds of Hebrew words, that the purpose is to express the *ideal* of the word. In other words, the pictogram of each letter in the Hebrew anchors the meaning of the word in the *ideal*.

The word Abba for example means father. But what kind of father? There are good fathers and there are wicked and horrible fathers.

The pictogram of each letter for the Hebrew word Abba expresses the meaning of the *ideal* Father. He is the one according to the picture meaning of the letters aleph and beyt that is the strong leader of the house that guides and protects.

The third language is the language of numbers. And why does God include numbers in His revelation? The answer, once again, is stunning.

The numbers, which have a meaning that can only be discovered by finding out how they are used in the Scriptures and the Scriptures alone more often that not reveal the *theology* of the Hebrew Word. So what is the theology of the word Abba? You will have to read the book to find out.

We always seek to understand what God has clearly revealed. This is the fruit we seek, not secret knowledge. We are not uncovering new secret doctrine or unknown truths.

Everything we discover will be additional testimony and witness to the truth that has already been revealed in the plain primary conventional text of Scripture.

And finally, everything we have discovered confirms the words of Jesus the Christ as reported in the Gospel of John.

John 5:39
Search the scriptures; for in them ye think ye have eternal life: and they are they which testify of me.

Those who grasp the concepts found in The Living Word In 3D will discover the amazing Messianic truths revealed in the ancient prophetic text.

Matthew 11:25-26
At that time Jesus answered and said, I thank thee, O Father, Lord of heaven and earth, because thou hast hid these things from the wise and prudent, and hast revealed them unto babes. Even so, Father: for so it seemed good in thy sight.

The Hebrew three-layered communication structure stands alone as a self-authenticating and self-identifying message. The code integrates pictographic and numeric meanings found in the primary conventional Hebrew letters.

Can the purpose of this tri-layered structure and architecture be deduced? Could it be the Almighty's signet ring stamped both upon and within His written testimony?

At the appointed time, as revealed precisely in the revelation, the Word exhibited itself supernaturally and became flesh, creating a seamless connection between the expression of words and the emergence of the Word into human flesh.

He became visible and He dwelt among us. He also became identifiable as to His unique nature and mission.

Did God create this code in order that the sincere seeker might have no doubt about the otherworldly source and supreme authority of His unique revelation to mankind? The truth will set you free!

Jeremiah 9:23-24

...Let not the wise man glory in his wisdom, neither let the mighty man glory in his might, let not the rich man glory in his riches: But let him that glorieth glory in this, that he under- standeth and knoweth me....

THE HEBREW ALEPH-BEYT . . .

Letter & Number	Name and pronunciation	Ancient pictogram (left) and its symbol	Meanings associated with the pictogram
א **1**	**Aleph** *aw'-lef*	ox, bull	Strong leader, strength, leading, the first , aloof or separate, gentle, the beginning, the head of the family, God the Father
ב **2**	**Beyt** *bayth*	tent, house	House, tent, son, family, dwelling place, the physical tent/body, inside, within, first letter in the Torah that identifies the Son of God
ג **3**	**Gimel** *ghee'-mel*	camel	To lift up, lifted up with pride, to lift up the name of the Lord, benefit, bounty, reward, to toil, exaltation
ד **4**	**Dalet** *daw'-let*	door	Doorway, gate, place of decision, entrance to life or death, moving into something, moving out of something, to open up, a place where change can take place

Number value of letter	Meanings associated with the number value
1	Deity, unity, sufficiency, independence, first, indivisible, **God the Father**
2	Difference, good or evil, division, Living Word, the second, second person of the Godhead, to come alongside to hinder, to come alongside for help, **God the Son**
3	Divine perfection, completeness, three attributes of God: omniscience - omnipresence - omnipotence, solid, substantial, the entirety, third commandment, lifting up the name of God, **God the Holy Spirit**
4	God's creative works, the world, four elements, four regions of Earth, four seasons, four divisions of day, four in contrast to seven, Earth (4) vs. Heaven (7), the fourth thing, first number that can be divided, material world that had a beginning, **creation**

Letter & Number	Name and pronunciation	Ancient pictogram (left) and its symbol	Meanings associated with the pictogram
ה 5	**Hey** *hay*	behold	Pay attention to what follows, to reveal, to unfold, to look upon, Holy Spirit as the revelator
ו 6	**Vav** *vawv*	iron nail, wooden hook	Add, to secure, to join together, to make secure, to bind together, to create a connection between two things that are separated from each other, wooden hook, wooden peg, to hold up
ז 7	**Zayin** *zah'-yin*	weapon	To cut off, cut, to pierce, to prune, harvest, ax, sword, weapon
ח 8	**Chet** *khayth*	fence, inner room	Private, to separate, to protect, place of protection, to be cut off, grace, favor, a place of refuge, a protected garden, quiet place, to be silent and still in security, fence, sanctuary, inner room
ט 9	**Tet** *tayt*	snake, surround	To surround, twist, entwine, encircle, ensnare, entrap, to spin, rolled together, snake
י 10	**Yood** *yode*	hand	To work, a mighty deed, a deed accomplished, to make, arm and hand accomplishing a purpose, divine deed, hand

16

Number value of letter	Meanings associated with the number value
5	Unmerited favor, God's goodness, Pentateuch, divine strength, the fifth, what follows creation, **grace**
6	Enmity with God, weakness of Man, manifestation of sin, evils of Satan, falling short, preservation, imperfection, labor, sorrow, number of Man, secular completeness, the sixth, **Man's world**
7	Completeness, resurrection, to be full, to be satisfied, good, perfect, the seventh day, millennial reign of Christ, eternal Sabbath and everlasting perfection, God the Father's perfection, inspiration of Holy Spirit, **spiritual perfection**
8	Eternity, new creation, first in new series, new birth, super abundance, follows seven and is the first in a new series, **new beginning**
9	Wrath, ensnared, entrapped, judgment of Man, (3x3) divine perfection magnified, fruits of the spirit, divine completeness, conclusion of a matter, last of the digits, **summation of Man's works**
10	Perfection of divine order, completeness of order, testimony, the law, Ten Commandments, responsibility, divinely ordered events, **ordinal perfection**

Letter & Number	Name and pronunciation	Ancient pictogram (left) and its symbol	Meanings associated with the pictogram
כ/ך 11	**Kaf** *caf*	palm	To cover, to open, to allow, atonement, palm
ל 12	**Lamed** *law'-med*	staff	Control, to shepherd, to have authority, to urge forward, the tongue, the voice of authority, staff
מ/ם 13	**Mem** *mame*	water	Liquid, mighty waters like the ocean, massive as the waves of the sea, chaotic and destructive like a tsunami, water coming down like a stream, rain water that makes the desert bloom, the Word of God that brings life, living water, waters
נ/ן 14	**Noon** *noon*	fish	Activity, life, fish
ס 15	**Samech** *saw'-mek*	prop	To support, twist slowly, to turn, to assist, prop
ע 16	**Ayin** *ah'-yin*	eye	To see, to know, to experience, eye

Number value of letter	Meanings associated with the number value
20	(10x2) concentrated meaning of ordinal perfection, expectancy, **redemption**
30	Blood of Christ, dedication, (3x10) magnified perfection of divine order marking the right moment, **blood sacrifice**
40	Trials, probation, chastisement but not judgment, action of grace resulting in revival, magnified renewal, (5x8) an extended period of rule or dominion, grace multiplied by renewal, **probationary period that results in renewal**
50	Holy Spirit, Pentecost, deliverance followed by rest, grace multiplied, **jubilee**
60	**Pride**
70	Punishment and restoration of Israel, universality, the seventy nations representing the nations of the world, **perfect spiritual order carried out with all spiritual power and significance**

Letter & Number	Name and pronunciation	Ancient pictogram (left) and its symbol	Meanings associated with the pictogram
כ/פ 17	**Pey** *pay*	mouth	To speak, a word, to open, mouth
ץ/צ 18	**Tsade** *tsaw-day'*	fishhook	To catch, to be caught, a harvest, to pull forward, unable to escape, trouble, to strongly desire, just or righteous, to need, fishhook
ק 19	**Qoof** *cofe*	back of the head	Behind, the last, the least, back of the head
ר 20	**Reysh** *raysh*	head	A person, the head, the highest, the sum, the supreme, the first, the most important, the top, master, leader, prince, head
ש/שׂ 21	**Seen Sheen** *sin* *shyn*	teeth	To consume, to destroy, sharp, to press, the one letter that God used to identify Himself, God's signature, letter that stands for God Almighty, teeth
ת 22	**Tav** *tawv*	sign	To seal, to covenant, a sign, crossed wooden sticks, cross

Number value of letter	Meanings associated with the number value
80	(10x8) magnified ordinal perfection resulting in eternality, **new beginning and new birth**
90	Signifies the conclusion of a matter that will be followed by judgment, same meaning as the number nine magnified by the multiplier ten, **combination of ordinal perfection and judgment at the conclusion of a series**
100	God's election of grace, children of the promise, **promise**
200	Inadequacy of the temporal, inadequate, the insufficiency of Man, insufficiency, deficient, the ineffective ransom, lacking what is necessary or required, inability to accomplish a purpose, (10x20) adequacy of the eternal, the complete sufficiency of God, redemption of body and soul, multiplied by ordinal perfection accomplished by the Son of God, sufficient to accomplish a purpose, ransom that is both efficient and sufficient to reclaim what was lost, to accomplish redemption, **insufficiency of man, sufficiency of God**
300	A divinely appointed period of time, number connected to the "children of promise," election, supernatural victory over enemies including death, number connected with the death, burial and resurrection of Messiah, **signifies final blood sacrifice made by the perfect Lamb of God.**
400	The last, the end, period of testing, period of probation to accomplish a divine purpose, Jubilee (50) multiplied by new birth or eternity (8), **a divinely ordained period of time that will bring about deliverance and renewal.**

NUMBERS IN THE BIBLE
AND WHAT THEY MEAN

Number	Hebrew number	Number value
1	א	Unity, sufficiency, independence, the first, the beginning, indivisible, **deity**
2	ב	Difference, good or evil, division, Living Word, second, to come alongside for help, to come alongside to hinder, second person of the Godhead, **God the Son**
3	ג	Divine perfection, completeness, three attributes of God – omniscience, omnipresence, omnipotence, solid, substantial, the entirety, Third Commandment, lifting up the name of God, **God the Holy Spirit**
4	ד	God's creative works, the world, four elements, four regions of Earth, four seasons, four divisions of day, four in contrast to seven – Earth (4) vs. Heaven (7), the fourth thing, first number that can be divided, material world that had a beginning, **creation**
5	ה	Unmerited favor, God's goodness, Pentateuch, divine strength, the fifth, what follows creation, **grace**
6	ו	Enmity with God, weakness of Man, imperfection, manifestation of sin, evils of Satan, falling short, preservation, labor, sorrow, the sixth, number of Man, secular completeness, **Man's world**
7	ז	Completeness, resurrection, to be full, to be satisfied, good, perfect, the seventh day, millennial reign of Christ, eternal Sabbath and everlasting perfection, God the Father's perfection, inspiration of Holy Spirit, **spiritual perfection**
8	ח	Eternity, new creation, first in new series, new birth, super abundance, follows seven and is the first in a new series, **new beginning**
9	ט	Wrath, ensnared, entrapped, judgment of Man, summation of Man's works, (3x3) divine perfection magnified, fruit of the Spirit, divine completeness, conclusion of a matter, last of the digits, **summation of Man's works**
10	י	Perfection of divine order, completeness of order, testimony, the law, Ten Commandments, responsibility, divinely ordered events, **ordinal perfection**

11	יא	Judgment, disorder, deliberate manifestation of chaos and disorganization, imperfection, the subversion of an order designed to bring about confusion, **consequences of deliberate rebellion against God's authority**
12	יב	The establishment of a perfect order which can only come about as a result of divine intervention and can only be maintained by divine governance and supervision, **governmental perfection**
13	יג	Apostasy, depravity and rebellion, ill omen, corruption, defection, revolution, **depravity**
14	יד	Deliverance, salvation, (2x7) **double perfection**
15	יה	(3x5) grace, brought about by the energy of divine grace and associated with perfect timing or a perfect time, (8+7) resurrection being a special mark of the energy of divine grace issuing in glory, **rest**
16	יו	**Love**
17	יז	Seventh number in a series – 1,3,5,7,11,13,17, union of spiritual perfection plus ordinal perfection, perfection of spiritual order, **victory**
18	יח	**Bondage**
19	יט	(10+9) perfection of divine order connected with judgment, **faith**
20	כ	(2x10) concentrated meaning of ordinal perfection, expectancy, **redemption**
21	כא	Exceeding sinfulness of sin, three sevens, **ultimate spiritual perfection**
22	כב	Number of letters in Hebrew aleph-beyt so 22 can have the idea of the complete word, **light**
23	כג	**Death**
24	כד	(12x2) concentrated meaning perfection of government, **the priesthood**

25	כה	Repentance, intercession, **the forgiveness of sins**
26	כו	Total letter count for YHVH is 26, **the Gospel of Christ**
27	כז	Preaching of the Gospel, cube of 3, **divine perfection connected with judgment**
28	כח	(4x7) creation and spiritual perfection, **eternal life**
29	כט	Departure, going away
30	ל	Blood of Christ, dedication, 3x10 magnified perfection of divine order marking the right moment, **blood sacrifice**
31	לא	Number of deity, 1+30 =31 aleph (1) lamed (12-30), **offspring**
32	לב	**Covenant**
33	לג	**Promise**
34	לד	**Naming of a son**
35	לה	**Hope**
36	לו	**Enemy**
37	לז	**The word of our Father**
38	לח	**Slavery**
39	לט	**Disease**
40	מ	Trials, probation, chastisement but not judgment, grace resulting in revival and renewal, (5x8) an extended period of rule or dominion, grace multiplied by renewal, **probationary period that results in renewal**
42	מב	Israel's oppression, first Advent, (42 months 30x42=1260) Antichrist, (6x7) connection between Christ and Antichrist, **between Man and Spirit of God**

44	מד	Judgment of the world, (4x11 = 44) **creation multiplies its corruption and sinfulness to the overflowing of the cup**
45	מה	Preservation, **judgment followed by grace**
50	נ	Holy Spirit, Pentecost, jubilee, deliverance followed by rest, grace multiplied, **Jubilee**
51	נא	**Divine revelation**
60	ס	**Pride**
65	סה	**Apostasy and judgment (Ephraim)**
66	סז	**Idol worship**
70	ע	Punishment and restoration of Israel, universality, the seventy nations representing the nations of the world, **perfect spiritual order carried out with all spiritual power and significance**
80	פ	(8x10) magnified ordinal perfection resulting in eternality, eternity, new beginning, **new birth**
90	צ	Conclusion of a matter that will be followed by judgment, same meaning as the number nine magnified, combination of ordinal perfection and judgment, **the conclusion of a series**
100	ק	God's election of grace, children of the promise, **promise**
200	ר	Inadequacy of the temporal, inadequate, deficient, the insufficiency of Man, insufficiency, ineffective, lacking what is necessary or required, inability to accomplish a purpose (10x20) adequacy of the eternal, the complete sufficiency of God, redemption of body and soul multiplied by ordinal perfection accomplished by the Son of God, sufficient to accomplish a purpose, ransom that is both efficient and sufficient to reclaim what was lost, to accomplish redemption, **insufficiency of Man, sufficiency of God**

300	שׁ	A divinely appointed period of time, election number connected to the "children of promise," supernatural victory over enemies including death, number connected with the death and burial and resurrection of Messiah, **signifies final blood sacrifice made by the perfect Lamb of God**
400	ת	The last, the end, period of testing period of probation in order to accomplish a divine purpose, Jubilee (50) multiplied by new birth or eternity (8), **a divinely ordained period of time that will bring about deliverance and renewal**
600	תר	**Warfare**
666	תרסו	The number of the beast Antichrist, the perfection of imperfection, culmination of human pride, independence from God, **opposition to His Christ**
700	תש	**Perfect period of rest brought about at exactly the right time by the sovereign ordinances of God**
777	תשעז	**The trinity of sevens signifies spiritual perfection multiplied in both power and completeness resulting in a rest found only in Yeshua Ha-Mashiach**
888	תתפח	The trinity of eights summed up in the first resurrection of the saints, **the tree of life and the new beginning brought about by the divine work of the Holy Spirit**
1000	תתר	Divine completeness and Father's glory

Aaron

noon	reysh	hey	aleph
50	200	5	1

Letters are right to left, original Hebrew

CONVENTIONAL USAGE OF **AARON**

Aaron was the older brother of Moses. Aaron served as his brother's spokesman in the confrontation with the Egyptian Pharoah regarding the release of Israel from the bondage of Egypt and the privilege to worship YHVH as directed by YHVH.

Moses received the Torah on Mt. Sinai and it was at this time that Aaron was granted the priesthood for himself and his descendants. He was the first High Priest of Israel.

FIRST USE OF **AARON** IN SCRIPTURES

Exodus 3:14
And the anger of the Lord was kindled against Moses, and he said, Is not Aaron the Levite thy brother? I know that he can speak well. And also, behold, he cometh forth to meet thee: and when he seeth thee, he will be glad in his heart.

Image left: Moses and Aaron before Pharaoh. 1866 print by Gustave Dore

Aaron

ן ר ה א
noon reysh hey aleph
50 200 5 1

PICTOGRAPHIC MEANINGS OF AARON

Strong leader, strength, leading, the first, aloof or separate, gentle, the beginning, the head of the family, God the Father

Pay attention to what follows, to reveal, to unfold, to look upon, Holy Spirit as the revelator

A person, the head, the highest, the sum, the supreme, the first, the most important, the top, master, leader, prince, head

Activity, life, fish

NUMERIC MEANINGS OF AARON

 1

Deity, unity, sufficiency, independence, first, indivisible, **God the Father**

ה 5

Unmerited favor, God's goodness, Pentateuch, divine strength, the fifth, what follows creation, **grace**

ר 200

Inadequacy of the temporal, inadequate, the insufficiency of Man, insufficiency, deficient, the ineffective ransom, lacking what is necessary or required, inability to accomplish a purpose, (10x20) adequacy of the eternal, the complete sufficiency of God, redemption of body and soul, multiplied by ordinal perfection accomplished by the Son of God, sufficient to accomplish a purpose, ransom that is both efficient and sufficient to reclaim what was lost, to accomplish redemption, **insufficiency of man, sufficiency of God**

ן 50

Holy Spirit, Pentecost, deliverance followed by rest, grace multiplied, **jubilee**

PICTOGRAPHIC TRANSLATION OF **AARON**

Ideal

Aaron is the **strong leader** who would **reveal** the **Prince** of **life.**

Aaron was the First High Priest of Israel. As High Priest it was his responsibility to make offerings on the altar to the God of Israel. Aaron was to first one to act out the rehearsal drama that was to prepare Israel to receive the one time offering that God the Father was going to make in order to atone for the sins of Israel and the World. Aaron's job in a nutshell was to perform the duties of the priesthood as directed by God in order to introduce His Son as the Perfect Lamb of God.

Hebrews 7:11
If therefore perfection were by the Levitical priesthood, (for under it the people received the law,) what further need was there that another priest should rise after the order of Melchisedec, and not be called after the order of Aaron?

NUMERIC TRANSLATION OF **AARON**

Theological and Prophetic

Man is insufficient to save himself. His sacrifices are insufficient as are his attempts to keep the law of God. The sacrifices instituted by God and carried out by Aaron and his descendants were not meant to save but to forecast the one sacrifice that was Sufficient. The blood sacrifice of the only Begotten Son of God, Yeshua Ha-Mashiach – Jesus the Christ.

SUMMARY TRANSLATION

God the Father shows **grace** that displays his **all
sufficiency in contrast to the insufficiency of Man**
in order to bring **deliverance** followed by **rest**.

Psalm 118:3

Let the house of Aaron now say, that his mercy endureth for ever.

Hebrews 10:1-14

1 For the law having a shadow of good things to come, and not the very image of the things, can never with those sacrifices which they offered year by year continually make the comers thereunto perfect.

2 For then would they not have ceased to be offered? because that the worshippers once purged should have had no more conscience of sins.

3 But in those sacrifices there is a remembrance again made of sins every year.

4 For it is not possible that the blood of bulls and of goats should take away sins.

5 Wherefore when he cometh into the world, he saith, Sacrifice and offering thou wouldest not, but a body hast thou prepared me:

6 In burnt offerings and sacrifices for sin thou hast had no pleasure.

7 Then said I, Lo, I come (in the volume of the book it is written of me,) to do thy will, O God.

8 Above when he said, Sacrifice and offering and burnt offerings and offering for sin thou wouldest not, neither hadst pleasure therein; which are offered by the law;

9 Then said he, Lo, I come to do thy will, O God. He taketh away the first, that he may establish the second.

10 By the which will we are sanctified through the offering of the body of Jesus Christ once for all.

11 And every priest standeth daily ministering and offering oftentimes the same sacrifices, which can never take away sins:

12 But this man, after he had offered one sacrifice for sins for ever, sat down on the right hand of God;

13 From henceforth expecting till his enemies be made his footstool.

14 For by one offering he hath perfected forever them that are sanctified.

Abba - Father

beyt   aleph

2   1

Letters are right to left, original Hebrew

CONVENTIONAL USAGE OF **ABBA**

The Hebrew word for Father is ABBA. This is probably the one Hebrew words that every New Testament Christian knows, because Jesus directly referenced the term and told his disciples to address God from that time forward using this title.

In the Conventional Hebrew, "father" is a word we all understand. If someone is the father, he has children. A father is the head of a family.

We think of God as the father of His people. It is a word that presupposes relationships that connect one person who is the head or chief person to other people by natural birth or adoption of national kinship.

FIRST USE OF HEBREW WORD
ABBA (FATHER) IN SCRIPTURES

Genesis 2:24
Therefore shall a man leave his father and his mother, and shall cleave unto his wife: and they shall be one flesh.

Abba - Father

ב
beyt
2

א
aleph
1

PICTOGRAPHIC MEANINGS OF ABBA

Strong leader, strength, leading, the first, aloof or separate, gentle, the beginning, the head of the family, God the Father

House, tent, son, family, dwelling place, the physical tent/body, inside, within, first letter in the Torah that identifies the Son of God

NUMERIC MEANINGS OF ABBA

 1

Deity, unity, sufficiency, independence, first, indivisible, **God the Father**

ב 2

Difference, good or evil, division, Living Word, second, second person of the Godhead, to come alongside to hinder, to come alongside for help, **God the Son**

IMPORTANT REVELATION REGARDING **ABBA**

Hebrew the letters are also numbers. Because of this, the first question we should ask is what number is A-B-B-A, or aleph beyt?

If aleph is 1 and beyt is 2, are we looking at the number 12? The answer is *no*.

The Hebrew method of numbers would add the value of the numbers together. So in Hebrew the number 1 (aleph) and the number 2 (beyt) is the sum of both numbers – 1+2=3.

Abba as a number is the *number three*!

The house of the Father has a *third resident* who makes the household complete and perfect.

And who is that person?

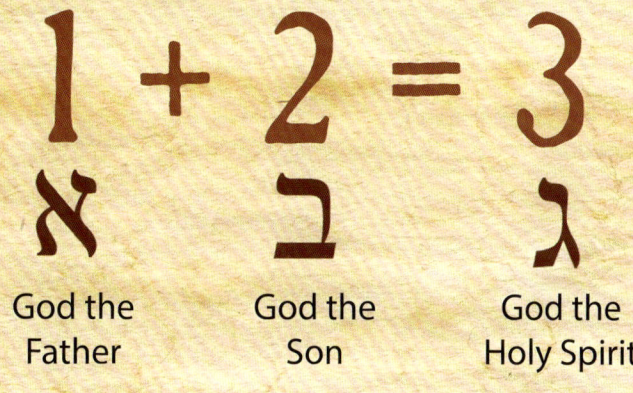

God the Father — God the Son — God the Holy Spirit

The pictographic meaning of gimel, the letter that is also the number 3, is to lift up or benefit – a picture of the Holy Spirit

SUMMARY TRANSLATION OF **ABBA** (FATHER)

Conventional – Father

Pictographic – Strong leader of the house

Numeric – Father, Son, and Holy Spirit

Adam - adm

mem   dalet   aleph
40   4   1

Letters are right to left, original Hebrew

CONVENTIONAL USAGE OF **ADAM**

Adam means human being or person.

Adam is also related to the words "red" and "earth."

"Adama" is earth.

"Adom" is red.

Adam literally means "Man."

FIRST USE OF **ADAM** IN SCRIPTURES

Genesis 2:19
And out of the ground the Lord God formed every beast of the field, and every fowl of the air; and brought them unto Adam to see what he would call them: and whatsoever Adam called every living creature, that was the name thereof.

Adam - adm

מ ד א

mem dalet aleph

40 4 1

PICTOGRAPHIC MEANINGS OF ADAM

Strong leader, strength, leading, the first, aloof or separate, gentle, the beginning, the head of the family, God the Father

Doorway, gate, place of decision, entrance to life or death, moving into something, moving out of something, to open up, a place where change can take place

Liquid, mighty waters like the ocean, massive as the waves of the sea, chaotic and destructive like a tsunami, water coming down like a stream, rain water that makes the desert bloom, the word of God that brings life, living water, waters

NUMERIC MEANINGS OF ADAM

 **1**

Deity, unity, sufficiency, independence, first, indivisible, God the Father

א **4**

God's creative works, the world, four elements, four regions of Earth, four seasons, four divisions of day, four in contrast to seven, Earth (4) vs. Heaven (7), the fourth thing, first number that can be divided, material world that had a beginning, creation

מ **40**

Trials, probation, chastisement but not judgment, action of grace resulting in revival, magnified renewal, an extended period of rule or dominion, (5x8) grace multiplied by renewal, probationary period that results in renewal

PICTOGRAPHIC TRANSLATION OF ADAM

Ideal

The **first** to open the **door** to the path that leads to **chaos and confusion.**

NUMERIC TRANSLATION OF ADAM

Theological and Prophetic

The **first man created** fails **probationary test**.

SUMMARY OF ADAM

Adam, the first man, who is the representative of God's creative works, fails the probationary test.

Adam enters the wrong door!

1 Corinthians 15:22
For as in Adam all die, even so in Christ shall all be made alive.

1 Corinthians 15:45
And so it is written, The first man Adam was made a living soul; the last Adam was made a quickening spirit.

Adonai - Lord

yood	noon	dalet	aleph
10	50	4	1

Letters are right to left, original Hebrew

CONVENTIONAL USAGE OF **ADONAI**

Adonai is the Hebrew word that means "lord."

Religious Jews are forbidden to speak or write the name of YHVH and have substituted the Hebrew title Adonai (Lord) for the name YHVH.

The English word Lord is a correct translation of the Hebrew word Adonai. Adonai is *not* a name, it is a title.

It should not be confused with the sacred name of YHVH which is also translated into the English as the title LORD.

Usually when YHVH is translated LORD in the English versions of the Scriptures, it is either emboldened or all the letters are capitalized.

Adonai is often used in Scripture in reference to God as a term meant to indicate subordination.

The name YHVH is used 6,820 times in Scripture. The title Adonai is used 439 times, and in almost all those cases it is used as a word to identify human princes or to indicate that all the lords of the Earth are under the authority of YHVH.

Deuteronomy 10:17
For YHVH your God is God of gods, and YHVH of lords (Adonai), a great God, a mighty, and a terrible, which regardeth not persons, nor taketh reward:

YHVH of Adonai, or as it says in English *LORD of Lords*.

FIRST USE OF **ADONAI** IN SCRIPTURES

Genesis 18:12
Therefore Sarah laughed within herself, saying, After I am waxed old shall I have pleasure, my lord being old also?

Adonai - Lord

<table>
<tr><td>י</td><td>נ</td><td>ד</td><td>א</td></tr>
<tr><td>yood</td><td>noon</td><td>dalet</td><td>aleph</td></tr>
<tr><td>10</td><td>50</td><td>4</td><td>1</td></tr>
</table>

PICTOGRAPHIC MEANINGS OF ADONAI

Strong leader, strength, leading, the first, aloof or separate, gentle, the beginning, the head of the family, God the Father

Doorway, gate, place of decision, entrance to life or death, moving into something, moving out of something, to open up, a place where change can take place

Activity, life, fish

 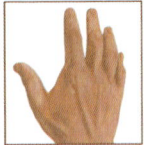

To work, a mighty deed, a deed accomplished, to make, arm and hand accomplishing a purpose, divine deed, hand

NUMERIC MEANINGS OF ADONAI

א 1

Deity, unity, sufficiency, independence, first, indivisible, **God the Father**

ד 4

God's creative works, the world, four elements, four regions of Earth, four seasons, four divisions of day, four in contrast to seven, Earth (4) vs. Heaven (7), the fourth thing, first number that can be divided, material world that had a beginning, **creation**

נ 50

Holy Spirit, Pentecost, deliverance followed by rest, grace multiplied, **jubilee**

י 10

Perfection of divine order, completeness of order, testimony, the law, Ten Commandments, responsibility, divinely ordered events, **ordinal perfection**

PICTOGRAPHIC TRANSLATION OF ADONAI

Ideal

The **strong leader** who does a **mighty deed** that opens the **door** to a place of **protection and safety.**

NUMERIC TRANSLATION OF ADONAI

Theological and Prophetic

God the Father is going to deliver and bring **life** to his **creation** after a **divinely ordered sequence of events, and at exactly the right time**.

SUMMARY OF ADONAI

At the precise time, and after a sequence of divinely ordained events, God is going to deliver His creation from the curse of sin and death.

Hebrew 1:1-3

1 God, who at sundry times and in divers manners spake in time past unto the fathers by the prophets,

2 Hath in these last days spoken unto us by his Son, whom he hath appointed heir of all things, by whom also he made the worlds;

3 Who being the brightness of his glory, and the express image of his person, and upholding all things by the word of his power, when he had by himself purged our sins, sat down on the right hand of the Majesty on high:

*The Church of the Nativity in Bethlehem is
one of the oldest surviving Christian churches.
It marks the traditional place of Christ's birth.*

Bethlehem

mem	chet	lamed	tav	yood	beyt
40	8	30	400	10	2

Bith Lehem

Letters are right to left, original Hebrew

CONVENTIONAL USAGE OF **BETHLEHEM**

Bethlehem is a small town located 10 kilometers south of Jerusalem. It is where David was crowned King of Israel, and is referred to in the New Testament as the City of David. Bethlehem is a combination of two Hebrew words. Beth means "the house" and the Hebrew word lehem means "of bread." The "House of Bread" was the birthplace of Yeshua Ha-Mashiach – Jesus the Christ. Micah the prophet forecast that Bethlehem of Ephratah was where Messiah "whose goings forth have been from of old, from everlasting" will come forth. Immanuel!

FIRST USE OF **BETHLEHEM** IN SCRIPTURES

Genesis 35:18
And Rachel died, and was buried in the way to Ephrath, which is Bethlehem.

COMMENTARY

Micah 5:2
But thou, Bethlehem Ephratah, though thou be little among the thousands of Judah, yet out of thee shall he come forth unto me that is to be ruler in Israel; whose goings forth have been from of old, from everlasting.

PICTOGRAPHIC MEANINGS OF BETHLEHEM

House, tent, son, family, dwelling place, the physical tent/body, inside, within, first letter in the Torah that identifies the Son of God

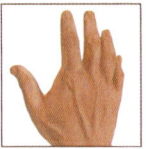

To work, a mighty deed, a deed accomplished, to make, arm and hand accomplishing a purpose, divine deed, hand

To seal, to covenant, a sign, crossed wooden sticks, cross

Control, to shepherd, to have authority, to urge forward, the tongue, the voice of authority, staff

Private, to separate, to protect, place of protection, to be cut off, grace, favor, a place of refuge, a protected garden, quiet place, to be silent and still in security, fence, sanctuary, inner room

Liquid, mighty waters like the ocean, massive as the waves of the sea, chaotic and destructive like a tsunami, water coming down like a stream, rain water that makes the desert bloom, the Word of God that brings life, living water, waters

Bethlehem

mem	chet	lamed	tav	yood	beyt
40	8	30	400	10	2

NUMERIC MEANINGS OF BETHLEHEM

 **2**

Difference, good or evil, division, Living Word, second, second person of the Godhead, to come alongside to hinder, to come alongside for help, **God the Son**

י 10

Perfection of divine order, completeness of order, testimony, the law, Ten Commandments, responsibility, divinely ordered events, **ordinal perfection**

ח 400

The last, the end, period of testing, period of probation to accomplish a divine purpose, Jubilee (50) multiplied by new birth or eternity (8), **a divinely ordained period of time that will bring about deliverance and renewal.**

ל 30

Blood of Christ, dedication, (3x10) magnified perfection of divine order marking the right moment, **blood sacrifice**

ת 8

Eternity, new creation, first in new series, new birth, super abundance, follows seven and is the first in a new series, **new beginning**

ב 40

Trials, probation, chastisement but not judgment, action of grace resulting in revival, magnified renewal, (5x8) an extended period of rule or dominion, grace multiplied by renewal, **probationary period that results in renewal**

PICTOGRAPHIC TRANSLATION OF BETHLEHEM
Ideal

The tent (God the Son who "tabernacled" among us) is going to do a **mighty deed**. This deed will **seal a covenant** and be identified with the **sign of the Cross**. The Son of God has the **authority** to provide **sanctuary** to those who have received. To them He promises the **waters of eternal life.**

John 1:14
And the Word was made flesh, and dwelt among us, (and we beheld his glory, the glory as of the only begotten of the Father,) full of grace and truth.

NUMERIC TRANSLATION OF BETHLEHEM
Theological and Prophetic

The Only Begotten **Son of God** is going to come after a sequence of **Divinely Ordained Events**. He will live a sinless life passing the **probationary test** that the first Adam failed. The Messiah will arrive at the **Appointed Time** to offer Himself as the **Perfect Lamb of God**, an atonement for the sins of mankind. Those that receive Him will be given a **new birth** and will upon their death or upon His coming will receive a newly created body. We will then live for Eternity in the presence of our Heavenly Father, Son and Holy Spirit. Maranatha!

SUMMARY TRANSLATION
The Son of God overcomes the insufficiency of Man with His all sufficiency, resulting in both atonement and redemption for fallen Mankind.

John 17:1-4

1 These words spake Jesus, and lifted up his eyes to heaven, and said, Father, the hour is come; glorify thy Son, that thy Son also may glorify thee:

2 As thou hast given him power over all flesh, that he should give eternal life to as many as thou hast given him.

3 And this is life eternal, that they might know thee the only true God, and Jesus Christ, whom thou hast sent.

4 I have glorified thee on the earth: I have finished the work which thou gavest me to do.

pey	vav	ayin
80	6	70

Flyers

Letters are right to left, original Hebrew

CONVENTIONAL USAGE OF **BIRDS**

The dictionary defines a bird as any warm-blooded vertebrate of the class Aves, having a body covered with feathers, forelimbs modified into wings, scaly legs, a beak, and no teeth, and bearing young in a hard-shelled egg.

The Bible introduces them as creatures that fly above the Earth in the expanse of the heavens that He created. In the original Hebrew they are simply called "flyers."

FIRST USE OF HEBREW WORD **BIRDS** IN SCRIPTURE

Genesis 1:20
And God said, "Let the waters swarm with swarms of living creatures, and let birds fly above the earth across the expanse of the heavens."

Birds – ouph

ף	ו	ע
pey	vav	ayin
80	6	70

PICTOGRAPHIC MEANINGS OF BIRDS

ע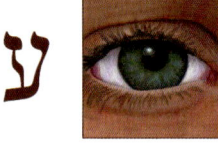

To see, to know, to experience, eye

ו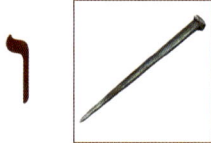

Add, to secure, to join together, to make secure, to bind together, to create a connection between two things that are separated from each other, wooden hook, wooden peg, to hold up

ף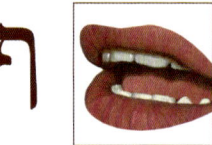

To speak, a word, to open,   mouth

PICTOGRAPHIC TRANSLATION OF BIRDS
Ideal

To *know or experience* two things that are *separated from each other* in order to *open up* our understanding.

We have all heard the expression "a birds-eye" view. Embedded in the root concept of the pictorial meaning of the Hebrew word "bird," or as it is literally translated "flyer," we have the concept of a "viewing" or "seeing" and "experiencing" the world below from the unique vantage point of an elevated perspective.

The Hebrew letter vav found in the middle of the Hebrew word between ayin and pey tells us that this vision and perspective is connected to *something*.

What is that something? It is the world that the bird flies above. The bird is placed in the first heaven where it can soar and view the world below, but it cannot rise above the boundaries set by the Lord.

In the book of Psalms the eighth chapter and verses 4-9, we are reminded that the birds were put under the dominion of man. The Lord saw the birds and said they were good. There is nothing inherently evil about birds.

Matthew 10:29
Are not two sparrows sold for a penny? And not one of them will fall to the ground apart from your Father.

Some have wondered why the bird is so often pictured allegorically in the parables and metaphors of the Scriptures as connected with the Demonic realm.

Matthew 13:4
And as he sowed, some seeds fell along the path, and the birds came and devoured them.

Could it be that the birds cited by the Lord on occasion as the physical representation of a spiritual and invisible reality that is literally swarming with dark and menacing flying spirits right over our heads?

Satan is the Prince of the Power of the Air. As such he has an advantage over those of us who only have a "terrestrial" perspective. Satan uses this widened and spacious perspective along with the long history through which he has viewed the sad history of mankind in order to destroy mankind. It is from this place where he is "lifted up" that he schemes to "steal and kill" the fallen pinnacles of God's creation.

Christians are given a heavenly perspective, far above the home of the birds and the domain of Satan. By faith we can soar to the very throne room of heaven where we can move the affairs of Earth with our Godly prayers.

Isaiah 40:31
But they that wait upon the LORD shall renew their strength; they shall mount up with wings as eagles; they shall run, and not be weary; and they shall walk, and not faint.

Birds – ouph

פ	ו	ע
pey	vav	ayin
80	6	70

NUMERIC MEANINGS OF BIRDS

ע 70

Punishment and restoration of Israel, universality, the seventy nations representing the nations of the world, **perfect spiritual order carried out with all spiritual power and significance**

ו 6

Enmity with God, weakness of Man, manifestation of sin, evils of Satan, falling short, preservation, imperfection, labor, sorrow, number of Man, secular completeness, the sixth, **Man's world**

ף 80

(10x8) magnified ordinal perfection resulting in eternality, **new beginning and new birth**

NUMERIC TRANSLATION OF BIRDS
Theological and Prophetic

In **God's perfect time** He will carry out His plan with all spiritual power and significance. This plan will be for the benefit of **Man** and will result in **perfection, a new beginning and eternity.**

COMMENTARY

The Hebrew word for birds reminds us that there is a higher perspective, a power that is far above the heavens in which the birds soar.

The picture of doom and gloom, which is the natural outcome of the tyrannical and diabolic plans of the Prince of the Power of the Air, is overshadowed by a perspective and sovereign power who has devised a better plan for Mankind. This plan results in life everlasting and joy unspeakable. It is a plan carried out with *all* spiritual power in order to redeem Mankind.

This glorious plan stands in direct opposition to the failed and insufficient plans of men and the diabolical plans of demons and fallen angels. It is a plan that abolishes the covenant that man has made with sin and death. It is a plan that will finally bring the Kingdom of Heaven to earth.

It is a plan that was conceived by the Heavenly Father, worked out in time and space by God the Son and made effective by the Holy Spirit.

Job 19:25-27
25 For I know that my redeemer liveth, and that he shall stand at the latter day upon the earth:
26 And though after my skin worms destroy this body, yet in my flesh shall I see God:
27 Whom I shall see for myself, and mine eyes shall behold, and not another; though my reins be consumed within me.

Bless – be-rach

kaf	reysh	beyt
20	200	2

Letters are right to left, original Hebrew

CONVENTIONAL USAGE OF **BLESS**

The dictionary defines the word bless as "to consecrate or sanctify by a religious rite; make or pronounce holy." Another meaning of bless is to request of God the bestowal of divine favor on a person, place or thing. It also means to extol as holy and to glorify.

MOST WELL-KNOWN USE OF HEBREW WORD **BLESS** IN SCRIPTURES

Genesis 12:3
And I will bless them that bless thee, and curse him that curseth thee: and in thee shall all families of the earth be blessed.

COMMENTARY

It is interesting that the most well-known time the word bless is used in the Scriptures it is in relationship to Abraham, the one to whom the promises were made. The promises were made to Abraham and his seed. And it was from Abraham that the genealogical progression that would gloriously conclude in the coming of the promised Messiah.

Messiah was destined to make atonement for fallen and sinful Mankind. The blessing given to Abraham would have its final and ideal fulfillment in the salvation of the world. Keep this in mind as we discover the amazing picture that is embedded in the Hebrew word translated into English as *bless*! You can read about this unconditional promise in the book of Genesis, found in 22:17-18.

כ	ר	ב
kaf	reysh	beyt
20	200	2

PICTOGRAPHIC MEANINGS OF BLESS

House, tent, son, family, dwelling place, the physical tent/body, inside, within, first letter in the Torah that identifies the Son of God

A person, the head, the highest, the sum, the supreme, the first, the most important, the top, master, leader, prince, head

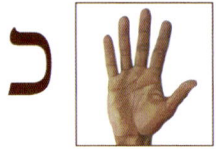

To cover, to open, to allow, atonement, palm

NUMERIC MEANINGS OF BLESS

ב 2

Difference, good or evil, division, Living Word, second, second person of the Godhead, to come alongside to hinder, to come alongside for help, **God the Son**

ר 200

Inadequacy of the temporal, inadequate, the insufficiency of Man, insufficiency, deficient, the ineffective ransom, lacking what is necessary or required, inability to accomplish a purpose, (10x20) adequacy of the eternal, the complete sufficiency of God, redemption of body and soul, multiplied by ordinal perfection accomplished by the Son of God, sufficient to accomplish a purpose, ransom that is both efficient and sufficient to reclaim what was lost, to accomplish redemption, **insufficiency of man, sufficiency of God**

כ 20

(10x2) concentrated meaning of ordinal perfection, expectancy, **redemption**

PICTOGRAPHIC TRANSLATION OF BLESS
Ideal

Beyt reysh is the pictogram of the prince who comes out of
the house. In other words, the beyt reysh is the Son. The Son
is in view as we discover the ideal picture meaning embedded
in the three Hebrew letters—it is the Son who is the Prince of
Heaven, coming to make atonement. He is coming to cover
the sin that keeps us from fellowship with our Heavenly Father.

SUMMARY TRANSLATION
The *Son of God* makes *atonement.*

NUMERIC TRANSLATION OF BLESS
Theological and Prophetic

The Hebrew word bless is crowned with the number 2.
Clearly the Son of God, the second person in the divine
Trinity is in view. The mission is also summarized in the
exponential meaning infused into the number two that has
the biblical significance of announcing both redemption
and atonement.

A Biblical priest – a direct descendant of Aaron – performs a sacrificial blood

Blood – dam

mem   dalet

40   4

Letters are right to left, original Hebrew

CONVENTIONAL USAGE OF **BLOOD**

The dictionary defines blood as the fluid that circulates in the principal vascular system of human beings and other vertebrates. In humans, blood consists of plasma in which the red blood cells, white blood cells, and platelets are suspended. Blood is the vital principle; life.

FIRST USE OF HEBREW WORD **BLOOD** IN SCRIPTURES

Genesis 4:10
And he said, What hast thou done? the voice of thy brother's blood crieth unto me from the ground.

SCRIPTURAL COMMENTARY

Leviticus 17:11
For the life of the flesh is in the blood: and I have given it to you upon the altar to make an atonement for your souls: for it is the blood that maketh an atonement for the soul.

Revelation 1:5
And from Jesus Christ, who is the faithful witness, and the first be-gotten of the dead, and the prince of the kings of the earth. Unto him that loved us, and washed us from our sins in his own blood,

Blood – dam

מ
mem
40

ד
dalet
4

PICTOGRAPHIC MEANINGS OF BLOOD

Doorway, gate, place of decision, entrance to life or death, moving into something, moving out of something, to open up, a place where change can take place

Liquid, mighty waters like the ocean, massive as the waves of the sea, chaotic and destructive like a tsunami, water coming down like a stream, rain water that makes the desert bloom, the Word of God that brings life, living water, waters

NUMERIC MEANINGS OF BLOOD

ד 4

God's creative works, the world, four elements, four regions of Earth, four seasons, four divisions of day, four in contrast to seven, Earth (4) vs. Heaven (7), the fourth thing, first number that can be divided, material world that had a beginning, **creation**

מ 40

Trials, probation, chastisement but not judgment, action of grace resulting in revival, magnified renewal, (5x8) an extended period of rule or dominion, grace multiplied by renewal, **probationary period that results in renewal**

PICTOGRAPHIC TRANSLATION OF BLOOD
Ideal

The *water* in the *pathway.*

NUMERIC TRANSLATION OF BLOOD
Theological and Prophetic

Created by God in order to test Man.

Man is given a period of probation in which he fails. It is ultimately the pure and undefiled blood of Jesus that demonstrates God's gracious plan for Mankind. A grace that is connected to blood that ultimately results in revival and renewal for all those who are covered and cleansed by the Savior's bloods and who are born again by its power.

Leviticus 17:11
For the life of the flesh is in the blood: and I have given it to you upon the altar to make an atonement for your souls: for it is the blood that maketh an atonement for the soul.

Romans 3:25
Whom God hath set forth to be a propitiation through faith in his blood, to declare his righteousness for the remission of sins that are past, through the forbearance of God;

Romans 5:9
Much more then, being now justified by his blood, we shall be saved from wrath through him.

Ephesians 1:7
In whom we have redemption through his blood, the forgiveness of sins, according to the riches of his grace;

dalet	yood	aleph
4	10	1

Letters are right to left, original Hebrew

CONVENTIONAL USAGE **CALAMITY**

The dictionary defines Calamity as a great misfortune or disaster, as a flood or serious injury. Also defined as a grievous affliction, adversity; and misery.

FIRST USE OF HEBREW WORD **CALAMITY** IN SCRIPTURES

Deuteronomy 32:35
To me belongeth vengeance and recompence; their foot shall slide in due time: for the day of their calamity is at hand, and the things that shall come upon them make haste.

Calamity – eyd

ד   י   א
dalet   yood   aleph
4   10   1

PICTOGRAPHIC MEANINGS OF CALAMITY

Strong leader, strength, leading, the first, aloof or separate, gentle, the beginning, the head of the family, God the Father

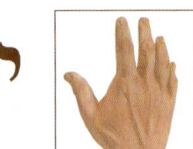

To work, a mighty deed, a deed accomplished, to make, arm and hand accomplishing a purpose, divine deed, hand

Doorway, gate, place of decision, entrance to life or death, moving into something, moving out of something, to open up, a place where change can take place

PICTOGRAPHIC TRANSLATION OF CALAMITY

In conventional Hebrew the aleph and yood mean *"where?"*

The question then arises: why does the pictogram of the Father (aleph) and the hand (yood) translate into the word *where*?

What picture did God have in mind when He revealed the meaning of the word calamity?

The answer is profound and once understood explains many of the other Hebrew words that begin with aleph yood. It also helps us understood how God uses the picture of His hand (yood) to communicate both the positive and negative aspects of His redemptive plan.

This is worth investigating and expending mental effort in order to understand the secrets that God wants His children to understand.

The Hebrew word for anger is the picture of the father (aleph) and son (beyt) separated by a hand (yood), which translates to *the son separated from the father*. Or to put it another way, *anger* is pictured by the son (beyt) crying "Where is my father?"

The meaning of calamity has the same idea and provokes the same question. In the same way that the picture translated as "where is the father?" is the quintessential picture of *anger*, the picture translated "where is the path or doorway?" is the essence of *calamity*.

The pictogram of calmity is literally a picture of the father (aleph) separating with his hand (yood) the way to the door or pathway (dalet). In other words it is: "Where is the path? Where is the doorway?"

To put it in the Hebrew ideal based on the pictographic meaning, the question is as follows:

"Where is the path to life?"

If we are separated from the doorway or the pathway to life we are not only experiencing *calamity* of the first magnitude, we are in a desperate condition that can only be described as both disastrous and eternally life threatening.

WHERE IS THE DOOR?

John 10:7-9
7 Then said Jesus unto them again, Verily, verily, I say unto you, I am the door of the sheep.
8 All that ever came before me are thieves and robbers: but the sheep did not hear them.
9 I am the door: by me if any man enter in, he shall be saved, and shall go in and out, and find pasture.

ד   י   א

dalet   yood   aleph

4   10   1

NUMERIC MEANINGS OF CALAMITY

א 1

Deity, unity, sufficiency, independence, first, indivisible, **God the Father**

י 10

Perfection of divine order, completeness of order, testimony, the law, Ten Commandments, responsibility, divinely ordered events, **ordinal perfection**

ד 4

God's creative works, the world, four elements, four regions of Earth, four seasons, four divisions of day, four in contrast to seven, Earth (4) vs. Heaven (7), the fourth thing, first number that can be divided, material world that had a beginning, **creation**

NUMERIC TRANSLATION OF CALAMITY
Theological and Prophetic

God at the appointed time is going to allow ***calamity*** to come upon his creation in order to bring about ***ultimate perfection***.

Acts 14:27
And when they were come, and had gathered the church together, they rehearsed all that God had done with them, and how he had opened the door of faith unto the Gentiles.

John 10:9
I am the door: by me if any man enter in, he shall be saved, and shall go in and out, and find pasture.

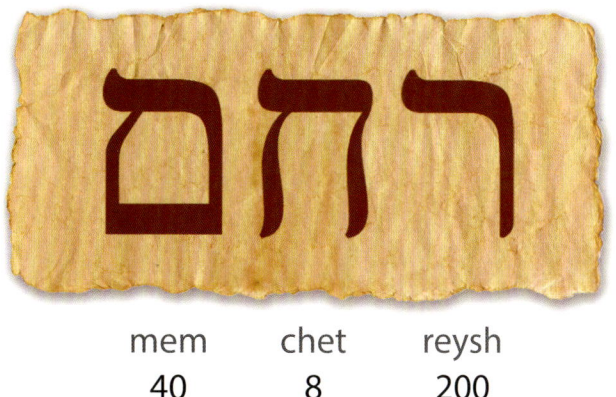

mem	chet	reysh
40	8	200

Letters are right to left, original Hebrew

CONVENTIONAL USAGE OF **COMPASSION**

The dictionary defines as compassion as a feeling of deep sympathy and sorrow for another who is stricken by misfortune, accompanied by a strong desire to alleviate the suffering.

FIRST USE OF HEBREW WORD TRANSLATED **COMPASSION** IN THE ENGLISH SCRIPTURES

Exodus 2:6
And when she had opened it, she saw the child: and, behold, the babe wept. And she had compassion on him, and said, This is one of the Hebrews' children.

In 1642, Dutch Master Rembrandt illustrated compassion with the story of the covenant of David and Jonathan from the Book of Samuel. After the death of Jonathan – David's presumed rival for the crown – David seated Jonathan's son Mephibosheth, at his own royal table instead of eradicating his rival's line.

Compassion - rachum

מ	ח	ר
mem	chet	reysh
40	8	200

PICTOGRAPHIC MEANINGS OF COMPASSION

A person, the head, the highest, the sum, the supreme, the first, the most important, the top, master, leader, prince, head

Private, to separate, to protect, place of protection, to be cut off, grace, favor, a place of refuge, a protected garden, quiet place, to be silent and still in security, fence, sanctuary, inner room

Liquid, mighty waters like the ocean, massive as the waves of the sea, chaotic and destructive like a tsunami, water coming down like a stream, rain water that makes the desert bloom, the word of God that brings life, living water, waters

NUMERIC MEANINGS OF COMPASSION

ר 200

Inadequacy of the temporal, inadequate, the insufficiency of Man, insufficiency, deficient, the ineffective ransom, lacking what is necessary or required, inability to accomplish a purpose, (10x20) adequacy of the eternal, the complete sufficiency of God, redemption of body and soul, multiplied by ordinal perfection accomplished by the Son of God, sufficient to accomplish a purpose, ransom that is both efficient and sufficient to reclaim what was lost, to accomplish redemption, **insufficiency of man, sufficiency of God**

ח 8

Eternity, new creation, first in new series, new birth, super abundance, follows seven and is the first in a new series, **new beginning**

מ 40

Trials, probation, chastisement but not judgment, action of grace resulting in revival, magnified renewal, an extended period of rule or dominion, (5x8) grace multiplied by renewal, **probationary period that results in renewal**

PICTOGRAPHIC TRANSLATION OF COMPASSION
Ideal

The **Prince of Heaven** will provide in Himself a **place of refuge**. A place found only in the **Living Word (Messiah)** that will bring forth the **living waters of eternal life.**

Psalm 145:
The Lord is gracious, and full of compassion; slow to anger, and of great mercy.

NUMERIC TRANSLATION OF COMPASSION
Theological and Prophetic

The **inadequacy and inefficiency of Man** will be overcome by the **adequacy and efficiency of God** who supernaturally gives **new birth to a new creation**. This happens after a **period of chastisement that ends in revival not judgment** as a result of God's grace.

Matthew 9:36
But when he saw the multitudes, he was moved with compassion on them, because they fainted, and were scattered abroad, as sheep having no shepherd.

aleph	reysh	beyt
1	200	2

Letters are right to left, original Hebrew

CONVENTIONAL USAGE OF **CREATED**

The Biblical Revelation that all matter came "from nothing" as a result of God speaking all things into existence. The *Word* of God then made all things.

The concept that matter comes "from nothing" is called *creatio ex nihilo* in the Latin, more directly "creation out of nothing."

The Biblical view is that in the beginning there was God and all creation has its beginning in Him.

FIRST USE OF HEBREW WORD
CREATED IN SCRIPTURES

Genesis 1:1
In the beginning God created the heaven and the earth.

COMMENTARY

Gods purpose in creation is revelation. What is it that God is revealing? The answer is found in the pictographic translation of creation.

א	ר	ב
aleph	reysh	beyt
1	200	2

PICTOGRAPHIC MEANINGS OF CREATED

House, tent, son, family, dwelling place, the physical tent/body, inside, within, first letter in the Torah that identifies the Son of God

Difference, good or evil, division, Living Word, second, second person of the Godhead, to come alongside to hinder, to come alongside for help, **God the Son**

Strong leader, strength, leading, the first, aloof or separate, gentle, the beginning, the head of the family, God the Father

NUMERIC MEANINGS OF CREATED

ב 2

A person, the head, the highest, the sum, the supreme, the first, the most important, the top, master, leader, prince, head

ר 200

Inadequacy of the temporal, inadequate, the insufficiency of Man, insufficiency, deficient, the ineffective ransom, lacking what is necessary or required, inability to accomplish a purpose, (10x20) adequacy of the eternal, the complete sufficiency of God, redemption of body and soul, multiplied by ordinal perfection accomplished by the Son of God, sufficient to accomplish a purpose, ransom that is both efficient and sufficient to reclaim what was lost, to accomplish redemption, **insufficiency of man, sufficiency of God**

א 1

Deity, unity, sufficiency, independence, first, indivisible, **God the Father**

PICTOGRAPHIC TRANSLATION OF CREATED
Ideal

The *person* who comes out of the *house* is the *son.*

The pictographic meaning of beyt reysh is *the son*. Beyt reysh is *bar* – as in Bar Jonah, the son of Jonah. The question is *whose son*?

God the Father
Creation is the revelation of the *Son of God.*

NUMERIC TRANSLATION OF CREATED
Theological and Prophetic

God the Son comes alongside to accomplish for *insufficient and inadequate Man* the sufficiency only found in *God!*

Romans 5:8
But God commendeth his love toward us, in that, while we were yet sinners, Christ died for us.

Matthew 9:13
But go ye and learn what that meaneth, I will have mercy, and not sacrifice: for I am not come to call the righteous, but sinners to repentance.

Romans 5:19
For as by one man's disobedience many were made sinners, so by the obedience of one shall many be made righteous.

I Timothy 1:15
This is a faithful saying, and worthy of all acceptation, that Christ Jesus came into the world to save sinners; of whom I am chief.

Created - bara

CREATION THEME BIBLE HELPS

Genesis 1:27
So God created man in his own image, in the image of God created he him; male and female created he them.

Psalm 148:5
Let them praise the name of the Lord: for he commanded, and they were created.

Isaiah 41:20
That they may see, and know, and consider, and understand together, that the hand of the Lord hath done this, and the Holy One of Israel hath created it.

Isaiah 42:5
Thus saith God the Lord, he that created the heavens, and stretched them out; he that spread forth the earth, and that which cometh out of it; he that giveth breath unto the people upon it, and spirit to them that walk therein:

Revelation 4:11
Thou art worthy, O Lord, to receive glory and honour and power: for thou hast created all things, and for thy pleasure they are and were created.

Colossians 1:16
For by him were all things created, that are in heaven, and that are in earth, visible and invisible, whether they be thrones, or dominions, or principalities, or powers: all things were created by him, and for him:

Ephesians 2:10
For we are his workmanship, created in Christ Jesus unto good works, which God hath before ordained that we should walk in them.

kaf	sheen	chet
20	300	8

Letters are right to left, original Hebrew

CONVENTIONAL USAGE OF DARKNESS

The opposite of light. The absence of light.

FIRST USE IN SCRIPTURES

Genesis 1:2
And the earth was without form, and void; and darkness was upon the face of the deep. And the Spirit of God moved upon the face of the waters.

ך	ש	ח
kaf	sheen	chet
20	300	8

PICTOGRAPHIC MEANINGS OF DARKNESS

Private, to separate, to protect, place of protection, to be cut off, grace, favor, a place of refuge, a protected garden, quiet place, to be silent and still in security, fence, sanctuary, inner room

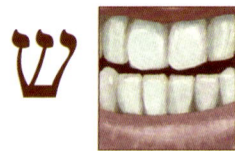

To consume, to destroy, sharp, to press, the one letter that God used to identify Himself, God's signature, letter that stands for God Almighty, teeth

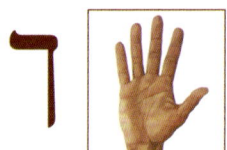

To cover, to open, to allow, atonement, palm

NUMERIC MEANINGS OF DARKNESS

ח **8**

Eternity, new creation, first in new series, new birth, super abundance, follows seven and is the first in a new series, **new beginning**

ש **300**

A divinely appointed period of time, number connected to the "children of promise," election, supernatural victory over enemies including death, number connected with the death, burial and resurrection of Messiah, **signifies final blood sacrifice made by the perfect Lamb of God.**

ך **20**

(10x2) concentrated meaning of ordinal perfection, expectancy, **redemption**

PICTOGRAPHIC TRANSLATION OF DARKNESS

Ideal

A **separate place** that is designed for **consumption and destruction** that is **covered up by the hand** of God.

NUMERIC TRANSLATION OF DARKNESS
Theological and Prophetic

Notice that in the theological and prophetic, God always provides a way of escape. In this case it is His Son who is the doorway to safety The numeric message is an answer that brings hope to the despair presented by the picture of darkness. The message is that God is going to open the doorway out of the darkness. God is going to start a new series of events that results in new birth and a new beginning. There is going to be victory over darkness and death provided by the blood sacrifice of Messiah who is going to bring redemption at the perfectly appointed time.

Genesis 1:4
And God saw the light, that it was good: and God divided the light from the darkness.

Revelation 16:10
And the fifth angel poured out his vial upon the seat of the beast; and his kingdom was full of darkness; and they gnawed their tongues for pain,

1 John 2:8
Again, a new commandment I write unto you, which thing is true in him and in you: because the darkness is past, and the true light now shineth.

1 John 1:5
This then is the message which we have heard of him, and declare unto you, that God is light, and in him is no darkness at all.

John 8:12
Then spake Jesus again unto them, saying, I am the light of the world: he that followeth me shall not walk in darkness, but shall have the light of life.

Disobey (bitter) – mar

hey	reysh	mem
5	200	40

Letters are right to left, original Hebrew

CONVENTIONAL USAGE OF **DISOBEY** (BITTER)

The dictionary defines disobey as to neglect or refuse to obey.

FIRST USE OF HEBREW WORD **DISOBEY** (BITTER) IN SCRIPTURES

Genesis 27:34
And when Esau heard the words of his father, he cried with a great and exceeding bitter cry, and said unto his father, Bless me, even me also, O my father.

COMMENTARY

The Hebrew word for disobey is embedded in the word for bitterness. The two are inseparable as they define each other. The experiential side of disobedience is bitterness. The root of bitterness is disobedience. The first image we are given of disobedience is Esau, who neglected the God of his Father Isaac and disobeyed the instructions of his father and mother. He was the picture of disobedience and his life was a portrait of bitterness.

הְ רֹ מֶ

hey
5

reysh
200

mem
40

PICTOGRAPHIC MEANINGS OF DISOBEY

Liquid, mighty waters like the ocean, massive as the waves of the sea, chaotic and destructive like a tsunami, water coming down like a stream, rain water that makes the desert bloom, the word of God that brings life, living water, waters

A person, the head, the highest, the sum, the supreme, the first, the most important, the top, master, leader, prince, head

Pay attention to what follows, to reveal, to unfold, to look upon, Holy Spirit as the revelator

NUMERIC MEANINGS OF DISOBEY

מ40

Trials, probation, chastisement but not judgment, action of grace resulting in revival, magnified renewal, an extended period of rule or dominion, (5x8) grace multiplied by renewal, **probationary period that results in renewal**

ר200

Inadequacy of the temporal, inadequate, the insufficiency of Man, insufficiency, deficient, the ineffective ransom, lacking what is necessary or required, inability to accomplish a purpose, (10x20) adequacy of the eternal, the complete sufficiency of God, redemption of body and soul, multiplied by ordinal perfection accomplished by the Son of God, sufficient to accomplish a purpose, ransom that is both efficient and sufficient to reclaim what was lost, to accomplish redemption, **insufficiency of man, sufficiency of God**

ה5

Unmerited favor, God's goodness, Pentateuch, divine strength, the fifth, what follows creation, **grace**

PICTOGRAPHIC TRANSLATION OF DISOBEY

Ideal

Massive **chaos and confusion** is what **follows** when you are in bondage to the **Prince of Darkness!**

NUMERIC TRANSLATION OF DISOBEY

Theological and Prophetic

God's amazing math is always holding out hope to sinful Mankind. Instead of judgment, God uses the numeric of the word that epitomizes separation from His presence and dooms us to eternal bitterness to announce that His Son has accomplished on our behalf. God has the remedy for disobedience, the cure that annuls the power and consequences of disobedience. And how is this miracle accomplished? It was accomplished by His Son's obedience to His will and purpose and displayed for our salvation on the cross of Calvary.

Job 3:20

Wherefore is light given to him that is in misery, and life unto the bitter in soul;

Philippians 2:8-11

8 And being found in fashion as a man, he humbled himself, and became obedient unto death, even the death of the cross.
9 Wherefore God also hath highly exalted him, and given him a name which is above every name:
10 That at the name of Jesus every knee should bow, of things in heaven, and things in earth, and things under the earth;
11 And that every tongue should confess that Jesus Christ is Lord, to the glory of God the Father.

(the) Earth – eretz

tsade	reysh	aleph	hey
90	200	1	5

Letters are right to left, original Hebrew

CONVENTIONAL USAGE OF **EARTH**

The word Earth is defined as the planet third in order from the sun, having an equatorial diameter of 7926 miles (12,755 km) and a polar diameter of 7900 miles (12,714 km), a mean distance from the sun of 92.9 million miles (149.6 million km), and a period of revolution of 365.26 days, and having one satellite.

The Earth is the planet inhabited by humans, often in contrast to Heaven and Hell.

FIRST USE OF HEBREW WORD TRANSLATED **EARTH** IN THE ENGLISH SCRIPTURES

Genesis 1:1
In the beginning God created the heavens and the earth.

Earth – eretz

צ	ר	א	ה
tsade	reysh	aleph	hey
90	200	1	5

PICTOGRAPHIC MEANINGS OF EARTH

Pay attention to what follows, to reveal, to unfold, to look upon, Holy Spirit as the revelator

Strong leader, strength, leading, the first, aloof or separate, gentle, the beginning, the head of the family, God the Father

A person, the head, the highest, the sum, the supreme, the first, the most important, the top, master, leader, prince, head

To catch, to be caught, a harvest, to pull forward, unable to escape, trouble, to strongly desire, just or righteous, to need, fishhook

NUMERIC MEANINGS OF EARTH

 **5**

Unmerited favor, God's goodness, Pentateuch, divine strength, the fifth, what follows creation, **grace**

1

Deity, unity, sufficiency, independence, first, indivisible, **God the Father**

200

Inadequacy of the temporal, inadequate, the insufficiency of Man, insufficiency, deficient, the ineffective ransom, lacking what is necessary or required, inability to accomplish a purpose, (10x20) adequacy of the eternal, the complete sufficiency of God, redemption of body and soul, multiplied by ordinal perfection accomplished by the Son of God, sufficient to accomplish a purpose, ransom that is both efficient and sufficient to reclaim what was lost, to accomplish redemption, **insufficiency of man, sufficiency of God**

90

Signifies the conclusion of a matter that will be followed by judgment, same meaning as the number nine magnified by the multiplier ten, **combination of ordinal perfection and judgment at the conclusion of a series**

PICTOGRAPHIC TRANSLATION OF EARTH

Ideal

Behold God the Father's Prince (His Son) and **strongly desire** Him!

NUMERIC TRANSLATION OF EARTH

Theological and Prophetic

It is meant for Man to understand that he has been placed on this Earth for a purpose. That purpose is to discover his insufficiency so that he might seek with all his heart and desire above everything else on Earth, the Son of God. The Earth is going to come to an end as we now know it. When that moment comes, there is going to be divine judgment. The only thing that will matter in the end is the answer to the following question:

How did you respond to the Lord Jesus Christ?

THE PURPOSE OF EARTH

It is meant for Man to understand that he has been placed on this Earth to discover his insufficiency so that he might seek with all his heart and desire above everything else on Earth, the Son of God, his Savior.

Elohim (God) – aleim

mem	yood	hey	lamed	aleph
40	10	5	30	1

Letters are right to left, original Hebrew

CONVENTIONAL USAGE OF **ELOHIM** (GOD)

Creator of all things!

FIRST USE OF HEBREW WORD **ELOHIM** (GOD) IN SCRIPTURES

Genesis 1:1
In the beginning God created the heavens and the earth.

Elohim (God) – aleim

PICTOGRAPHIC MEANINGS OF ELOHIM

Strong leader, strength, leading, the first, aloof or separate, gentle, the beginning, the head of the family, God the Father

Control, to shepherd, to have authority, to urge forward, the tongue, the voice of authority, staff

Pay attention to what follows, to reveal, to unfold, to look upon, Holy Spirit as the revelator

To work, a mighty deed, a deed accomplished, to make, arm and hand accomplishing a purpose, divine deed, hand

 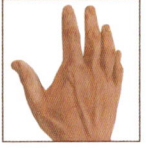

Liquid, mighty waters like the ocean, massive as the waves of the sea, chaotic and destructive like a tsunami, water coming down like a stream, rain water that makes the desert bloom, the word of God that brings life, living water, waters

NUMERIC MEANINGS OF ELOHIM

 **1**

Deity, unity, sufficiency, independence, first, indivisible, **God the Father**

ל 30

Blood of Christ, dedication, (3x10) magnified perfection of divine order marking the right moment, **blood sacrifice**

ה 5

Unmerited favor, God's goodness, Pentateuch, divine strength, the fifth, what follows creation, **grace**

י 10

Perfection of divine order, completeness of order, testimony, the law, Ten Commandments, responsibility, divinely ordered events, **ordinal perfection**

מ 40

Trials, probation, chastisement but not judgment, action of grace resulting in revival, magnified renewal, an extended period of rule or dominion, (5x8) grace multiplied by renewal, **probationary period that results in renewal**

aleph	lamed	hey	yood	mem
1	30	5	10	40

PICTOGRAPHIC TRANSLATION OF ELOHIM

Ideal

God the Father, The Son Who speaks with **authority** and the Holy Spirit will **reveal** a **mighty deed** that will create springs of **living waters.**

NUMERIC TRANSLATION OF ELOHIM

Theological and Prophetic

God the Father will bring about **deliverance through His Anointed One** and by His **grace** bring about a **divinely ordained plan**, testing Man to show his weakness, and then **reviving and renewing Man by His grace.**

Elijah and Enoch represented on a seventeenth century icon.

kaf	vav	noon	chet
20	6	50	8

Letters are right to left, original Hebrew

CONVENTIONAL USAGE **ENOCH**

Enoch was the seventh from Adam. Enoch was the first man to enter into the presence of God without first dying. Enoch is the father of the longest living man in the world, Methuselah. Enoch walked with the Lord!

FIRST USE OF HEBREW WORD **ENOCH** IN SCRIPTURES

Genesis 4:17
And Cain knew his wife; and she conceived, and bare Enoch: and he builded a city, and called the name of the city, after the name of his son, Enoch.

COMMENTARY ON NAME OF **ENOCH**

The "Enoch" mentioned in Genesis 4:17 is not the same Enoch who was translated to Heaven. The first Enoch mentioned in the Scriptures was the son of Cain who was the son of Adam.

The name Enoch in the conventional Hebrew means teacher or teaching.

kaf	vav	noon	chet
20	6	50	8

PICTOGRAPHIC MEANINGS IN ENOCH

Private, to separate, to protect, place of protection, to be cut off, grace, favor, a place of refuge, a protected garden, quiet place, to be silent and still in security, fence, sanctuary, inner room

Activity, life, fish

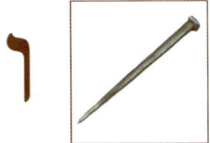

Add, to secure, to join together, to make secure, to bind together, to create a connection between two things that are separated from each other, wooden hook, wooden peg, to hold up

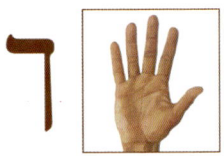

To cover, to open, to allow, atonement, palm

NUMERIC MEANINGS IN ENOCH

ח 8

Eternity, new creation, first in new series, new birth, super abundance, follows seven and is the first in a new series, **new beginning**

נ 50

Holy Spirit, Pentecost, deliverance followed by rest, grace multiplied, **jubilee**

ו 6

Enmity with God, weakness of Man, manifestation of sin, evils of Satan, falling short, preservation, imperfection, labor, sorrow, number of Man, secular completeness, the sixth, **Man's world**

ך 20

(10x2) concentrated meaning of ordinal perfection, expectancy, **redemption**

PICTOGRAPHIC TRANSLATION OF ENOCH

Ideal

A private sanctuary where life is both created and protected. This miracle happens as a result of a connection between two things that have been separated from each other. Those two things are sinful Man and a holy God. The breach is healed by way of an iron nail that is connected somehow with the redemptive work of atonement.

We can now see clearly what God had in mind in the naming of Enoch as a harbinger of His redemptive plan. Yeshua Ha-Mashiach is the solution to the puzzle. Praise God!

NUMERIC TRANSLATION OF ENOCH

Theological and Prophetic

The numeric translation is very much like the pictographic revelation. This is unusual, which means it is important—something we need to pay attention to.

God has a plan to deliver Man from the bondage of sin and the consequences of His wrath. This plan will demonstrate His grace by overcoming the weakness and imperfection of Man through an act of redemption that is hinted at by the pictogram of an iron nail. A nail that pictures the removal of our enmity with God. An iron nail that is the picture of an act of mercy that heals the breach and joins us together with our Heavenly Father. This divine favor is not temporal but eternal. The consequences of the atonement once received is eternal and literally life changes as it results in a new birth and a new beginning.

NUMERIC TRANSLATION OF EVENING

Theological and Prophetic

The numeric meaning of ayin, the first letter in the Hebrew word evening, begins with two concepts. The first is that all the nations of the world, or all the people of the world, are in view.

The second concept is that there is a final judgment or accounting that takes place. Embedded in this idea is the further concept that this judgment is going to happen at a perfect time, and it will be perfect judgment carried out with spiritual power, authority and significance.

The numeric meaning of the second letter in the Hebrew word reysh carries a double meaning. On the one hand it reminds us of the insufficiency of Man. This is positioned against the other meaning, which is clearly the sufficiency of God.

When you put this together with the meaning of the first letter in the word evening, you begin to get the picture of a *judgment* in which Man is always insufficient. Things do not look good for Mankind until you consider the third letter in the Hebrew word evening. Two concepts jump out: one is the concept of division, and the other is the revelation of the Son of God.

In summary, the numeric meaning of evening is a theological and prophetic revelation that the time is coming when all men from all nations will be judged. The outcome of that judgment will result in two verdicts. One verdict is death and destruction. The other verdict is an undeserved deliverance as a result of the intervention of the Son of God who by His grace forgives us and repurposes us by His Spirit so that we might enter the pathway that leads to eternal life.

Revelation 20:12
And I saw the dead, small and great, stand before God; and the books were opened: and another book was opened, which is the book of life: and the dead were judged out of those things which were written in the books, according to their works. And the sea gave up the dead which were in it; and death and hell delivered up the dead which were in them: and they were judged every man according to their works.

mem	vav	yood
40	6	10

Letters are right to left, original Hebrew

CONVENTIONAL USAGE OF **DAY**

Day is defined in the dictionary as the interval of light between two successive nights – the time between sunrise and sunset.

FIRST USE OF HEBREW WORD TRANSLATED **DAY** IN THE ENGLISH SCRIPTURES

Genesis 1:5
God called the light "day," and the darkness he called "night." And there was evening, and there was morning—the first day.

מ	ו	י
mem	vav	yood
40	6	10

PICTOGRAPHIC MEANINGS OF DAY

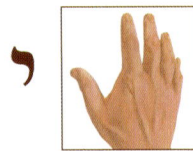

To work, a mighty deed, a deed accomplished, to make, arm and hand accomplishing a purpose, divine deed, hand

Add, to secure, to join together, to make secure, to bind together, to create a connection between two things that are separated from each other, wooden hook, wooden peg, to hold up

Liquid, mighty waters like the ocean, massive as the waves of the sea, chaotic and destructive like a tsunami, water coming down like a stream, rain water that makes the desert bloom, the word of God that brings life, living water, waters

NUMERIC MEANINGS OF DAY

י 10

Perfection of divine order, completeness of order, testimony, the law, Ten Commandments, responsibility, divinely ordered events, **ordinal perfection**

ו 6

Enmity with God, weakness of Man, manifestation of sin, evils of Satan, falling short, preservation, imperfection, labor, sorrow, number of Man, secular completeness, the sixth, **Man's world**

מ 40

Trials, probation, chastisement but not judgment, action of grace resulting in revival, magnified renewal, an extended period of rule or dominion, (5x8) grace multiplied by renewal, **probationary period that results in renewal**

PICTOGRAPHIC TRANSLATION OF DAY

Ideal

A **mighty deed** that is **connected** to **creation**.

The Messianic picture is a variation of this revelation. A mighty deed that is secured by an iron nail that brings both destruction and life. Destruction, pictured as a tsunami wave to those who refuse to trust in Messiah, and eternal life pictured as living water for those who do put their faith and trust in Messiah.

NUMERIC TRANSLATION OF DAY

Theological and Prophetic

At the appointed time after a divinely ordained sequence of events Mankind will end his period of probation. Those who have put their faith and trust in Messiah will, after a period of testing, be renewed and revived. This is all as a result of God's grace.

noon	dalet	ayin
50	4	70

Letters are right to left, original Hebrew

CONVENTIONAL USAGE OF **EDEN**

Biblical garden that God planted for Man as described in the book of Genesis.

FIRST USE OF HEBREW WORD **EDEN** IN SCRIPTURES

Genesis 2:8
And the Lord God planted a garden eastward in Eden; and there he put the man whom he had formed.

Left: Sculpture at the Cimitero Monumentale in Milan, Italy.

ן   ד   ע

noon   dalet   ayin
50   4   70

PICTOGRAPHIC MEANINGS OF EDEN

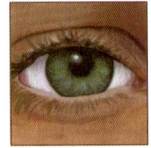

To see, to know, to experience, eye

Doorway, gate, place of decision, entrance to life or death, moving into something, moving out of something, to open up, a place where change can take place

Activity, life, fish

NUMERIC MEANINGS OF EDEN

ע **70**

Punishment and restoration of Israel, universality, the seventy nations representing the nations of the world, **perfect spiritual order carried out with all spiritual power and significance**

ד **4**

God's creative works, the world, four elements, four regions of Earth, four seasons, four divisions of day, four in contrast to seven, Earth (4) vs. Heaven (7), the fourth thing, first number that can be divided, material world that had a beginning, **creation**

ן **50**

Holy Spirit, Pentecost, deliverance followed by rest, grace multiplied, **jubilee**

PICTOGRAPHIC TRANSLATION OF EDEN

Ideal

Eden is where man first **saw with his eyes**, experienced in his heart, and knew with his mind the **pathway or doorway** that leads to **life!**

While in Eden experiencing the unimaginable bliss resulting from fellowship with his Creator, Adam turned away from life and chose the doorway that leads to death and destruction.

NUMERIC TRANSLATION OF EDEN

Theological and Prophetic

From **every nation of the world,** God is going to call out a people for Himself. He will accomplish this with unmatched **spiritual power.** God is going to **restore** Mankind to **life** at exactly the right moment. The captive will go free, and those in bondage will be delivered. This **Jubilee** will come about as a result of the finished work of Messiah and is only available to those who choose to put their faith and trust in Him and Him alone.

Revelation 5:9

And they sung a new song, saying, Thou art worthy to take the book, and to open the seals thereof: for thou wast slain, and hast redeemed us to God by thy blood out of every kindred, and tongue, and people, and nation;

beyt	reysh	ayin
2	200	70

Letters are right to left, original Hebrew

CONVENTIONAL USAGE OF **EVENING**

The latter part of the day. The early part of the night. The period from sunset to bedtime.

FIRST USE OF **EVENING** IN ENGLISH SCRIPTURES

Genesis 1:5
And God called the light Day, and the darkness he called Night. And the evening and the morning were the first day.

PROPHETIC SIGNIFICANCE OF **EVENING** IN SCRIPTURE

Genesis 8:11
And the dove came in to him in the evening; and, lo, in her mouth was an olive leaf pluckt off: so Noah knew that the waters were abated from off the earth.

1 Kings 18:36
And it came to pass at the time of the offering of the evening sacrifice, that Elijah the prophet came near, and said, Lord God of Abraham, Isaac, and of Israel, let it be known this day that thou art God in Israel, and that I am thy servant, and that I have done all these things at thy word.

Daniel 9:21
Yea, whiles I was speaking in prayer, even the man Gabriel, whom I had seen in the vision at the beginning, being caused to fly swiftly, touched me about the time of the evening oblation.

Zechariah 14:7
But it shall be one day which shall be known to the Lord, not day, nor night: but it shall come to pass, that at evening time it shall be light.

Mark 14:17
And in the evening he cometh with the twelve.

John 20:19
Then the same day at evening, being the first day of the week, when the doors were shut where the disciples were assembled for fear of the Jews, came Jesus and stood in the midst, and saith unto them, Pcacc be unto you.

Acts 28:23
And when they had appointed him a day, there came many to him into his lodging; to whom he expounded and testified the kingdom of God, persuading them concerning Jesus, both out of the law of Moses, and out of the prophets, from morning till evening.

ב	ר	ע
beyt	reysh	ayin
2	200	70

PICTOGRAPHIC MEANINGS OF EVENING

 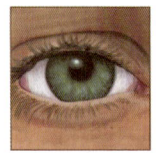

To see, to know, to experience, eye

A person, the head, the highest, the sum, the supreme, the first, the most important, the top, master, leader, prince, head

House, tent, son, family, dwelling place, the physical tent/body, inside, within, first letter in the Torah that identifies the Son of God

PICTOGRAPHIC TRANSLATION OF EVENING

Ideal

I believe that the pictograph for the word evening is actually a question. I believe we are being asked to consider two choices that are contained in the two possible interpretations of the pictographic meaning of the word evening.

On the one hand it could be translated as follows:
To see, know and experience the Prince from Heaven the Son of God.
On the other hand it could be translated to mean the following:
To see, know and experience the Prince of the power of the Air, Satan.

Is this picture of evening telling us that there are two choices that can be made? One is to worship the Son of God, and the other is to worship the world system that Satan has set up and by so doing to actually worship him? The concept of evening is the concept of ending one period of time and beginning another. Could evening be a metaphor for a time of transition when we are faced with the doorway that opens to life or death, and the choice of which door will open has been made in whatever period of time God has given us up to that point? You may discover the answer to this question as you consider the numeric meaning of the word evening.

SCRIPTURAL COMMENTARY ON THE WORD EVENING

Matthew 26:64
Jesus saith unto him, Thou hast said: nevertheless I say unto you, Hereafter shall ye see the Son of man sitting on the right hand of power, and coming in the clouds of heaven.

Daniel 7:13
I saw in the night visions, and, behold, one like the Son of man came with the clouds of heaven, and came to the Ancient of days, and they brought him near before him.

John 9:4
I must work the works of him that sent me, while it is day: the night cometh, when no man can work.

Luke 14:35
Behold, your house is left unto you desolate: and verily I say unto you, Ye shall not see me, until the time come when ye shall say, Blessed is he that cometh in the name of the Lord.

ב   ר   ע

beyt   reysh   ayin

2   200   70

NUMERIC MEANINGS OF EVENING

ע 70

Punishment and restoration of Israel, universality, the seventy nations representing the nations of the world, **perfect spiritual order carried out with all spiritual power and significance**

ר 200

Inadequacy of the temporal, inadequate, the insufficiency of Man, insufficiency, deficient, the ineffective ransom, lacking what is necessary or required, inability to accomplish a purpose, (10x20) adequacy of the eternal, the complete sufficiency of God, redemption of body and soul, multiplied by ordinal perfection accomplished by the Son of God, sufficient to accomplish a purpose, ransom that is both efficient and sufficient to reclaim what was lost, to accomplish redemption, **insufficiency of man, sufficiency of God**

ב 2

Difference, good or evil, division, Living Word, second, second person of the Godhead, to come alongside to hinder, to come alongside for help, **God the Son**

PICTOGRAPHIC TRANSLATION OF DELUGE

Ideal

The Flood or Deluge was the first demonstration of God's wrath. Notice that this severe and deadly judgment only came after hundreds of years of warning and pleading.

The longsuffering nature of God is undeniable. The wrath of God once unleashed is unstoppable. The entire world, except for eight souls, was lost in a watery judgment.

The most often overlooked reason for the flood can be found by reading Genesis 6:1-6 with special attention to verse 4. The corruption of Man was not just limited to the wickedness of Man alone, it included the contamination of Man's DNA by fallen angels.

The Great Flood is a demonstration of God's forbearance. The contamination and corruption of His creation could have just as easily resulted in a do over, with no surviving souls.

This a good place to be reminded of the promise that God made in Genesis 3:15. If it were not for that promise it is doubtful that any of us would be here today. The pictographic translation of deluge includes the following messages to Mankind. The first message contained in the picture meaning of the letter hey is to be observant. We are commanded to look and view with understanding not only our own lives but also the condition of our world and community. Is there reason to be alarmed? Are we inviting God's judgment with our disobedience and rebellion or are we welcoming God's ways and instructions that are designed for our welfare?

The second message is contained in the letter mem. It is a two-pronged message. On the one hand we are encouraged that if we are filling our hearts with the living words of God, pictured as living water, we will be blessed.

On the other hand if we are disrespecting God and his purposes and the plans that He has designed for our benefit, then the only water we can look forward to is the tsunami flood that will sweep us away. Unrighteousness cannot abide for long in the presence of a Holy God and will eventually be swept away.

The third pictographic message is contained in the three letters beyt, vav and lamed.

This picture contains layers of revelation. The most obvious is that (beyt) Man's physical welfare is directly (vav) connected to our obedience to the shepherding (lamed) authoritative voice of God. Deny that authority, or try and live independent of that authority, and destruction will soon follow.

ל	ו	ב	מ	ה
lamed	vav	beyt	mem	hey
30	6	2	40	5

NUMERIC MEANINGS OF FLOOD

ה 5

Unmerited favor, God's goodness, Pentateuch, divine strength, the fifth, what follows creation, **grace**

מ 40

Trials, probation, chastisement but not judgment, action of grace resulting in revival, magnified renewal, an extended period of rule or dominion, (5x8) grace multiplied by renewal, **probationary period that results in renewal**

ב 2

Difference, good or evil, division, Living Word, second, second person of the Godhead, to come alongside to hinder, to come alongside for help, **God the Son**

ו 6

Enmity with God, weakness of Man, manifestation of sin, evils of Satan, falling short, preservation, imperfection, labor, sorrow, number of Man, secular completeness, the sixth, **Man's world**

ל 30

Blood of Christ, dedication, (3x10) magnified perfection of divine order marking the right moment, **blood sacrifice**

NUMERIC TRANSLATION OF DELUGE

Theological and Prophetic

God's Grace will be demonstrated after a **period of probationary testing**. **God the Son** will enter into **Man's world** and at the right moment provide an **atoning blood sacrifice.**

SUMMARY

Mankind has become so wicked and so enslaved by Satan that God destroys Mankind in a flood. But in order that His promise to redeem man through His Messiah, God graciously preserves Noah and his family. God's promise is preserved and at exactly the right time Messiah will redeem Man through His perfect blood sacrifice on the Cross of Calvary.

Genesis 6:13
And God said unto Noah, The end of all flesh is come before me; for the earth is filled with violence through them; and, behold, I will destroy them with the earth.

Hebrews 11:7
By faith Noah, being warned of God of things not seen as yet, moved with fear, prepared an ark to the saving of his house; by the which he condemned the world, and became heir of the righteousness which is by faith.

Hebrews 13:20-21
Now the God of peace, that brought again from the dead our Lord Jesus, that great shepherd of the sheep, through the blood of the everlasting covenant, make you perfect in every good work to do his will, working in you that which is wellpleasing in his sight, through Jesus Christ; to whom be glory for ever and ever. Amen

The story of David and Goliath on the Gates of Paradise, Florence Baptistery.
Gilded bronze relief by Lorenzo Ghiberti

PICTOGRAPHIC TRANSLATION OF FRUIT

Ideal

The pictorial meaning of the Hebrew word fruit would be completely lost on anyone trying to understand it outside the lens of Scripture. Fruit in the Scriptures has an allegorical and metaphorical meaning. Fruit refers to the works of a Man or women and is used as a means of identifying the true motivations of an individual. The Scriptures tell us that by their fruit you will know them.

The three pictures that are embedded in the Hebrew word fruit transport us back to the Garden of Eden, where we are told how the Serpent tempted Eve to eat the forbidden fruit. It was by this first act of disobedience that man lost his innocence and was separated from his creator.

The first letter in the Hebrew word fruit is pey and is the pictogram of an open mouth. The meaning can be to speak and to open. The speaker in view is none other that Satan. The open mouth in view is the man who has opened himself up to the words that are being spoken.

The second letter in the Hebrew word fruit is reysh. Reysh is the pictogram of a prince or a leader. The leader in view is Satan, the Prince of the power of the air. He is the one doing the speaking.

The third letter in the Hebrew word fruit is yood. Yood is the pictogram of a hand doing a mighty deed. This deed can be divine or in this case a mighty deed that accomplished a purpose, an evil purpose.

The simple picture meaning of fruit is a reminder that Man not only opened his mouth to receive the forbidden fruit, but that he opened his mind and heart to the Prince of the Power of the Air. The result was a mighty deed that brought Man into a sinful state of separation from his Creator.

י	ר	פ
yood	reysh	pey
10	200	80

NUMERIC MEANINGS OF FRUIT

פ 80

(10x8) magnified ordinal perfection resulting in eternality, **new beginning and new birth**

ר 200

Inadequacy of the temporal, inadequate, the insufficiency of Man, insufficiency, deficient, the ineffective ransom, lacking what is necessary or required, inability to accomplish a purpose, (10x20) adequacy of the eternal, the complete sufficiency of God, redemption of body and soul, multiplied by ordinal perfection accomplished by the Son of God, sufficient to accomplish a purpose, ransom that is both efficient and sufficient to reclaim what was lost, to accomplish redemption, **insufficiency of man, sufficiency of God**

י 10

Perfection of divine order, completeness of order, testimony, the law, Ten Commandments, responsibility, divinely ordered events, **ordinal perfection**

NUMERIC TRANSLATION OF FRUIT

Theological and Prophetic

The first number in the Numeric revelation contained in the Hebrew word fruit is the number 80. Eighty is a combination of two numbers that both have a clear purpose.

The number 8 is the number that means eternity and new beginnings. The number 10 is multiplied by 8 to get the product of 80. Ten is the number of ordinal perfection. What is being expressed is the certainty of eternal life in God's perfect timing and based on a sequence of events that He alone sovereignly ordains.

The second number is the number 200. Two hundred is the number of Man's insufficiency in contrast to the all sufficiency of God.

The final number is the number 10. As stated earlier, 10 is the number of ordinal perfection.

The summary is clear. God will accomplish something Man cannot accomplish on his own. This event will take place in order that Man might live eternally with his Creator.

This event will take place at exactly the right time. What is in view? There is no question that the mighty deed done by Satan to undo Man and put him into a state or mortal dread and death will be undone by the mightier work of the Savior, who will accomplish what Man cannot accomplish.

By the mighty work done on the Cross of Calvary, God has secured salvation, deliverance and eternal life for all those who put their faith and trust in the Messiah.

PICTOGRAPHIC TRANSLATION OF GENTILE
Ideal
The pictogram of the Gentiles is indeed glorious.

The promise that the pagan nations that will be ***lifted up*** and ***added and secured*** to the ***mighty work*** of salvation that provides streams of ***living water.***

Colossians 1:27
To whom God would make known what is the riches of the glory of this mystery among the Gentiles; which is Christ in you, the hope of glory:

Ephesians 3:6
That the Gentiles should be fellowheirs, and of the same body, and partakers of his promise in Christ by the gospel:

Romans 3:29
Is he the God of the Jews only? is he not also of the Gentiles? Yes, of the Gentiles also:

Acts 28:28
Be it known therefore unto you, that the salvation of God is sent unto the Gentiles, and that they will hear it.

Gentile – goy

מ	י	ו	ג
mem	yood	vav	gimel
40	10	6	3

NUMERIC MEANINGS OF GENTILE

ג 3

Divine perfection, completeness, three attributes of God: omniscience - omnipresence - omnipotence, solid, substantial, the entirety, third commandment, lifting up the name of God, **God the Holy Spirit**

ו 6

Enmity with God, weakness of Man, manifestation of sin, evils of Satan, falling short, preservation, imperfection, labor, sorrow, number of Man, secular completeness, the sixth, **Man's world**

י 10

Perfection of divine order, completeness of order, testimony, the law, Ten Commandments, responsibility, divinely ordered events, **ordinal perfection**

מ 40

Trials, probation, chastisement but not judgment, action of grace resulting in revival, magnified renewal, an extended period of rule or dominion, (5x8) grace multiplied by renewal, **probationary period that results in renewal**

NUMERIC TRANSLATION OF GENTILE

Theological and Prophetic

God the Holy Spirit is going to do a work of regeneration at precisely the right time after a **divinely ordained sequence of events**. The Gentile world of **Man** is going to emerge from a **period of probation that will begin with separation from God and chastisement, but will end in a period of grace and revival and renewal.**

Today we call this the Age of Grace or the Church Age and it has lasted almost 2,000 years.

Acts 13:47

For so hath the Lord commanded us, saying, I have set thee to be a light of the Gentiles, that thou shouldest be for salvation unto the ends of the earth.

American folk painter Edward Hicks painted The Peaceable Kingdom in 1826. He took his theme from Isaiah 11:6-8, which tells of the
world's animals gathering in harmony.

PICTOGRAPHIC TRANSLATION OF GRACE

Ideal

God produces *life* in us and then puts a *fence or wall of protection* around that life so that is may not be destroyed or removed.

NUMERIC TRANSLATION OF GRACE

Theological and Prophetic

The *new birth* that God graciously initiates in every believer *delivers us* from the bondage of sin and by God's Holy Spirit produces eternal life.

Ephesians 2:8-9

For by grace are ye saved through faith; and that not of yourselves: it is the gift of God: Not of works, lest any man should boast.

Happy – ashri

yood	reysh	sheen	aleph
10	200	300	1

Letters are right to left, original Hebrew

CONVENTIONAL USAGE OF **HAPPY**

The English KJV translation of the word that literally means happy is an unfortunate translation.

The KJV has translated the Hebrew word that literally means happy as *blessed*. Although the meanings for happy and blessed are very similar, the literal translation of happy is much more instructive and precise in revealing what the Scriptures had in mind. So why did the Holy Spirit reveal a Hebrew word that literally means happy? The primary definition of happy is to be delighted or pleased and glad over a particular thing.

The secondary meanings of happy are in line with the word blessed. The word blessed is used all throughout the Scriptures, but it was not until I reached the Psalms that I found the Hebrew word for Blessed that is literally translated *happy* in Hebrew. When you look at those verses where happy is the literal meaning you begin to understand what the Holy Spirit meant to be revealed. Whenever the Scripture are translated into English as "Blessed by the Lord" or "Blessed be the Lord" the Hebrew word used is not the same Hebrew word used to literally mean happy. The reason for that will become clear as you understand this teaching.

USE IN SCRIPTURE

The Hebrew word for Blessed literally translated as happy – Notice what all these verses have in common:

Psalm 1:1
Blessed (Happy) is the man that walketh not in the counsel of the ungodly, nor standeth in the way of sinners, nor sitteth in the seat of the scornful.

Psalm 2:12
Kiss the Son, lest he be angry, and ye perish from the way, when his wrath is kindled but a little. Blessed (Happy) are all they that put their trust in him.

Psalm 32:1
Blessed (Happy) is he whose transgression is forgiven, whose sin is covered.

Psalm 32:2
Blessed (Happy) is the man unto whom the Lord imputeth not iniquity, and in whose spirit there is no guile.

Happy – ashri

COMMENTARY

In order to understand the meaning and force behind the word happy, all you need to do is ask yourself the following questions:

Who is happy?
Why are they happy?

The answer to these two questions clearly illustrate why the word Happy is used. Happy is he whose sins are forgiven!

yood	reysh	sheen	aleph
10	200	300	1

PICTOGRAPHIC MEANINGS OF **HAPPY**

Strong leader, strength, leading, the first, aloof or separate, gentle, the beginning, the head of the family, God the Father

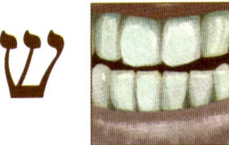

To consume, to destroy, sharp, to press, the one letter that God used to identify Himself, God's signature, letter that stands for God Almighty, teeth

A person, the head, the highest, the sum, the supreme, the first, the most important, the top, master, leader, prince, head

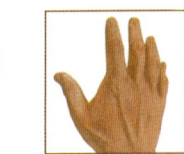

To work, a mighty deed, a deed accomplished, to make, arm and hand accomplishing a purpose, divine deed, hand

Heaven – shmim

mem	yood	mem	sheen	hey
40	10	40	300	5

Letters are right to left, original Hebrew

CONVENTIONAL USAGE OF **THE HEAVEN**

The dictionary defines Heaven as the abode of God, the angels, and the spirits of the righteous after death; the place or state of existence of the blessed after the mortal life.

The dictionary also defines heavens as the sky, firmament, or expanse of space surrounding the Earth.

FIRST USE OF HEBREW WORD **THE HEAVEN** IN SCRIPTURES

Genesis 1:1
In the beginning God created the heaven and the earth.

Heaven – shmim

מ	י	מ	ש	ה
mem	yood	mem	sheen	hey
40	10	40	300	5

PICTOGRAPHIC MEANINGS OF HEAVEN

Pay attention to what follows, to reveal, to unfold, to look upon, Holy Spirit as the revelator

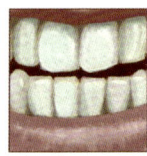

To consume, to destroy, sharp, to press, the one letter that God used to identify Himself, God's signature, letter that stands for God Almighty, teeth

Liquid, mighty waters like the ocean, massive as the waves of the sea, chaotic and destructive like a tsunami, water coming down like a stream, rain water that makes the desert bloom, the word of God that brings life, living water, waters

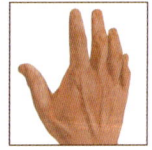

To work, a mighty deed, a deed accomplished, to make, arm and hand accomplishing a purpose, divine deed, hand

Liquid, mighty waters like the ocean, massive as the waves of the sea, chaotic and destructive like a tsunami, water coming down like a stream, rain water that makes the desert bloom, the word of God that brings life, living water, waters

PICTOGRAPHIC TRANSLATION OF HEAVEN
Ideal

The first message contained in the pictographic meaning of Heaven is provided by the letter hey which reminds up to be observant. We are commanded to look and view with understanding.

The second message is contained in the Hebrew word Heaven is the letter shin. Clearly in view is God Almighty.

The third message contained in the Hebrew word for Heaven is mem yood mem. The message is clear. Water separated by God's mighty hand from water. The water below separated from the water above.

The summary is simple:

Behold God Almighty separating the waters.

ם	י	מ	שׁ	ה
mem	yood	mem	sheen	hey
40	10	40	300	5

NUMERIC MEANINGS OF HEAVEN

ה 5

Unmerited favor, God's goodness, Pentateuch, divine strength, the fifth, what follows creation, **grace**

שׁ 300

A divinely appointed period of time, number connected to the "children of promise," election, supernatural victory over enemies including death, number connected with the death, burial and resurrection of Messiah, **signifies final blood sacrifice made by the perfect Lamb of God**

מ 40

Trials, probation, chastisement but not judgment, action of grace resulting in revival, magnified renewal, an extended period of rule or dominion, (5x8) grace multiplied by renewal, **probationary period that results in renewal**

י 10

Perfection of divine order, completeness of order, testimony, the law, Ten Commandments, responsibility, divinely ordered events, **ordinal perfection**

ם 40

Trials, probation, chastisement but not judgment, action of grace resulting in revival, magnified renewal, an extended period of rule or dominion, (5x8) grace multiplied by renewal, **probationary period that results in renewal**

NUMERIC TRANSLATION OF HOLY
Theological and Prophetic

It takes little imagination to assemble the numerical meaning of
Holy. Man is separated from God by his sin and rebellion. God's
holiness and Man's sinfulness have created a division that cannot
be cured by Man. Only God, out of an abundance of grace and
at great cost to Himself, is able to heal the breach and bring Man
back into fellowship with Himself. Those who receive the promise
of life and believe in God's Son, who came down from Heaven and
offered Himself as a perfect blood sacrifice, can receive eternal life.
All others are lost forever. And it is in this way that the holiness of
God is both comforting and terrifying.

Revelation 15:4
Who shall not fear thee, O Lord, and glorify thy name? for thou
only art holy: for all nations shall come and worship before thee;
for thy judgments are made manifest.

A golden calf, from an ancient Assyrian mozaic.

Image – tselem

mem	lamed	ayin
40	30	70

Letters are right to left, original Hebrew

CONVENTIONAL USAGE OF **IMAGE**

The first time we find the Hebrew word translated image in the English is in the first book of the Bible.

Genesis 1:27
So God created man in his own image, in the image of God created he him; male and female created he them.

It is clear that the sin of Adam and Eve resulted in the alteration and corruption of the image that God originally created in Man. It is also clear that the altered and corrupted the image of God, which was defaced when Adam and Eve believed the lies of the Serpent, continues in the DNA of Mankind to this day.

Sin plunged the entire creation into a state of brokenness and sorrow that is the state of affairs to this very day. The next reference to image in the Bible, apart from the revelation that Man was created in the image of God, is also found in Genesis.

Genesis 31:19
And Laban went to shear his sheep: and

Rachel had stolen the images that were her father's.

We can see chronicled in Scriptures the downward progression of Mankind as he first alters and defaces the image of God through the act of rebellion and disobedience, and then exacerbates the crime by worshiping other gods whose images Man replicates in wood, stone and metal carvings.

The first two commandments that were memorialized on Mt. Sinai revealed the true and living God's attitude toward images.

All these images were designed to magnify fallen angels, who are referred to in Scripture as "lesser gods." All these demi-gods and lesser gods fall into one category that condemns them to failure and judgment.

They are all but mere "creatures", fallen from their original state of sinlessness by the willful act of rebellion and disobedience against the One True God. This is the repeating revelation we see all through the Scriptures. In the last days we are told that there will be a great deception that will result in mass idol worship. We read about this in the final book of the Bible.

Revelation 13:14
And deceiveth them that dwell on the earth by the means of those miracles which he had power to do in the sight of the beast; saying to them that dwell on the earth, that they should make an image to the beast, which had the wound by a sword, and did live.

The modern English dictionary defines the word image as follows:

An image is a physical likeness or representation of a person, animal, or thing, photographed, painted, sculptured, or otherwise made visible.

An image is an optical counterpart or appearance of an object, as is produced by reflection from a mirror, refraction by a lens, or the passage of luminous rays through a small aperture and their reception on a surface.

Image – tselem

mem	lamed	ayin
40	30	70

PICTOGRAPHIC MEANINGS OF IMAGE

 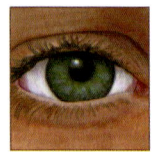

To see, to know, to experience, eye

Control, to shepherd, to have authority, to urge forward, the tongue, the voice of authority, staff

Liquid, mighty waters like the ocean, massive as the waves of the sea, chaotic and destructive like a tsunami, water coming down like a stream, rain water that makes the desert bloom, the word of God that brings life, living water, waters

Isaac – Itzchq

qoof	chet	tsade	yood
100	8	90	10

Letters are right to left, original Hebrew

CONVENTIONAL USAGE OF **ISAAC**

Isaac is the name of Abraham's son, born of his wife Sarah. Isaac was the second son of Abraham.

The first born son of Abraham was Ishmael, who was born by Hagar the Egyptian bondservant.

Abraham was 100 years old when Isaac was born and Sarah was in her 90's.

Abraham brought Isaac his beloved son to the Mount of Moriah to sacrifice him on an altar of wood as YHVH had commanded him.

This was a test from YHVH that was interrupted before Abraham sacrificed Isaac. God provided a ram whose horns were caught in the thicket as a substitute sacrifice.

This drama was a picture of the coming Messiah who will be sacrificed for the sins of the world.

Isaac was the only one of the three Patriarchs (Abraham, Isaac & Jacob) whose name was not changed. Isaac lived to be 180 years old.

The name Isaac means "laughter" or "will laugh."

FIRST USE IN SCRIPTURES

Genesis 17:19
And God said, Sarah thy wife shall bear thee a son indeed; and thou shalt call his name Isaac: and I will establish my covenant with him for an everlasting covenant, and with his seed after him.

ק	ח	צ	י
qoof	chet	tsade	yood
100	8	90	10

PICTOGRAPHIC MEANINGS OF ISAAC

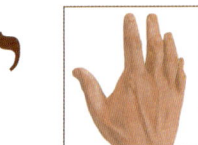

To work, a mighty deed, a deed accomplished, to make, arm
and hand accomplishing a purpose, divine deed, hand

To catch, to be caught, a harvest, to pull forward, unable to escape, trouble, to
strongly desire, just or righteous, to need, fishhook

Private, to separate, to protect, place of protection, to be cut off,
grace, favor, a place of refuge, a protected garden, quiet place,
to be silent and still in security, fence, sanctuary, inner room

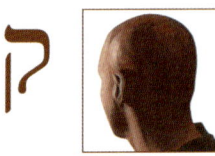

Behind, the last, the least, back of the head

PICTOGRAPHIC TRANSLATION OF ISAAC
Ideal
The Word of God translates this picture with grand precision.

Deuteronomy 7:6-8
For thou art an holy people unto the Lord thy God: the Lord thy God hath chosen thee to be a special people unto himself, above all people that are upon the face of the earth. The Lord did not set his love upon you, nor choose you, because ye were more in number than any people; **for ye were the fewest of all people**: But because the Lord loved you, and because he would keep the oath which he had sworn unto your fathers, hath the Lord brought you out with a mighty hand, and redeemed you out of the house of bondmen, from the hand of Pharaoh king of Egypt.

Matthew 20:16
So the **last shall be first**, and the first last: for many be called, but few chosen.

1 Corinthians 1:27-28
But God hath chosen the **foolish things of the world** to confound the wise; and God hath chosen the **weak things** of the world to confound the things which are mighty; And **base things** of the world, and things which are **despised**, hath God chosen, yea, and things which are not, to bring to nought things that are.

ק	ח	צ	י
qoof	chet	tsade	yood
100	8	90	10

NUMERIC MEANINGS OF ISAAC

י 10

Perfection of divine order, completeness of order, testimony, the law, Ten Commandments, responsibility, divinely ordered events, **ordinal perfection**

צ 90

Signifies the conclusion of a matter that will be followed by judgment, same meaning as the number nine magnified by the multiplier ten, **combination of ordinal perfection and judgment at the conclusion of a series**

ח 8

Eternity, new creation, first in new series, new birth, super abundance, follows seven and is the first in a new series, **new beginning**

ק 100

God's election of grace, children of the promise, **promise**

NUMERIC TRANSLATION OF JOSEPH

After a **divinely ordered sequence of events and at exactly the right time**, the Messiah will enter **Man's world** and accomplish for Man what he cannot accomplish for himself because of his sinfulness, weakness and **pride**. Messiah will secure for Man **eternal life.**

Moses, a biblical judge, destroys the Ten Commandment tablets in response

Judge – dun

noon   vav   dalet

50   6   4

Letters are right to left, original Hebrew

CONVENTIONAL USAGE OF **JUDGE**

As a noun, the word Judge is defined in the dictionary as a public officer authorized to hear and decide cases in a court of law; a magistrate charged with the administration of justice.

A Judge is a person qualified to pass a critical judgment.

The biblical use of the word Judge was used to describe the administrative head of Israel in the period between the death of Joshua and the accession to the throne by Saul.

As a verb, Judge is defined as one appointed and authorized to pass legal judgment passing a sentence on another person or a matter in dispute.

FIRST USE OF HEBREW WORD TRANSLATED **JUDGE** IN THE ENGLISH SCRIPTURES

Genesis 15:14
And also that nation, whom they shall serve, will I judge: and afterward shall they come out with great substance.

COMMENTARY

Our modern concept of a judge has been so corrupted that it is hard for us to understand the biblical meaning and the Ideal for this high office, as illustrated by the two letters that underpin the beautiful picture of *a judge*.

Judge – dun

noon   vav   dalet

50   6   4

PICTOGRAPHIC MEANINGS OF **JUDGE**

Doorway, gate, place of decision, entrance to life or death, moving into something, moving out of something, to open up, a place where change can take place

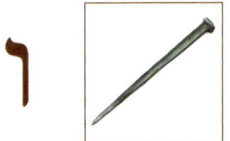

Add, to secure, to join together, to make secure, to bind together, to create a connection between two things that are separated from each other, wooden hook, wooden peg, to hold up

Activity, life, fish

NUMERIC MEANINGS OF **JUDGE**

4

God's creative works, the world, four elements, four regions of Earth, four seasons, four divisions of day, four in contrast to seven, Earth (4) vs. Heaven (7), the fourth thing, first number that can be divided, material world that had a beginning, **creation**

6

Enmity with God, weakness of Man, manifestation of sin, evils of Satan, falling short, preservation, imperfection, labor, sorrow, number of Man, secular completeness, the sixth, **Man's world**

50

Holy Spirit, Pentecost, deliverance followed by rest, grace multiplied, **jubilee**

dalet   samech   chet

4   60   8

Letters are right to left, original Hebrew

CONVENTIONAL USAGE OF **KINDNESS**

The dictionary defines kindness and the state or quality of being kind. To show favor and to behave in a way that is friendly and supportive.

FIRST USE OF HEBREW WORD **KINDNESS** IN SCRIPTURES

Genesis 20:13
And it came to pass, when God caused me to wander from my father's house, that I said unto her, This is thy kindness which thou shalt shew unto me; at every place whither we shall come, say of me, He is my brother.

COMMENTARY

The first use of the word kindness in Scriptures describes the act of concealing or covering up information in order that someone else, Abraham in this first example, is spared from death. Abraham feared that if it was known that the beautiful Sarai was actually his wife that he would be killed and she would be kidnapped. By pretending to be her brother, Abraham by his own human wisdom sought to avoid something he feared. This was the original half-truth since Sarai was actually Abrams half sister. The result of this deception, which Abraham described as a kindness, had its natural consequences. The result was at first heart breaking for Abram, but in the end it was tragic for the Pharaoh of Egypt. The natural conclusion of the matter was turned around to be a great benefit to Abram who was ultimately sent home with his un-molested wife. That would have been a great kindness by itself, but Abram also went home with great treasures from Egypt including gold, silver, cattle, camels and servants. This amazing ending to what might have been a bad situation was brought about by God's direct intervention. The Lord put fear into the heart of Pharaoh and that dramatic revelation provoked both the release of Sarah and great generosity. The motivations for these acts by the Pharaoh of Egypt emerged out of fear and self-interest, provoked out of a terror brought about by a revelation from the Lord Man's kindness is feeble and ineffective. God's kindness is always sufficient to accomplish its purpose. Abraham who sought kindness from his wife was ill conceived and actually created what would have been in the natural a personal tragedy.

God's kindness redeemed the situation and resulted in a blessing. You can read this entire amazing story in Genesis 12:10 – Genesis 13:2.

ד   ס   ח

dalet   samech   chet

4   60   8

Letters are right to left, original Hebrew

PICTOGRAPHIC MEANINGS OF KINDNESS

Private, to separate, to protect, place of protection, to be cut off, grace, favor, a place of refuge, a protected garden, quiet place, to be silent and still in security, fence, sanctuary, inner room

To support, twist slowly, to turn, to assist, prop

Doorway, gate, place of decision, entrance to life or death, moving into something, moving out of something, to open up, a place where change can take place

PICTOGRAPHIC TRANSLATION OF KINDNESS

Ideal

Kindness is pictured as entering into a doorway that leads to a sanctuary where you are held up and protected.

The ideal kindness that God puts before us by way of a picture is no mere platitude, it is love in action. Kindness is not a feeling, it is love wrapped in a deed. The kindest deed that can ever be experienced by Man is to be rescued from death and given new and bountiful life. This is the true ideal of kindness that undergirds all God's gracious dealings with Man.

David declares in the Psalms that God's loving kindness is better than (this) *life*. Jesus came to give us life eternal. The kindness of the cross is the doorway that leads to eternal life, eternal bliss and eternal joy.

Psalm 63:3

Because thy loving kindness is better than life, my lips shall praise thee.

John 6:40

And this is the will of him that sent me, that every one which seeth the Son, and believeth on him, may have everlasting life: and I will raise him up at the last day.

Kindness - checed

ד   ס   ח
dalet   samech   chet
4   60   8

Letters are right to left, original Hebrew

NUMERIC MEANINGS OF KINDNESS

ח **8**

Eternity, new creation, first in new series, new birth, super abundance, follows seven and is the first in a new series, **new beginning**

ס **60**

Pride

ד **4**

God's creative works, the world, four elements, four regions of Earth, four seasons, four divisions of day, four in contrast to seven, Earth (4) vs. Heaven (7), the fourth thing, first number that can be divided, material world that had a beginning, **creation**

Love – ahavah

hey	beyt	hey	aleph
5	2	5	1

Letters are right to left, original Hebrew

CONVENTIONAL USAGE OF **LOVE**

The Hebrew word "ahavah" translated "love" in English is used to describe intimate or romantic feelings or relationships, such as the love between a husband and wife. It also means a love that selflessly serves the other person, such as the love that a father and mother have for a child.

It is no coincidence that the first time the word love is revealed in the ancient prophetic Scriptures is when God tested Abraham. Abraham was prevented by God from sacrificing his only son. The drama was meant to be a prophetic picture of our loving Heavenly Father who would offer up His own Son as a sacrifice for our sins.

Consider the depths of our sin and despair in light of the preciousness of the price that was paid to redeem us. God the Father *loves* each one of us and has gone to extraordinary lengths to deliver us from the curse of sin and death. Think about it!

The KJV says that "God did tempt Abraham." This is an unfortunate and completely wrong translation of the original Hebrew. The Hebrew word translated "tempt" literally means to *probe* or to *test*. God tempts no man.

James 1:13
Let no man say when he is tempted, I am tempted of God: for God cannot be tempted with evil, neither tempteth he any man:

FIRST USE OF **LOVE** IN SCRIPTURES

Genesis 22:1-2
And it came to pass after these things, that God did tempt Abraham, and said unto him, Abraham: and he said, Behold, here I am. And he said, Take now thy son, thine only son Isaac, whom thou lovest, and get thee into the land of Moriah; and offer him there for a burnt offering upon one of the mountains which I will tell thee of.

ה   ב   ה   א
hey   beyt   hey   aleph
5   2   5   1

PICTOGRAPHIC MEANINGS OF LOVE

Strong leader, strength, leading, the first, aloof or separate, gentle, the beginning, the head of the family, God the Father

Pay attention to what follows, to reveal, to unfold, to look upon, Holy Spirit as the revelator

House, tent, son, family, dwelling place, the physical tent/body, inside, within, first letter in the Torah that identifies the Son of God

Pay attention to what follows, to reveal, to unfold, to look upon, Holy Spirit as the revelator

PICTOGRAPHIC TRANSLATION OF LOVE
Ideal

There are two ways of interpreting the revelation in the picture God has given us of love.

The first translation is that **God the Father reveals** Himself to the **Son**.

John 5:19

Then answered Jesus and said unto them, Verily, verily, I say unto you, The Son can do nothing of himself, but what he seeth the Father do: for what things soever he doeth, these also doeth the Son likewise.

The second translation is that **God the Father reveals** Himself **to us** through **His Only Begotten Son.**

John 1:18

No man hath seen God at any time, the only begotten Son, which is in the bosom of the Father, he hath declared him.

John 5:20

I can of mine own self do nothing: as I hear, I judge: and my judgment is just; because I seek not mine own will, but the will of the Father which hath sent me.

Love – ahavah

הבהא

hey   beyt   hey   aleph
5   2   5   1

NUMERIC MEANINGS OF LOVE

 א **1**

Deity, unity, sufficiency, independence, first, indivisible, **God the Father**

 ה **5**

Unmerited favor, God's goodness, Pentateuch, divine strength, the fifth, what follows creation, **grace**

 ב **2**

Difference, good or evil, division, Living Word, second, second person of the Godhead, to come alongside to hinder, to come alongside for help, **God the Son**

ה **5**

Unmerited favor, God's goodness, Pentateuch, divine strength, the fifth, what follows creation, **grace**

Obey – shmo

ayin	mem	sheen
70	40	300

Listen, you!

Letters are right to left, original Hebrew

CONVENTIONAL USAGE OF **OBEY**

The dictionary definition of obey is to comply with or follow the commands, restrictions, wishes, or instructions.

FIRST USE OF HEBREW WORD **OBEY** IN SCRIPTURES

Genesis 27:8
Now therefore, my son, obey my voice as I command you.

Obey – shmo

ע   מ   ש
ayin   mem   sheen
70   40   300

 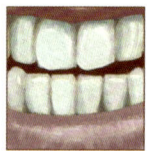

To consume, to destroy, sharp, to press, the one letter that God used to identify Himself, God's signature, letter that stands for God Almighty, teeth

Liquid, mighty waters like the ocean, massive as the waves of the sea, chaotic and destructive like a tsunami, water coming down like a stream, rain water that makes the desert bloom, the word of God that brings life, living water, waters

 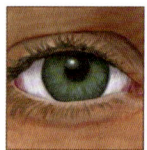

To see, to know, to experience, eye

ש 300

A divinely appointed period of time, number connected to the "children of promise," election, supernatural victory over enemies including death, number connected with the death, burial and resurrection of Messiah, **signifies final blood sacrifice made by the perfect Lamb of God**

מ 40

Trials, probation, chastisement but not judgment, action of grace resulting in revival, magnified renewal, an extended period of rule or dominion, (5x8) grace multiplied by renewal, **probationary period that results in renewal**

ע 70

Punishment and restoration of Israel, universality, the seventy nations representing the nations of the world, **perfect spiritual order carried out with all spiritual power and significance**

PICTOGRAPHIC TRANSLATION OF OBEY
Ideal

The ideal translation of obey based on the meaning of the three pictures that are embedded in the Hebrew word are stunningly simple. To obey is to know and experience the life giving word of God. That may sound strange but it actually conforms to the conventional and literal meaning of the word translated into English as obey. The literal Hebrew meaning is: *listen you.*

NUMERIC TRANSLATION OF OBEY
Theological and Prophetic

The numeric meaning of the Hebrew word obey is absolutely amazing. Do you see it? Let me help make it clear. This is not about human obedience, it is about the Son of God *listening* to the Father and carrying out His wishes here on Earth at exactly the right moment in order to bring about redemption and renewal to Mankind. This is about the Cross of Calvary and the Blood Sacrifice of the Lamb of God. This is indeed *amazing.*

Matthew 26:39
And he went a little further, and fell on his face, and prayed, saying, O my Father, if it be possible, let this cup pass from me: nevertheless not as I will, but as thou wilt.

John 5:30
I can of mine own self do nothing: as I hear, I judge: and my judgment is just; because I seek not mine own will, but the will of the Father which hath sent me.

Aren't you glad the Son of God listened to the Father? Your salvation is only possible because the Son listened and obeyed. Why? Because He loved the Father, and He loved us!

How do you love God back?

Jesus told us how. The same way He did. We first *listen* and then we respond to the *words* we hear with obedience. So, *listen up!*

Scepter (sceptre) – shbt

tet	beyt	sheen
9	2	300

Letters are right to left, original Hebrew

CONVENTIONAL USAGE OF **SCEPTER**

According to the dictionary, the word scepter used as a noun or a verb conveys the same meaning. It is a rod or wand held in the hand as an emblem of regal authority. To give a scepter is to invest the recipient with imperial power and authority. The scepter is a symbol of sovereignty.

Scepter is a good translation of the Hebrew word shbt, but the orgin of the term comes from Middle English (ceptre). The Hebrew picture of a scepter would be closer to the picture of a rod or a staff.

FIRST USE OF HEBREW WORD TRANSLATED **SCEPTER** IN THE ENGLISH SCRIPTURES

Genesis 49:10
The sceptre shall not depart from Judah, nor a lawgiver from between his feet, until Shiloh come; and unto him shall the gathering of the people be.

Now let's look at the pictographic and numeric meaning of the Hebrew word scepter in order to collect clues about how this word fits into the story of Jesus.

ט	ב	ש
tet	beyt	sheen
9	2	300

PICTOGRAPHIC MEANINGS IN SCEPTER

 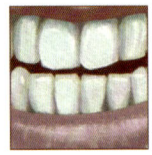

To consume, to destroy, sharp, to press, the one letter that God used to identify Himself, God's signature, letter that stands for God Almighty, teeth

House, tent, son, family, dwelling place, the physical tent/body, inside, within, first letter in the Torah that identifies the Son of God

To surround, twist, entwine, encircle, ensnare, entrap, to spin, rolled together, snake

NUMERIC MEANINGS IN SCEPTER

 300

A divinely appointed period of time, number connected to the "children of promise," election, supernatural victory over enemies including death, number connected with the death, burial and resurrection of Messiah, **signifies final blood sacrifice made by the perfect Lamb of God**

 2

Difference, good or evil, division, Living Word, second, second person of the Godhead, to come alongside to hinder, to come alongside for help, **God the Son**

ט **9**

Wrath, ensnared, entrapped, judgment of Man, (3x3) divine perfection magnified, fruits of the spirit, divine completeness, conclusion of a matter, last of the digits, **summation of Man's works**

PICTOGRAPHIC TRANSLATION OF SCEPTER
Ideal
To *destroy* the *dwelling place* of the *serpent*.

Notice that the pictographic translation gives us the *ideal*. The scepter is ideally the authoritative instrument that represents the destruction of everything that has is origin in sin and rebellion. In short, the works of Satan the Serpent manifest in the world and in the hearts of fallen Man. The scepter is ultimately a sign of the warfare that exists between God and Satan, between good and evil.

NUMERIC TRANSLATION OF SCEPTER
Theological and Prophetic
At the *appointed time* the *Messiah* will *judge* his creation including Man.

Notice that the numeric translation gives us the *theological*. It is the Messiah who will come and destroy the works of the Serpent. It is the Messiah who makes atonement for the sins of fallen Man and promises to be the King of Righteousness throughout all eternity. Until that day comes the war between good and evil rages on. The holy Messianic scepter is a divine symbol of hope for all who put their faith and trust in the Messiah – Yeshua Ha Mashiach – Jesus the Christ! It is also a terrible warning to those who refuse to receive the freely offered and precious gift of God.

The summary translation of both the pictographic and the numeric meaning of Scepter clearly elevate the term into the realm of the Messianic hope.

NUMERIC TRANSLATION OF SHALOM
Theological and Prophetic

God is going to do a work that is literally energized by His Grace and manifest itself as a victory over death. It is connected with the death, burial and resurrection of Messiah.

ל

This work is going to involve the sacrifice of the Perfect Lamb of God. This event will happen at exactly the right moment in time.

ו

This event is going to be displayed so that those that look upon it will recognize it as a Divinely Prophetic event by viewing the sign of the Wooden Peg and the Iron Nail.

Man has been tested and found to be in an utterly hopeless state of rebellion, apostasy and corruption. He has been tested and found incapable of redeeming himself, let alone the world he inhabits. Ultimately this probationary period of testing will last for a short season, in which the wicked will be destroyed and the covenant people of God will be chastened and revived. This revival and renewal will culminate in a new beginning and a resurrection that will be based on the substitutionary atonement of the Messiah, who was also tested and found to be perfect.

The works of The Prince of Chaos are going to be destroyed by the True Prince of Peace!

John 14:27
Peace I leave with you, my peace I give unto you: not as the world giveth, give I unto you. Let not your heart be troubled, neither let it be afraid.

Pieter Bruegel the Elder depicted the land of Shinar in this 1563 oil on panel painting of the construction of the Tower of Babel. The person receiving bows in the foreground left is likely Nimrod, who was said to have ordered the tower to be built.

Shinar – shnor

reysh	ayin	noon	sheen
200	70	50	300

Letters are right to left, original Hebrew

CONVENTIONAL USAGE OF **SHINAR**

Babyononish! Nimrod's kingdom is said to have been "Babel [Babylon] in the land of Shinar." Genesis 11:2 states that Shinar enclosed the plain that became the site of the Tower of Babel.

FIRST USE OF **SHINAR** IN SCRIPTURES

Genesis 10:10
And the beginning of his kingdom was Babel,
and Erech, and Accad, and Calneh, in the land of Shinar.

COMMENTARY

While the name of Shinar is to be understood as Babylonian, it is emblematic of an older power than the world-empire of Babylon. "In the land of Shinar" was that first attempt to unify a world-empire against God.

Shinar is a picture of the anti-Christian world, employing witchcraft, sorcery, violence, and falsehood war against God the Father, God the Son and the Holy Spirit.

Shinar is both a geographical place and a byword for the kingdom of the "god and prince of this world" who, by deception and imitation, seeks to deceive men and overthrow the Kingdom of God. Shinar reminds us that there is a war against the Kingdom of God by a usurper who goes by the name of Lucifer – aka the Devil and Satan.

Shinar – shnor

reysh	ayin	noon	sheen
200	70	50	300

PICTOGRAPHIC MEANINGS OF SHINAR

 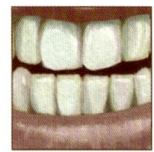

To consume, to destroy, sharp, to press, the one letter that God used to identify Himself, God's signature, letter that stands for God Almighty, teeth

Activity, life, fish

 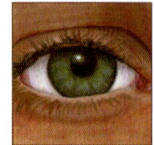

To see, to know, to experience, eye

A person, the head, the highest, the sum, the supreme, the first, the most important, the top, master, leader, prince, head

YHVH - Lord

hey	vav	hey	yood
5	6	5	10

Letters are right to left, original Hebrew

CONVENTIONAL USAGE OF **YHVH**

YHVH is the Sacred Name of God that is revealed more than 6,000 times in the Old Testament. Almost all English versions of the Scripture have replaced the Sacred Name YHVH with the title (not a name) *LORD.*

The commonly held view of what the name YHVH is a name that may have been derived from a verb that means to "be," "exist," "become," or "come to pass."

FIRST USE OF THE SACRED NAME
YHVH IN SCRIPTURE

Genesis 2:4
These are the generations of the heavens and of the earth when they were created, in the day that the YHVH God made the earth and the heavens.

(KJV with title LORD replaced by the Sacred Name of God)

הey	וav	הey	יood
ה	ו	ה	י
hey	vav	hey	yood
5	6	5	10

PICTOGRAPHIC MEANINGS OF YHVH

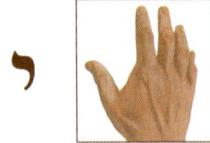

To work, a mighty deed, a deed accomplished, to make, arm and hand accomplishing a purpose, divine deed, hand

Pay attention to what follows, to reveal, to unfold, to look upon, Holy Spirit as the revelator

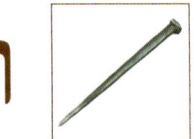

Add, to secure, to join together, to make secure, to bind together, to create a connection between two things that are separated from each other, wooden hook, wooden peg, to hold up

Pay attention to what follows, to reveal, to unfold, to look upon, Holy Spirit as the revelator

NUMERIC MEANINGS OF YHVH

י 10

Perfection of divine order, completeness of order, testimony, the law, Ten Commandments, responsibility, divinely ordered events, **ordinal perfection**

ה 5

Unmerited favor, God's goodness, Pentateuch, divine strength, the fifth, what follows creation, **grace**

ו 6

Enmity with God, weakness of Man, manifestation of sin, evils of Satan, falling short, preservation, imperfection, labor, sorrow, number of Man, secular completeness, the sixth, **Man's world**

ה 5

Unmerited favor, God's goodness, Pentateuch, divine strength, the fifth, what follows creation, **grace**

PICTOGRAPHIC TRANSLATION OF YHVH
Ideal

Behold the **Hand!**
Behold the **Nail!**

NUMERIC TRANSLATION OF YHVH
Theological and Prophetic

At a Divinely Appointed **time**
God will show **favor**
to the world of fallen and helpless **Mankind**,
and it will be a divine manifestation of **grace!**

COMMENTARY

—

Prior to the sacrificial death of the Messiah (Ha-Mashiach –The Christ), this is the mystery message that sounded forth with each utterance and each textual reference to YHVH! The pictures and the numbers announced the coming Redeemer.

SUMMARY
YHVH

Behold the mystery of the hand and the nail!

Psalms 113:3
From the rising of the sun unto the going down of the same the name YHVH is to be praised.

(KJV with title LORD replaced by the Sacred Name of God)

About the Author

OTHER BOOKS BY C.J. LOVIK

The Living Word in 3D, Vol. 1:
The Mystery of the Aleph and
the Tav

·

The Living Word in 3D, Vol. 2:
The Mysteries of Adam to Noah

·

Rest: Your Heavenly Reward

CHILDREN'S SERIES

Theodore Bump: What's in Your
trunk?

·

Theodore Bump: You're Late for
Church!

C. J. Lovik graduated from Westmont College California with a degree in Education and Communication and taught elementary school in Southern California.

After teaching and writing children's books for many years, he started a manufacturing business and developed an online family-friendly Internet search engine. In 2015, C.J. launched Rock Island Books, which supplies Christian resources for adults and children.

Volume One of *The Living Word in 3D Series* was published in 2014. Volume Two of *The Living Word in 3D Series* was published in 2016. The first reprinted and newly illustrated version of his *Theodore Bump* children's book series from the 1980s was published in 2015. The first in a series of meditations, *Rest,* was also published in 2015.

An edited and updated version of John Bunyan's classic, The Pilgrim's Progress: From This World to That Which Is to Come, published in 2009, was C.J.'s first book for adults.

In 2004, C.J. produced an eight-part website, *The Story of Jesus,* that combines the four biographies written by Matthew, Mark, Luke and John into a single story line. The site has been viewed by untold millions, many of whom were encountering the story of Jesus for the first time. The Story of Jesus is also available as a full-color hardcover book on www.rockislandbooks.com.

A SPORTING CHANCE

You don't have to wait for London's big events to enjoy your favourite sport.

The **Wimbledon Lawn Tennis Museum** shows the history of lawn tennis with fashions, trophies and other memorabilia. A trip to the museum includes a view of the famous Centre Court. As you might expect, the museum is not open during the big event.

Rugby fans, young and old, will enjoy the **Museum of Rugby** and **Twickenham Stadium Tours**. This multi-media museum brings the history and game of rugby alive.

Visit the home ground of 2000's FA Cup winners, **Chelsea Football Club**. Call in advance to arrange a behind-the-scenes tour of Stamford Bridge.

Cricket fans can take in a tour of the **Lord's** ground, including the Long Room, MCC Museum, the Ashes Urn and the NatWest Media Centre.

...take the millennium trail along the South Bank...

OUTDOOR LONDON

One of the best ways to enjoy London is on foot and there are any number of walking trails to help you make the most of the city. On the South Bank you can take either the **Millennium Mile** or the **Jubilee Walkway**, which takes in the City and West End as well.

London offers more than 1,800 open spaces, a vast range of leafy venues to enjoy a picnic or a quiet stroll away from the city. **St James's Park**, **Hyde Park** and **Kensington Gardens** are some of the big central parks. Further out of the centre is **Richmond Park** where, with deer roaming wild, you can forget that you are in one of the world's biggest cities.

top Jubilee Walkway
bottom above Wimbledon Lawn Tennis Museum
below Richmond Park

For more information about London's attractions and events call **09068 66 33 44** (calls are charged at 60p per minute) or visit **www.LondonTown.com.**

Eltham Palace
& Gardens

more
style

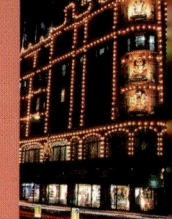

London is one of the world's great shopping destinations. Whatever your budget, whatever your style, whatever you're looking for – you'll find it here.

shopping heaven

OXFORD STREET

Oxford Circus, Marble Arch, Bond Street

This is the place for value and diversity – high street fashion stores and chain stores such as **Marks & Spencer**, line the street, along with shoe shops and record stores such as **HMV**. It's a mecca for department store shoppers with **Selfridges**, **Debenhams** and **John Lewis** all situated on Oxford Street.

REGENT STREET AND BOND STREET

Oxford Circus, Piccadilly Circus, Bond Street

Regent Street is well known for high quality British labels including **Jaeger**, **Austin Reed**, **Burberry** and **Aquascutum**. Elegant buildings are a feature, particularly the mock Tudor lines of **Liberty**, a department store famed for its fine fabrics. Kids and the young at heart must visit **Hamleys**, one of the world's finest toy stores.

At the bottom of Regent Street, on Piccadilly Circus, is **Lillywhites**, a one-stop shop for sporting goods. **Carnaby Street**, just off Regent Street, is just as funky now as in its 60s heyday. Here you'll find cutting edge fashion from shops such as **Sun Sun**, as well as jewellery and record stores.

Nearby Bond Street is divided into 'Old' and 'New' and both streets are the place for designer labels and luxury goods. **Prada**, **Gucci**, **Donna Karan** and **Versace** are just some of the names to be found in the area. If fine jewellery is on your shopping list, **Tiffany & Co**. and **Asprey & Garrard** can be found on Old Bond Street.

KNIGHTSBRIDGE

Knightsbridge

Many of the high street fashion stores can be found here but the area is best known for department store, **Harrods**. This London icon has 300 departments and three royal warrants, with merchandise ranging from domestic pets to fine fragrances. Nearby **Scotch House** is the place to purchase the best selection of high quality Scottish merchandise. The collection includes cashmere and lambswool knitwear, rugs, throws and shawls as well as tartan clothing and accessories.

FOR MORE INFORMATION

Call London Tourist Board's Visitorcall shopping line on **09068 505 478** (calls charged at 60p per minute at all times, as at September 2000, plus any hotel/payphone surcharge)
or visit **www.Shop-London.net.**
For a full list of London's shops, buy the *Time Out Shopping and Services Guide*, available at bookshops.

this page top Harrods at Christmas
opposite page bottom Columbia Road Flower Market

...a mecca for department store shoppers...

KING'S ROAD

◉ Sloane Square

Situated in the heart of Chelsea, King's Road is an intriguing blend of high street chain stores, antiques and cutting edge fashion. This is a great place to purchase something old, with **Antiquarius** providing an 'Aladdin's Cave' experience. Contemporary homeware can be found at the **Conran Shop** and fine furniture at **David Linley** in nearby Pimlico.

COVENT GARDEN

◉ Covent Garden/Leicester Square

This used to be a busy fruit and flower market and it still retains that feel today, with street performers and buskers entertaining shoppers as they browse the wide variety of shops and enjoy coffee at any number of cafés in the area.

Urban wear shops and craft markets are to be found alongside designer labels – **Paul Smith**, **Agnés B** and **Nicole Farhi**, to name a few.

MARKETS GALORE

One of London's greatest features is its unique and diverse markets. Make sure you visit at least one of the following.

Columbia Road – the place to buy flowers but on Sunday only. The sea of colour makes a great photo.

Spitalfields – arts, crafts and food. Open daily but best on a Sunday.

Camden Markets – Possibly the busiest markets in London, offering everything from fashion and food to arts and ethnic jewellery. Open daily and busiest at the weekends.

Portobello Road – more than 2,000 stalls selling antiques and bric-à-brac. Open daily, except Sunday.

Greenwich Market – a lively market packed with arts and crafts. Open Friday to Sunday.

OPENING HOURS

Most West End shops open from 0930 and close at 1800 from Monday to Saturday. Shops rarely close at lunchtime. Late night opening varies. In Oxford Street and Regent Street it's Thursday, in Knightsbridge it's Wednesday. Many shops open on Sunday, usually for five to six hours from 1100 or 1200.

In the lead up to Christmas, major stores usually extend their shopping hours. And many stores extend hours at the start of the sales in January and June/July.

London
entertains

When the evening arrives there is nowhere like London for being entertained...

THEATRE FOR EVERYONE

World class theatre is one of London's greatest trademarks. There are more than 50 theatres in the West End alone and more than 100 across the city in total. At any time of the year you can choose from blockbuster musicals, comedy, cabaret, fringe theatre and classic productions in the finest British tradition. You'll find some of the greatest names in film and theatre treading the boards in London. Appearances over the last few years include Kathleen Turner in *The Graduate*, Cate Blanchett in *Plenty*, Nicole Kidman in *The Blue Room* and Kevin Spacey in *The Iceman Cometh*.

There are usually matinees on Wednesdays and Saturdays and some theatres have shows on Sundays.

For an interesting look at the history of British theatre, visit the Theatre Museum in Covent Garden.

There are more than 50 theatres in the West End alone

To find out more about what's on at London's theatres, pick up a copy of the free *Official London Theatre Guide* in arts venues, see the *Evening Standard* newspaper, or visit **www.OfficialLondonTheatre.co.uk.**

SHOREDITCH

FINSBURY

BLOOMSBURY

CITY

STRAND

RIVER THAMES

SOUTHWARK

WESTMINSTER

St James's Park

LAMBETH

PLICO

R THAMES

WANDSWORTH

Theatre and Cinema

NEW OXFORD STREET

HIGH HOLBORN

CHARING CROSS ROAD

SHAFTESBURY

STRAND

TRAFALGAR SQ.

NORTHUMBERLAND AVE.

WHITEHALL

GLOBALVISION

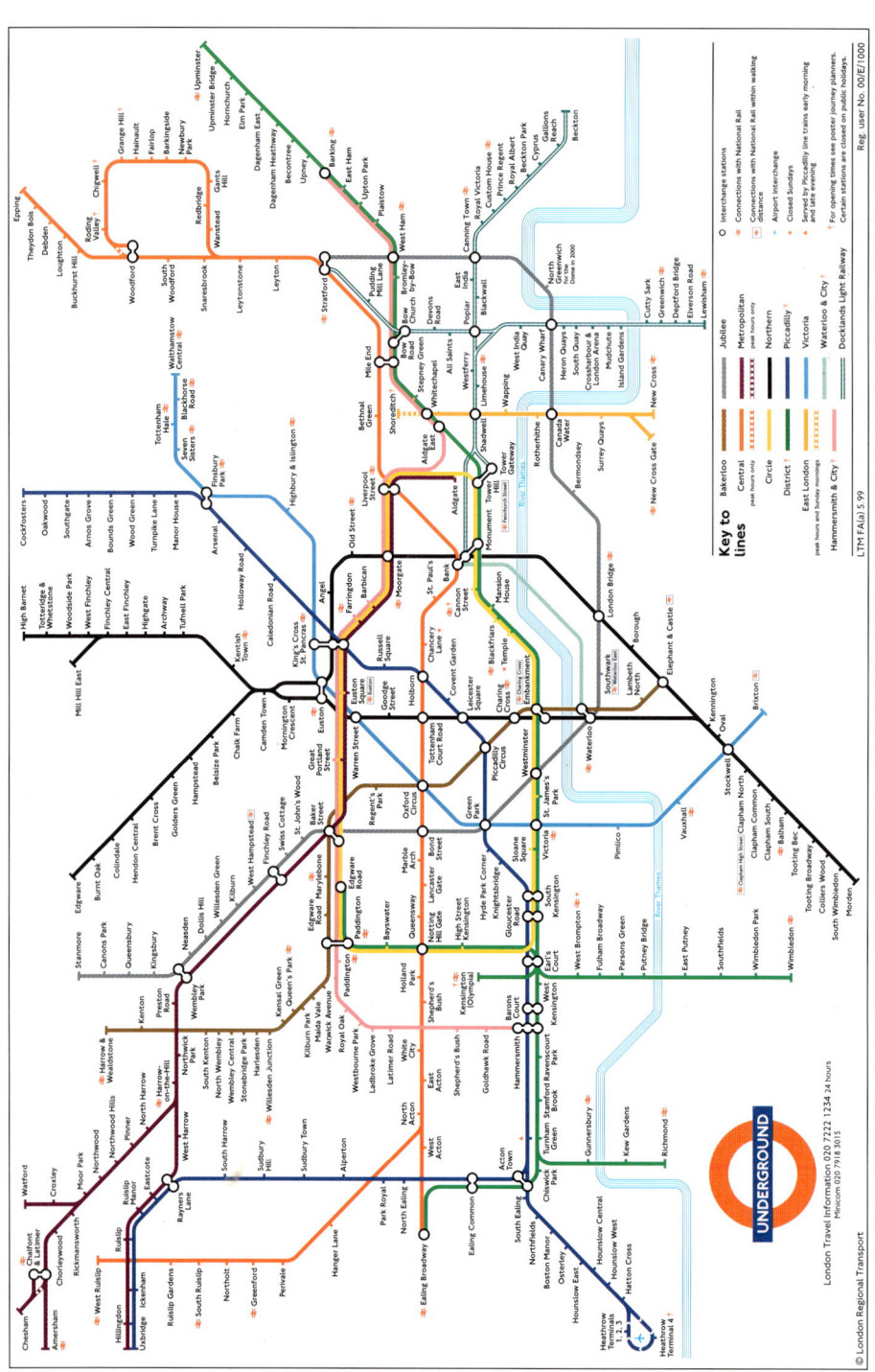

Good Value Accommodation
in Central London

Central Reservations Telephone (020) 7402 0202

Abbey Court and Westpoint Hotel

- ✓ Pleasant central location
- ✓ Convenient location 2 minutes from Paddington Station & Heathrow Express, & 4 minutes from Airbus
- ✓ Easy access to all London's important tourist sights, shopping districts, theatres, Oxford Street and Piccadilly Circus
- ✓ En-Suite shower & w.c. in all rooms
- ✓ Lift to all floors
- ✓ Each room with colour T.V., radio & telephone
- ✓ Car parking by arrangement

Abbey Court and Westpoint Hotel
170-174 Sussex Gardens
Hyde Park London W2 1TP
Tel **(020) 7402 0704**
Fax **(020) 7262 2055**
www.westpointhotel.com
e-mail info@westpointhotel.com
Tel **(020) 7402 0281**
Fax **(020) 7224 9114**
www.abbeycourt.com
e-mail info@abbeycourt.com

RATES	LOW SEASON	HIGH SEASON
Singles	from £48.00	from £56.00
Doubles *pp*	from £32.00	from £37.00
Triples *pp*	from £26.00	from £28.00
Family Room *pp*	from £22.00	from £24.00

Sass House Hotel

Central London hotel located within two minutes walk from Hyde Park. Most rooms with private showers/toilets. All rooms have colour TV and radio. Easy access to all tourist attractions – within 5 minutes walking distance of Lancaster Gate and Paddington underground/mainline stations and Heathrow Express.

RATES	LOW SEASON	HIGH SEASON
Twin *pp*	from £26.00	from £29.00
Doubles *pp*	from £24.50	from £28.00
Triples *pp*	from £22.00	from £24.00
Family Room *pp*	from £19.50	from £21.50

Sass House Hotel
11 Craven Terrace,
Hyde Park, London W2 3QT
Tel **(020) 7262 2325**
Fax **(020) 7262 0889**
www.sasshotel.com
e-mail info@sasshotel.com

choosing and booking accommodation

USING THIS GUIDE

London's hotels span all price bands and range from the luxurious properties of international hotel chains to small private hotels and guest houses.

Check the **number of rooms** given for each hotel in this guide as an indication of its size and use the symbols (see explanation on page 30) to see what facilities it offers.

Serviced and **self-catering apartments** are also available throughout London at price levels from budget to luxury, and a wide selection is listed in this guide.

Staying with a family is an increasingly popular option for visitors wanting to experience the real London lifestyle, so you will find information on agencies that organise this kind of accommodation on page 94.

If you are travelling on a **tight budget**, it is useful to know that London's universities and colleges make their halls of residence available to visitors of all ages throughout the vacation period (roughly July-September). See the Group and Youth section for details, page 97.

Accommodation in **central London** is listed in this guide by postal area (WC2, SW1, etc), as shown on the map on page 28.

Remember, too, that London's excellent public transport system gives easy access to **accommodation outside the central area**, which can be less expensive and more relaxing than a city centre hotel. Suburban commercial centres such as Croydon, Greenwich, Bromley, Richmond, Kingston and Harrow provide a choice of accommodation for visitors who wish to explore central London, as well as those doing business with local companies in those areas. They are particularly suitable if you are arriving by car.

OFFICIAL CLASSIFICATIONS

Serviced Accommodation

All establishments displaying a rating have been visited by a Quality Assurance assessor, ensuring that they meet or exceed **minimum standards**. Visits are made annually and are designed to monitor and maintain accommodation standards. Look out for establishments with ratings – they are your sign of quality assurance, giving you the confidence to book the accommodation that's right for you.

The English Tourism Council, the AA and the RAC have developed a new system for rating serviced accommodation based on the quality and the range of services. There are two categories – Hotels, including townhouses, and Guest Accommodation, which includes guesthouses, bed and breakfasts, inns and farmhouses.

★ Hotels are rated from one to five *Stars* – the more Stars, the higher the quality and greater the provision of facilities and services.

◆ The rating system for Guest Accommodation emphasises quality, to reflect the unique character of guesthouses, bed and breakfasts, inns and farmhouses. Areas such as cleanliness, service and hospitality, bedrooms, bathrooms and food are assessed for quality and combine to give a rating from one to five *Diamonds*.

Travel Accommodation establishments are also visited by Quality Assurance assessors to ensure that they meet or exceed Minimum Standards. Establishments which participate in the rating system are awarded the designator of *Travel Accommodation*.

Gold and Silver Awards

The English Tourism Council's *Gold* and *Silver Awards* are **special accolades** for Hotels and Guest Accommodation.

Gold and Silver Awards for Hotels are awarded to properties achieving the highest levels of quality within their Star rating. While the ratings are based on a combination of quality, range of facilities and level of services offered, the Gold and Silver Awards for Hotels are based solely on the quality aspect.

Gold and Silver Awards for Guest Accommodation are awarded to properties which not only achieve the overall quality required for their Diamond rating but also reach the highest levels of quality in those specific areas which guests tell us are really important to them. The awards reflect the quality of comfort provided in the bedrooms and bathrooms and the quality of service throughout a guest's stay.

Self-catering Accommodation

In autumn 2000 a new rating scheme for Self-catering Accommodation was launched. The new Star Ratings reflect the quality of the accommodation. All properties have to meet a list of minimum requirements to take part in the scheme. The more stars, the higher the overall level of quality. Establishments at higher rating levels also have to meet some additional requirements for facilities.

★ Acceptable overall level of quality. Adequate provision of furniture, furnishings and fittings.

★★ As for ★ plus: Improved overall level of quality. All units self-contained – two bathrooms where there are eight guests or more.

★★ As for ★★ plus: Good overall level of
★ quality. Good standard of maintenance and decoration. Ample space and good quality furniture. All double beds with access from both sides. Microwave.

★★ As for ★★★ plus: Very good overall level
★★ of quality. Very good care and attention to detail will be obvious throughout. Either access to washing machine and dryer, if not provided in the unit, or a 24 hour laundry service.

★★ As for ★★★★ plus: Excellent overall level
★★ of quality. High levels of décor, fixtures and
★ fittings, together with excellent standards of management efficiency and guest services. Excellent range of accessories and personal touches. Video player, telephone. Fully controllable heating.

DISABLED VISITORS

Schemes to check **accessibility** have been developed throughout the UK as part of the nationwide Tourism for All campaign in conjunction with the Hotel and Holiday Consortium, and are designed to provide disabled travellers with reliable information on standards and facilities.

The criteria used by inspecting agencies are standard. All properties denoted as being accessible for disabled visitors in this publication have been inspected by London Tourist Board.

There are three categories of accessibility:

 Category 1 Accessible to a wheelchair user travelling independently

 Category 2 Accessible to a wheelchair user travelling with assistance

 Category 3 Accessible to someone with limited mobility, able to walk a few paces and up a maximum of three steps.

The Holiday Care Service can provide information on other accommodation that has been inspected using the same criteria of accessibility as the accessible accommodation contained within this guide. They can be contacted at:
Holiday Care Service, Second Floor, Imperial Buildings, Victoria Road, Horley, Surrey RH6 7PZ. Tel. (01293) 774535.

DEPOSITS AND ADVANCE PAYMENTS

For reservations made weeks or months ahead a **deposit** is usually payable and the amount will vary according to the length of booking, time of year and number in the party. The deposit is then deducted from the total bill at the end of the stay.

Many hotels, particularly the larger ones, now require **payment for the room on arrival** if a prior reservation has not been made – especially when a guest arrives late and/or with very little luggage. Major credit cards are usually accepted. Regrettably this practice has become necessary because of the number of guests who have left without paying their bills. If you are asked to pay on

hotels & b&bs

Bed & Breakfast: single £270.13-
£364.13, double £317.00-£411.00
Evening meal: 1900 (l.o. 2315)
Parking for: 70
Methods of payment: Mastercard/
Visa/Barclaycard/American Express/
JCB/Diners/Switch/Delta/Eurocheque
❏ ❖ ⌑ ✗ ▣ ◑ ⌻ ♨ ⚑ ☎

Knightsbridge Green Hotel
♦♦♦♦

159 Knightsbridge, London
SW1X 7PD
Tel: (020) 7584 6274
Fax: (020) 7225 1635
E-mail: thekghotel@aol.com
✛ KNIGHTSBRIDGE
Small, family-run hotel close to
Harrods.
Bedrooms: 7 single, 4 double, 5 twin,
12 triple
Bathrooms: 28 en suite
Bed & Breakfast: single £115.50-
£125.50, double £161.00-£168.00
Non-smoking establishment
Methods of payment: Mastercard/
Visa/Barclaycard/American Express/
Diners
❏ ❖ ⌑ ✗ ▣ ⌻

The Lowndes Hyatt Hotel

21 Lowndes Street, Belgravia,
London SW1X 9ES
Tel: (020) 7823 1234/
(020) 7823 0003
Fax: (020) 7235 1154
E-mail: lowndes@hyattintl.com
✛ KNIGHTSBRIDGE
Contemporary English boutique
hotel, featuring 78 newly refurbished
rooms, including four Junior suites
and 1 Executive suite. In one of
London's most exclusive residential
areas, Belgravia Village, close to
Harrods and Harvey Nichols.
Bedrooms: 49 double, 24 twin,
5 family
Bathrooms: 78 en suite
Evening meal: 1800 (l.o. 2300)
Methods of payment: Mastercard/
Visa/Barclaycard/American Express/
JCB/Eurocard/Diners/Delta/
Eurocheque
❏ ⌑ ✗ ▣ ◑ ⌻ ♨ ☎

Luna-Simone Hotel
♦♦

47 Belgrave Road, London
SW1V 2BB
Tel: (020) 7834 5897

Fax: (020) 7828 2474
E-mail: lunasimone@talk21.com
❖/⇌ VICTORIA
Friendly, good-value bed and
breakfast hotel within easy walking
distance of Victoria rail, underground
and coach stations.
Bedrooms: 3 single, 11 double,
11 twin, 10 triple
Bathrooms: 19 en suite, 5 shower
only, 4 shared
Bed & Breakfast: single £45.00-
£60.00, double £60.00-£80.00
Methods of payment: Mastercard/
Visa/Barclaycard/JCB
❏ ⌑ ⌻ ⒰ ◑ ♨

Melita House Hotel   ♦♦♦

35 Charlwood Street, Victoria,
London SW1V 2DU
Tel: (020) 7828 0471/
(020) 7834 1387
Fax: (020) 7932 0988
E-mail: reserve@melita.co.uk
❖/⇌ VICTORIA, ❖ PIMLICO
Elegant, good-value, newly
refurbished, family-run hotel, close
to Victoria station. Rooms are well
equipped.
Bedrooms: 4 single, 10 double,
2 twin, 3 triple, 3 family
Bathrooms: 22 en suite, 1 shared
Bed & Breakfast: single £50.00-
£60.00, double £70.00-£85.00
Methods of payment: Mastercard/
Visa/Barclaycard/American Express/
JCB/Eurocard/Switch/Delta/
Eurocheque
❏ ⌑ ⌻ ⒰ ✗ ◑ ♨ ⚱

Millennium Knightsbridge

17 Sloane Street, London SW1X 9NU
Tel: (020) 7235 4377
Fax: (020) 7235 3705
✛ KNIGHTSBRIDGE
Located in the heart of Knightsbridge,
close to Harrods and Hyde Park.
Bedrooms: 22 single, 129 double,
71 twin
Bathrooms: 222 en suite
Bed & Breakfast: single £210.50-
£269.50, double £227.00-£286.00
Evening meal: 1830 (l.o. 2230)
Parking for: 7
Methods of payment: Mastercard/
Visa/Barclaycard/American Express/
Diners/Switch/Delta/Eurocheque
❏ ⌑ ⌻ ✗ ▣ ◑ ♨ ☎ ⚑

Oxford House Hotel   ♦

92 Cambridge Street, Victoria,
London SW1V 4QG
Tel: (020) 7834 6467
Fax: (020) 7834 0225
E-mail: oxfordhouse@breathemail.net
❖/⇌ VICTORIA
Small, friendly, family-run bed and
breakfast hotel within walking
distance of Westminster. (Five per
cent surcharge for Mastercard and
Visa bookings.)
Bedrooms: 2 single, 5 double, 4 twin
5 triple, 1 family
Bathrooms: 4 shared
Bed & Breakfast: single £36.00-
£38.00, double £48.00-£50.00
Methods of payment: Mastercard/
Visa/JCB/Switch/Eurocheque
⒰ ◑ ♨

Quality Hotel Westminster

Eccleston Square, London SW1V 1PS
Tel: (020) 7834 8042
Fax: (020) 7630 8942
E-mail: admin@gb614.u-net.com
❖/⇌ VICTORIA
Quietly located close to Buckingham
Palace. Ideal for Victoria coach and
rail stations. Hotel overlooks a
garden square.
Bedrooms: 15 single, 43 double,
46 twin, 3 triple
Bathrooms: 107 en suite
Bed & Breakfast: single £94.50-
£107.50, double £117.50-£130.50
Evening meal: 1800 (l.o. 2145)
Methods of payment: Mastercard/
Visa/American Express/Diners/Switch
❏ ⌑ ⌻ ✗ ▣ ◑ ♨ ☎

Royal Horseguards

2 Whitehall Court, London SW1A 2E
Tel: (020) 7839 3400
Fax: (020) 7930 3269
E-mail: royal.horseguards@thistle.
co.uk
❖/⇌ CHARING CROSS,
❖ EMBANKMENT
A unique château-style Victorian
building overlooking the Thames.
Situated close to Trafalgar Square,
Big Ben, the Houses of Parliament
and Westminster Abbey.
Bedrooms: 9 single, 175 double,
96 twin
Bathrooms: 280 en suite

Bed & Breakfast: single £165.00-£239.00, double £180.00-£349.00
Methods of payment: Mastercard/Visa/Barclaycard/American Express/JCB/Eurocard/Diners/Switch/Delta
☐ ♨ ↳ ⚒ ⊞ ◐ ☗

The Rubens at the Palace

39-41 Buckingham Palace Road, London SW1W 0PS
Tel: (020) 7834 6600
Fax: (020) 7828 5401
E-mail: reservations@rubens.redcarnationhotels.com
⊖/⇄ VICTORIA
Traditional hotel opposite the Royal Mews of Buckingham Palace and close to Westminster.
Bedrooms: 12 single, 128 double, 28 twin, 6 triple
Bathrooms: 174 en suite
Bed & Breakfast: single £165.00-£220.00, double £195.00-£295.00
Evening meal: 1800 (l.o. 2000)
Methods of payment: Mastercard/Visa/Barclaycard/American Express/Eurocard/Diners/Switch/Delta/Eurocheque
☐ ♨ ↳ ⚒ ⊞ ◐ 🛏 ☗

Sanctuary House Hotel

33 Tothill Street, London SW1H 9LA
Tel: (020) 7799 4044
Fax: (020) 7799 3657
E-mail: sanctuary.house@fullers.co.uk
⊖ ST JAMES'S PARK
Fully air-conditioned hotel and pub opened in September 1998.
Excellent value en suite bedrooms.
Traditional pub serving good home cooking and full range of drinks.
Bedrooms: 21 double, 13 twin
Bathrooms: 34 en suite
Evening meal: 1800 (l.o. 2130)
Methods of payment: Mastercard/Visa/Barclaycard/American Express/Eurocard/Diners/Switch/Delta/Eurocheque
☐ ♨ ↳ ⚒ ⊞ ◐

Sheraton Belgravia

20 Chesham Place, London SW1X 8HQ
Tel: (020) 7235 6040
Fax: (020) 7259 6243
E-mail: reservations_centrallondon@sheraton.com
⊖ KNIGHTSBRIDGE
Intimate townhouse hotel tucked away in a leafy square in Belgravia.

Close to Harrods and Knightsbridge shopping.
Bedrooms: 89 double
Bathrooms: 89 en suite
Bed & Breakfast: single £250.00-£425.00, double £362.00-£450.00
Evening meal: 1830 (l.o. 2230)
Methods of payment: Mastercard/Visa/Barclaycard/American Express/Diners/Switch/Delta/Eurocheque
☐ ↳ ⚒ ⊞ ◐ 🛏 ☗

Sheraton Park Tower

★★★★★ Silver Award

101 Knightsbridge, London SW1X 7RN
Tel: (020) 7235 8050
Fax: (020) 7235 8231
E-mail: morten_ebbesen@sheraton.com
⊖ KNIGHTSBRIDGE
Conveniently situated hotel in the élite shopping area of Knightsbridge, four minutes from Harrods and opposite Hyde Park.
Bedrooms: 198 double, 44 twin, 23 family
Bathrooms: 265 en suite, 2 shared
Bed only: single £351.33, double £374.83
Evening meal: 1900 (l.o. 2230)
Parking for: 100
Methods of payment: Mastercard/Visa/Barclaycard/American Express/JCB/Eurocard/Diners/Eurocheque
☐ ↳ ⚒ ⊞ ◐ ☗ 🚗 ▨

Stakis London St Ermin's Hotel

Caxton Street, London SW1H 0QW
Tel: (020) 7222 7888
Fax: (020) 7222 6914
E-mail: sales.director@stakis.stermins.co.uk
⊖ ST JAMES'S PARK
An elegant Edwardian property.
Traditional furnishings add charm in relaxing atmosphere.
Bedrooms: 54 single, 114 double, 110 twin, 4 triple
Bathrooms: 282 en suite
Bed only: single £190.00-£230.00, double £210.00-£254.00
Evening meal: 1800 (l.o. 2130)
Parking for: 23
Methods of payment: Mastercard/Visa/Barclaycard/American Express/JCB/Eurocard/Diners/Switch/Delta
☐ ♨ ↳ ⚒ ⊞ ◐ 🛏 ☗ 🚗

Stanley House Hotel ◆

19-21 Belgrave Road, London SW1V 1RB
Tel: (020) 7834 5042/ (020) 7834 7292
Fax: (020) 7834 8439
E-mail: cmahotel@aol.com
⊖/⇄ VICTORIA
Located in elegant Belgravia only a few minutes' walk from Victoria station. Within easy access of London's most famous sights and the West End for theatre and shopping.
Bedrooms: 4 single, 23 double, 7 twin, 5 triple, 5 family
Bathrooms: 44 en suite, 8 shared
Bed & Breakfast: single £45.00-£55.00, double £55.00-£65.00
Methods of payment: Mastercard/Visa/Barclaycard/American Express/Diners/Switch/Delta/Eurocheque
☐ ↳ ◐ 🛏 ♿

Thistle Victoria

101 Buckingham Palace Road, London SW1W 0SJ
Tel: (020) 7834 9494
Fax: (020) 7630 1978
E-mail: victoria@thistle.co.uk
⊖/⇄ VICTORIA
Elegant and spacious in the great Victorian tradition, offering modern facilities. Ideal for London sightseeing.
Bedrooms: 96 single, 53 double, 206 twin, 5 triple, 6 family
Bathrooms: 366 en suite
Evening meal: 1730 (l.o. 2200)
Methods of payment: Mastercard/Visa/Barclaycard/American Express/JCB/Eurocard/Diners/Switch/Delta/Eurocheque
☐ ♨ ↳ ⚒ ⊞ ◐ 🛏 ☗

Thistle Westminster

49 Buckingham Palace Road, Victoria, London SW1W 0QT
Tel: (020) 7834 1821
Fax: (020) 7931 7542
E-mail: royalwestminster@thistle.co.uk
⊖/⇄ VICTORIA
Air-conditioned hotel close to Buckingham Palace, St James's Park, Victoria station and the Houses of Parliament.
Bedrooms: 7 single, 43 double, 14 twin, 54 triple, 15 family
Bathrooms: 133 en suite
Evening meal: 1200 (l.o. 2300)

hotels & b&bs

Methods of payment: Mastercard/ Visa/Barclaycard/American Express/ Eurocard/Diners/Switch/Delta/ Eurocheque

Victor Hotel ◆ ◆ ◆

51 Belgrave Road, London SW1V 2BB
Tel: (020) 7592 9853
Fax: (020) 7592 9854
⊖/⇌ VICTORIA
Small, modern bed and breakfast hotel. Located in Victoria.
Bedrooms: 4 single, 11 double, 4 twin, 1 triple
Bathrooms: 20 en suite
Bed & Breakfast: single £65.00, double £90.00
Methods of payment: Mastercard/ Visa/Barclaycard/Switch/Delta

The Victoria Inn ◆ ◆ ◆

65-67 Belgrave Road, London SW1V 2BG
Tel: (020) 7834 6721/ (020) 7834 0182
Fax: (020) 7931 0201
E-mail: info@victoriainn.co.uk
⊖/⇌ VICTORIA
Modern hotel situated in the heart of Victoria within five minutes' walk of the coach and rail stations.
Bedrooms: 8 single, 11 double, 16 twin, 7 triple, 1 family
Bathrooms: 43 en suite
Bed & Breakfast: single £64.00-£69.00, double £72.00-£83.00
Methods of payment: Mastercard/ Visa/Barclaycard/American Express/ Diners

Windermere Hotel

◆ ◆ ◆ ◆ Silver Award

142-144 Warwick Way, Victoria, London SW1V 4JE
Tel: (020) 7834 5163/ (020) 7834 5480
Fax: (020) 7630 8831
E-mail: windermere@compuserve.com
⊖/⇌ VICTORIA
Small, well-maintained hotel with a restaurant and bar within a welcoming atmosphere, providing home comforts in an elegant setting.
Bedrooms: 4 single, 10 double, 5 twin, 1 triple, 2 family

Bathrooms: 20 en suite, 2 shared
Bed & Breakfast: single £67.00-£88.00, double £84.00-£136.00
Evening meal: 1730 (l.o. 2230)
Methods of payment: Mastercard/ Visa/Barclaycard/American Express/ JCB/Eurocard/Switch/Delta/ Eurocheque

W1
West End/Mayfair/Oxford Street

Athenaeum Hotel and Apartments

116 Piccadilly, London W1V 0BJ
Tel: (020) 7499 3464
Fax: (020) 7493 1860
E-mail: info@athenaeumhotel.com
⊖ GREEN PARK
Located on Piccadilly, overlooking Green Park, the Athenaeum Hotel and Apartments have recently been refurbished. Luxury apartments are also available. There is a free health club for guests' use and the famous Malt Whisky Bar.
Bedrooms: 27 single, 85 double, 44 twin
Bathrooms: 156 en suite
Bed & Breakfast: single £323.45-£840.45, double £364.90-£858.40
Evening meal: 1800 (l.o. 2300)
Methods of payment: Mastercard/ Visa/Barclaycard/American Express/ JCB/Diners/Switch/Delta/Eurocheque

Bentinck House Hotel ◆ ◆

20 Bentinck Street, London W1M 5RL
Tel: (020) 7935 9141
Fax: (020) 7224 5903
⊖ BOND STREET
Friendly, family-run hotel in the heart of the West End. Close to Bond Street underground and Oxford Street.
Bedrooms: 9 single, 2 double, 4 twin, 5 triple
Bathrooms: 9 en suite, 4 shared
Bed & Breakfast: single £49.00-£69.00, double £79.00-£98.00
Evening meal: 1930 (l.o. 2130)
Methods of payment: Mastercard/ Visa/Barclaycard/American Express/ JCB/Eurocard/Diners/Switch/Delta/ Eurocheque

Berkeley Court Hotel ◆ ◆

22 Upper Berkeley Street, London W1H 7PF
Tel: (020) 7262 3091
Fax: (020) 7258 0290
⊖ MARBLE ARCH
Friendly, newly refurbished hotel in a prime location, convenient for shops, theatres and business. Two minutes' walk from Marble Arch, Hyde Park and Oxford Street. Budget hotel in the heart of London's West End.
Bedrooms: 4 single, 6 double, 3 twin, 4 triple, 2 family
Bathrooms: 13 en suite, 1 private, 1 shower only, 4 shared
Bed & Breakfast: single £45.00-£60.00, double £50.00-£75.00
Methods of payment: Mastercard/ Visa/Barclaycard/American Express/ JCB/Eurocard/Diners/Switch/Delta/ Eurocheque

The Berners Hotel

★ ★ ★ ★ Silver Award

10 Berners Street, London W1A 3BE
Tel: (020) 7666 2000
Fax: (020) 7666 2001
E-mail: berners@berners.co.uk
⊖ OXFORD CIRCUS
Edwardian building restored to its original beauty and elegance, a few minutes' walk from Oxford Circus and Soho.
Bedrooms: 37 single, 135 double, 45 twin
Bathrooms: 217 en suite
Bed & Breakfast: single £186.00-£256.00, double £221.00-£266.00
Evening meal: 1730 (l.o. 2230)
Methods of payment: Mastercard/ Visa/Barclaycard/American Express/ JCB/Diners/Switch/Delta/Eurocheque

Blandford Hotel ◆ ◆ ◆

80 Chiltern Street, London W1M 1PS
Tel: (020) 7486 3103
Fax: (020) 7487 2786
E-mail: blandfordhotel@dial.pipex.com
⊖ BAKER STREET
The Blandford Hotel is a small quality hotel situated in the heart of London. The hotel offers comfortable en suite bedrooms at affordable prices.

hotels & b&bs

Bedrooms: 8 single, 10 double, 4 twin, 7 triple, 4 family
Bathrooms: 33 en suite
Bed & Breakfast: single £50.00-£65.00, double £70.00-£85.00
Non-smoking establishment
Methods of payment: Mastercard/Visa/Barclaycard/American Express/JCB/Eurocard/Switch/Delta/Eurocheque
▢ ✿ ☎ ⅏ ▤ ◐ ▰ ♨

Brown's Hotel

Albemarle Street, Mayfair, London W1X 4BP
Tel: (020) 7493 6020
Fax: (020) 7493 9381
E-mail: brownshotel@brownshotel.com
❋ GREEN PARK
In the heart of Mayfair, one of London's most distinguished hotels. Prices quoted are valid for 1999 and are subject to change.
Bedrooms: 29 single, 54 double, 15 twin, 12 triple, 9 family
Bathrooms: 119 en suite
Bed & Breakfast: single £325.50-£425.35, double £360.75-£445.35
Evening meal: 1900 (l.o. 2230)
Methods of payment: Mastercard/Visa/Barclaycard/American Express/JCB/Eurocard/Switch/Delta/Eurocheque
▢ ☎ ✂ ▤ ◐ ♨ ▰ ▾

The Chesterfield Mayfair

35 Charles Street, Mayfair, London W1X 8LX
Tel: (020) 7491 2622
Fax: (020) 7491 4793
E-mail: reservations@chesterfield.redcarnationhotels.com
❋ GREEN PARK
The Chesterfield is ideal for both business and pleasure and is centrally located in the heart of Mayfair.
Bedrooms: 19 single, 34 double, 7 twin, 37 triple, 13 family
Bathrooms: 110 en suite
Bed & Breakfast: single £168.75-£245.12, double £192.25-£256.87
Evening meal: 1830 (l.o. 2300)
Methods of payment: Mastercard/Visa/Barclaycard/American Express/JCB/Diners/Switch/Delta/Eurocheque
▢ ✿ ☎ ✂ ▤ ◐ ▰ ▦ ▾

Churchill Inter-Continental London

30 Portman Square, London W1A 4ZX
Tel: (020) 7486 5800
Fax: (020) 7485 1255
E-mail: churchill@interconti.com
❋ MARBLE ARCH
Bedrooms: 36 single, 220 double, 88 twin
Bathrooms: 344 en suite
Evening meal: 1800 (l.o. 2300)
Parking for: 48
Methods of payment: Mastercard/Visa/Barclaycard/American Express/JCB/Eurocard/Diners/Switch/Delta/Eurocheque
▢ ☎ ✂ ▤ ◐ ▾ ♨

Claridge's

Brook Street, Mayfair, London W1A 2JQ
Tel: (020) 7629 8860/ (020) 7409 6262
Fax: (020) 7499 2210
E-mail: info@claridges.co.uk
❋ BOND STREET
In the heart of Mayfair with its fashionable boutiques. A favourite of London society and distinguished visitors for over 100 years.
Bedrooms: 45 single, 88 double, 6 triple
Bathrooms: 136 en suite
Evening meal: 1730 (l.o. 2300)
Methods of payment: Mastercard/Visa/Barclaycard/American Express/JCB/Eurocard/Diners/Switch/Delta/Eurocheque
▢ ☎ ▤ ◐ ▰ ▾

The Connaught Hotel

16 Carlos Place, Mayfair, London W1Y 6AL
Tel: (020) 7499 7070
Fax: (020) 7495 3262
E-mail: info@the-connaught.co.uk
❋ GREEN PARK
Set in a picturesque part of Mayfair. A haven of cosiness, tranquility and supreme comfort; a gastronomic experience.
Bedrooms: 29 single, 37 twin
Bathrooms: 66 en suite
Bed only: single £340.75, double £434.75
Evening meal: 1830 (l.o. 2245)
Parking for: 3

Methods of payment: Mastercard/Visa/Barclaycard/American Express/Eurocard/Diners/Switch/Delta/Eurocheque
▢ ☎ ▤ ◐ ▰ ▾ ♨

The Cumberland Hotel

Marble Arch, London W1A 4RF
Tel: 0870 400 8701
Fax: (020) 7724 3343
E-mail: beverly.king@forte-hotels.com
❋ MARBLE ARCH
Situated at the heart of one of the world's most exciting cities, overlooking Marble Arch and Hyde Park. Great shopping on the doorstep with Oxford Street, Bond Street and Regent Street.
Bedrooms: 167 single, 345 double, 373 twin, 21 triple
Bathrooms: 906 en suite
Bed & Breakfast: single £205.00-£235.00
Methods of payment: Mastercard/Visa/Barclaycard/American Express/JCB/Eurocard/Diners/Switch/Delta/Eurocheque
▢ ✿ ☎ ◐ ▾

The Dorchester

★ ★ ★ ★ ★ Gold Award

Park Lane, London W1A 2HJ
Tel: (020) 7629 8888
Fax: (020) 7409 0114
E-mail: reservations@dorchesterhotel.com
❋ HYDE PARK CORNER
A five-star, traditional English, country-house-style hotel, with all modern facilities including a spa and three restaurants.
Bedrooms: 32 single, 125 double, 40 twin
Bathrooms: 197 en suite
Bed & Breakfast: single £370.13-£414.13, double £405.38-£449.38
Evening meal: 1800 (l.o. 2330)
Parking for: 24
Methods of payment: Mastercard/Visa/Barclaycard/American Express/JCB/Eurocard/Diners/Switch/Delta
▢ ☎ ✂ ▤ ◐ ♨ ▰ ▾ ♨

The Edward Lear Hotel ◆ ◆

30 Seymour Street, Marble Arch, London W1H 5WD
Tel: (020) 7402 5401
Fax: (020) 7706 3766
E-mail: edwardlear@aol.com

Good Value Accommodation
in Central London
Central Reservations Telephone (020) 7402 0202

Abbey Court and Westpoint Hotel

- ✓ Pleasant central location
- ✓ Convenient location 2 minutes from Paddington Station & Heathrow Express, & 4 minutes from Airbus
- ✓ Easy access to all London's important tourist sights, shopping districts, theatres, Oxford Street and Piccadilly Circus
- ✓ En-Suite shower & w.c. in all rooms

- ✓ Lift to all floors
- ✓ Each room with colour T.V., radio & telephone
- ✓ Car parking by arrangement

Abbey Court and Westpoint Hotel
170-174 Sussex Gardens
Hyde Park London W2 1TP
Tel (020) 7402 0704
Fax (020) 7262 2055
www.westpointhotel.com
e-mail info@westpointhotel.com
Tel (020) 7402 0281
Fax (020) 7224 9114
www.abbeycourt.com
e-mail info@abbeycourt.com

RATES	LOW SEASON	HIGH SEASON
Singles	from £48.00	from £56.00
Doubles *pp*	from £32.00	from £37.00
Triples *pp*	from £26.00	from £28.00
Family Room *pp*	from £22.00	from £24.00

Sass House Hotel

Central London hotel located within two minutes walk from Hyde Park. Most rooms with private showers/toilets. All rooms have colour TV and radio. Easy access to all tourist attractions – within 5 minutes walking distance of Lancaster Gate and Paddington underground/ mainline stations and Heathrow Express.

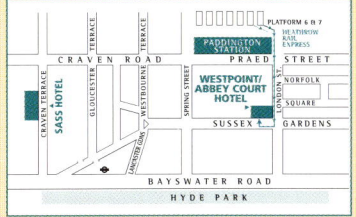

RATES	LOW SEASON	HIGH SEASON
Twin *pp*	from £26.00	from £29.00
Doubles *pp*	from £24.50	from £28.00
Triples *pp*	from £22.00	from £24.00
Family Room *pp*	from £19.50	from £21.50

Sass House Hotel
11 Craven Terrace,
Hyde Park, London W2 3QT
Tel (020) 7262 2325
Fax (020) 7262 0889
www.sasshotel.com
e-mail info@sasshotel.com

hotels & b&bs

Methods of payment: Mastercard/
Visa/Barclaycard/JCB/Eurocard/
Switch/Delta/Eurocheque

Allandale Hotel ◆◆

3 Devonshire Terrace, Lancaster
Gate, London W2 3DN
Tel: (020) 7723 8311/
(020) 7723 7807
Fax: (020) 7723 8311
E-mail: info@allandalehotel.co.uk
⊖ **LANCASTER GATE,**
⊖/⇌ **PADDINGTON**
Small, family-run hotel, close to the
West End and many of London's
attractions.
Bedrooms: 2 single, 8 double, 5
twin, 2 triple, 3 family
Bathrooms: 18 en suite, 1 shared
Bed & Breakfast: single £45.00-
£50.00, double £60.00-£65.00
Methods of payment: Mastercard/
Visa/Barclaycard/American Express/
JCB/Eurocard/Diners/Delta/
Eurocheque

Athena Hotel

110-114 Sussex Gardens, London
W2 1UA
Tel: (020) 7706 3866
Fax: (020) 7262 6143
⊖/⇌ **PADDINGTON**
The Athena Hotel is a newly
completed hotel in a restored
Victorian Listed building. Lift to all
floors. Ideally located in a tree-lined
avenue seven minutes' walk from
Hyde Park. Ideal for leisure or
business travellers.
Bedrooms: 8 single, 8 double,
4 twin, 4 triple, 2 family
Bathrooms: 26 en suite
Bed & Breakfast: single £50.00-
£70.00, double £70.00-£99.00
Methods of payment: Mastercard/
Visa/Barclaycard/American Express/
JCB/Eurocard/Diners/Switch/Delta/
Maestro/Visa Electron/Solo/
Eurocheque

Barry House Hotel ◆◆

12 Sussex Place, London W2 2TP
Tel: (020) 7723 7340/
(020) 7723 0994
Fax: (020) 7723 9775

E-mail: bh-hotel@bigfoot.com
⊖/⇌ **PADDINGTON,**
⊖ **LANCASTER GATE**
Friendly, family-run bed and
breakfast close to Paddington
station and Hyde Park. En suite
rooms with TV, telephone and tea
and coffee making facilities.
Bedrooms: 4 single, 4 double, 7 twin,
2 triple, 1 family
Bathrooms: 14 en suite, 1 shower
only, 2 shared
Bed & Breakfast: single £42.00,
double £82.00
Methods of payment: Mastercard/
Visa/Barclaycard/American Express/
JCB/Eurocard/Diners/Switch/Delta/
Eurocheque

Bayswater Inn

8-16 Princes Square, London W2 4NT
Tel: (020) 7727 8621/
(020) 7792 3536
Fax: (020) 7727 3346
E-mail: bayswaterinn@btinternet.com
⊖ **BAYSWATER/QUEENSWAY**
In a quiet residential square in close
proximity to Portobello Road market,
Oxford Street, Marble Arch and
many tourist attractions.
Bedrooms: 8 single, 17 double,
58 twin, 31 triple, 16 family
Bathrooms: 130 en suite
Bed & Breakfast: single £50.00-
£70.00, double £65.00-£95.00
Evening meal: 1800 (l.o. 2200)
Methods of payment: Mastercard/
Visa/Barclaycard/American Express/
JCB/Eurocard/Diners/Switch/Delta/
Eurocheque

Berjaya Eden Park Hotel

35-39 Inverness Terrace, London
W2 3JS
Tel: (020) 7221 2220
Fax: (020) 7221 2286
E-mail: edenpark@dircon.co.uk
⊖ **BAYSWATER**
Victorian-style building built in 1860,
with 136 en suite bedrooms, a bar
and restaurant.
Bedrooms: 48 single, 28 double,
52 twin, 7 triple, 1 family
Bathrooms: 136 en suite
Bed & Breakfast: single £110.00,
double £136.00

Evening meal: 1700 (l.o. 2300)
Methods of payment: Mastercard/
Visa/Barclaycard/American Express
JCB/Diners/Switch/Delta/Eurocheque

Beverley House Hotel ◆◆◆

142 Sussex Gardens, London W2 1U
Tel: (020) 7723 3380
Fax: (020) 7262 0324
E-mail: beverleyhousehotel@easy
net.co.uk
⊖/⇌ **PADDINGTON**
A completely refurbished hotel, close
to Paddington and Lancaster Gate
stations and within walking distance
of Hyde Park and Oxford Street.
Bedrooms: 6 single, 5 double, 6 twin
6 triple
Bathrooms: 23 en suite
Bed & Breakfast: single £53.00-
£59.00, double £64.00-£79.00
Parking for: 2
Methods of payment: Mastercard/
Visa/Barclaycard/JCB/Eurocard/
Diners/Switch/Delta/Eurocheque

The Blakemore Hotel

30 Leinster Gardens, London W2 3A
Tel: (020) 7262 4591
Fax: (020) 7724 1472
E-mail: reservations@starcrown.com
⊖/⇌ **PADDINGTON,**
⊖ **BAYSWATER**
The hotel is situated close to Hyde
Park and Oxford Street and has a
bar, coffee lounge, restaurant and
three conference rooms.
Bedrooms: 58 single, 27 double,
59 twin, 16 triple, 3 family
Bathrooms: 163 en suite
Bed & Breakfast: single £80.00-
£120.00, double £120.00-£240.00
Evening meal: 1730 (l.o. 2130)
Methods of payment: Mastercard/
Visa/Barclaycard/American Express
Diners/Switch

Caring Hotel ◆◆

24 Craven Hill Gardens, London
W2 3EA
Tel: (020) 7262 8708
Fax: (020) 7262 8590
E-mail: caring@lineone.net
⊖/⇌ **PADDINGTON**
Small bed and breakfast hotel within
easy access of Marble Arch and the

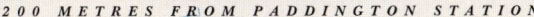

hotels & b&bs

West End. Close to Paddington underground station.
Bedrooms: 11 double, 7 twin, 4 triple, 4 family
Bathrooms: 9 en suite, 4 private, 7 shower only, 4 shared
Bed & Breakfast: single £40.00-£49.00, double £48.00-£72.00
Methods of payment: Mastercard/Visa/Barclaycard/American Express/Eurocard/Switch/Delta/Eurocheque
□ ♥ ☎ 📺 ◑ 🍴

Central Park Hotel ★★★

49 Queensborough Terrace, London W2 3SS
Tel: (020) 7229 2424
Fax: (020) 7229 2904
E-mail: cph@centralparklondon.co.uk
✆ QUEENSWAY/BAYSWATER
Modern hotel in a central, yet quiet location, close to many attractions and well served by public transport.
Bedrooms: 39 single, 33 double, 134 twin, 36 triple, 9 family
Bathrooms: 251 en suite
Bed & Breakfast: single £95.00-£110.00, double £115.00-£140.00
Evening meal: 1745 (l.o. 2045)
Parking for: 22
Methods of payment: Mastercard/Visa/Barclaycard/American Express/JCB/Diners/Switch/Delta/Eurocheque
□ ♥ ☎ ◑ 🍴 🚗

Classic Hotel ◆◆

92 Sussex Gardens, Hyde Park, London W2 1UH
Tel: (020) 7706 7776
Fax: (020) 7706 8136
E-mail: bookings@classic-hotel.com
✆/⇄ PADDINGTON
Listed Grade II building. Exclusive front garden with trees on either side.
Bedrooms: 2 single, 3 double, 4 twin, 3 triple, 1 family
Bathrooms: 13 en suite
Bed & Breakfast: single £45.00-£52.00, double £70.00-£76.00
Parking for: 2
Methods of payment: Mastercard/Visa/Barclaycard/American Express/JCB/Eurocard/Diners/Switch/Delta/Eurocheque
□ ☎ 📺 ◑ 🚗

Commodore Hotel

50 Lancaster Gate, Hyde Park, London W2 3NA

Tel: (020) 7402 5291/
(020) 7402 8010
Fax: (020) 7262 1088
E-mail: reservations@commodore-hotel.com
✆ LANCASTER GATE
In a quiet Victorian square opposite Hyde Park, comprising three townhouses, built 1850.
Bedrooms: 9 single, 28 double, 34 twin, 9 triple, 8 family
Bathrooms: 88 en suite
Bed & Breakfast: single £105.00-£120.00, double £129.00-£148.00
Evening meal: 1900 (l.o. 2200)
Methods of payment: Mastercard/Visa/Barclaycard/American Express/Eurocard/Diners/Switch/Delta/Eurocheque
□ ♥ ☎ ✂ 📺 ◑ 🍴

Cordova House Hotel

14-16 Craven Hill, London W2 3DU
Tel: (020) 7723 1065/
(020) 7262 0111
Fax: (020) 7262 7772
✆/⇄ PADDINGTON,
✆ LANCASTER GATE
Most of London's many colourful attractions are within easy reach, including the famous department stores and London's bustling nightlife.
Bedrooms: 4 single, 6 double, 39 twin, 8 triple, 2 family
Bathrooms: 59 en suite
Methods of payment: Mastercard/Visa/Barclaycard/American Express/Diners/Eurocheque
□ ♥ ☎ 📺 ◑ 🍴

The Delmere Hotel ★★

128-130 Sussex Gardens, Hyde Park, London W2 1UB
Tel: (020) 7706 3344
Fax: (020) 7262 1863
E-mail: delmerehotel@compuserve.com
✆/⇄ PADDINGTON
A quality, Victorian townhouse close to Marble Arch and Hyde Park. La Perla Restaurant at the Delmere is also open in the evenings to non-residents.
Bedrooms: 10 single, 13 double, 12 twin, 3 triple
Bathrooms: 38 en suite
Bed & Breakfast: single £73.50-£82.00, double £92.00-£103.00

Evening meal: 1800 (l.o. 2200)
Parking for: 2
Methods of payment: Mastercard/Visa/Barclaycard/American Express/JCB/Eurocard/Diners/Switch/Delta/Eurocheque
□ ♥ ☎ 📺 ◑ 🍴 🚗

Duke of Leinster ◆◆

34 Queen's Gardens, London W2 3AA
Tel: (020) 7258 0079/
(020) 7258 1839
Fax: (020) 7262 0741
E-mail: dukeshotel@aol.com
✆/⇄ PADDINGTON
All rooms are en suite. Ideally situated opposite Hyde Park and near Marble Arch and Oxford Street. Close to Bayswater and Queensway underground stations and within easy reach of the Heathrow Express at Paddington.
Bedrooms: 8 single, 13 double, 13 twin, 7 triple
Bathrooms: 41 en suite
Bed & Breakfast: single £54.00, double £74.00
Methods of payment: Mastercard/Visa/Barclaycard/American Express/Switch
□ ♥ ☎ 📺 ◑ 🍴

Europa House Hotel ◆◆

151 Sussex Gardens, London W2 2RY
Tel: (020) 7723 7343/
(020) 7402 1923
Fax: (020) 7224 9331
E-mail: europahouse@enterprise.net
✆/⇄ PADDINGTON,
✆ LANCASTER GATE
Small, family-run hotel convenient for Hyde Park, the Heathrow Airbus stop and the Paddington rail link to Heathrow.
Bedrooms: 3 single, 3 double, 6 twin, 4 triple, 2 family
Bathrooms: 18 en suite, 1 shared
Bed & Breakfast: single £40.00-£50.00, double £60.00-£70.00
Parking for: 1
Non-smoking establishment
Methods of payment: Mastercard/Visa/Barclaycard/American Express/Eurocard/Diners/Switch/Delta/Eurocheque
□ ♥ ☎ 📺 ✂ ◑ 🍴 🚗

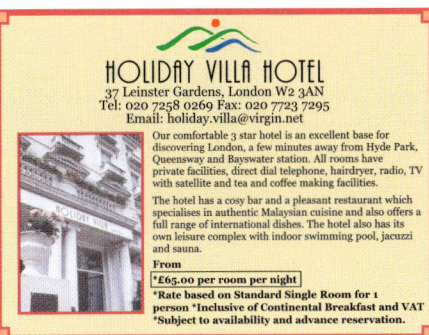

hotels & b&bs

Forum Hotel London ★★★★

97 Cromwell Road, London SW7 4DN
Tel: (020) 7370 5757
Fax: (020) 7373 1448
E-mail: forumlondon@interconti.com
✪ **GLOUCESTER ROAD**
All 932 rooms are en suite with colour television, telephone and facilities for making tea and coffee. The hotel has three restaurants, two bars, fitness room, business centre and car park.
Bedrooms: 448 double, 448 twin, 36 triple
Bathrooms: 932 en suite
Bed & Breakfast: single £193.50, double £227.50
Evening meal: 1730 (l.o. 2330)
Parking for: 80
Methods of payment: Mastercard/ Visa/Barclaycard/American Express/ JCB/Eurocard/Diners/Switch/Delta/ Eurocheque
▢ ✿ ☎ ✄ ▦ ● ☏ ⬟

Half Moon Hotel ◆◆

10 Earls Court Square, London SW5 9DP
Tel: (020) 7373 9956
Fax: (020) 7373 8456
✪ **EARL'S COURT**
In a central position two minutes' walk from the underground station and with easy access to the M4 and Heathrow.
Bedrooms: 10 single, 8 twin, 7 triple, 2 family
Bathrooms: 9 en suite, 2 shower only, 5 shared
Methods of payment: Mastercard/ Visa/Barclaycard/Eurocard/Delta/ Eurocheque
▢ ✿ ☎ ▦ ●

Harrington Hall

5-25 Harrington Gardens, London SW7 4JW
Tel: (020) 7396 9696
Fax: (020) 7396 9090
E-mail: harringtonsales@compu serve.com
✪ **GLOUCESTER ROAD**
All 200 bedrooms are spacious and fully air-conditioned with trouser press, mini-bar and tea and coffee tray. Satellite television and personalised telephones.
Bedrooms: 125 double, 70 twin, 5 triple
Bathrooms: 200 en suite

Bed & Breakfast: single £120.00, double £135.00
Evening meal: 1730 (l.o. 2230)
Methods of payment: Mastercard/ Visa/Barclaycard/American Express/ JCB/Eurocard/Diners/Switch/Delta/ Eurocheque
▢ ✿ ☎ ✄ ▦ ● ☏ ⬟

Hotel Earls Court ◆

28 Warwick Road, Earls Court, London SW5 9UD
Tel: (020) 7373 7079/
(020) 7373 0302
Fax: (020) 7912 0582
E-mail: hotelearlscourt@virgin.net
✪ **EARL'S COURT**
Small, friendly and comfortable centrally located bed and breakfast, opposite Earl's Court Exhibition Hall and 50 yards from Earl's Court underground station (Warwick Road exit).
Bedrooms: 6 single, 4 double, 2 twin, 5 triple
Bathrooms: 6 private, 3 shower only, 4 shared
Bed & Breakfast: single £30.00-£45.00, double £45.00-£60.00
Methods of payment: Mastercard/ Visa/Barclaycard/American Express/ JCB/Eurocard/Diners/Eurocheque
▢ ✿ ☎ ● ▦

Hotel Europe

131-137 Cromwell Road, London SW7 4DU
Tel: (020) 7598 7979
Fax: (020) 7598 7981
E-mail: reservations@hoteleurope. co.uk
✪ **GLOUCESTER ROAD**
Close to the Natural History, Science and V&A museums. Also close to Hyde Park, the West End, theatreland and Knightsbridge shopping district.
Bedrooms: 13 single, 8 double, 56 twin, 14 triple, 2 family
Bathrooms: 93 en suite
Bed & Breakfast: single £70.00-£90.00, double £85.00-£100.00
Evening meal: 1800 (l.o. 2000)
Methods of payment: Mastercard/ Visa/American Express/Eurocard
▢ ☎ ▦ ● ▦ ⬟

Hotel Oliver ◆◆

198 Cromwell Road, London SW5 0SN
Tel: (020) 7370 6881

Fax: (020) 7370 6556
E-mail: reservations@hoteloliver.free serve.co.uk
✪ **EARL'S COURT**
Hotel with 48 bedrooms, all en suite. All rooms have colour TV, radio, hairdryer and telephone. Lift to all floors. Situated close to Harrods, the South Kensington museums and shops. All major credit cards are accepted.
Bedrooms: 20 single, 11 double, 11 twin, 2 triple, 4 family
Bathrooms: 48 en suite
Bed & Breakfast: single £45.00-£60.00, double £70.00-£80.00
Methods of payment: Mastercard/ Visa/Barclaycard/American Express/ JCB/Eurocard/Diners/Eurocheque
▢ ✿ ☎ ▦ ▦ ● ▦ ⬟

Hotel Number Sixteen
◆◆◆◆ Gold Award

16 Sumner Place, London SW7 3EG
Tel: (020) 7589 5232
Fax: (020) 7584 8615
E-mail: reservations@numbersixteen hotel.co.uk
✪ **SOUTH KENSINGTON**
A comfortable townhouse with atmosphere, in four adjoining Victorian houses in an attractive street with award-winning gardens.
Bedrooms: 9 single, 23 double, 4 triple
Bathrooms: 32 en suite, 2 private
Bed & Breakfast: single £100.00-£140.00, double £175.00-£200.00
Methods of payment: Mastercard/ Visa/Barclaycard/American Express/ Eurocard/Diners/Switch/Delta/ Eurocheque
▢ ☎ ▦ ● ▦ ⬟

Jarvis Kensington ★★★

31-33 Queen's Gate, London SW7 5JA
Tel: (020) 7584 7222
Fax: (020) 7589 3910
✪ **GLOUCESTER ROAD**
The hotel is ideally situated for the Royal Albert Hall, the South Kensington museums, Hyde Park, Harrods and Earls Court.
Bedrooms: 7 single, 32 double, 22 twin, 13 triple, 6 family
Bathrooms: 80 en suite
Bed & Breakfast: single £105.00-£164.00, double £109.00-£174.00

Methods of payment: Mastercard/
Visa/Barclaycard/American Express/
JCB/Eurocard/Diners/Switch/Delta/
Eurocheque

K + K Hotel George

1-15 Templeton Place, Earls Court,
London SW5 9NB
Tel: (020) 7598 8700
Fax: (020) 7370 2285
E-mail: hotelgeorge@kkhotels.co.uk
�$ EARL'S COURT
Hotel with large, private garden and
car park. Easy access to Heathrow
and the attractions of Kensington
and Knightsbridge.
Bedrooms: 7 single, 24 double,
36 twin, 35 triple, 2 family
Bathrooms: 154 en suite
Bed & Breakfast: single £150.00,
double £180.00
Evening meal: 1700 (l.o. 2200)
Parking for: 36
Methods of payment: Mastercard/
Visa/Barclaycard/American Express/
JCB/Eurocard/Diners/Switch/Delta/
Eurocheque

Kensington Court Hotel ◆◆◆

33-35 Nevern Place, Earls Court,
London SW5 9NP
Tel: (020) 7370 5151
Fax: (020) 7370 3499
E-mail: kensington.court.hotel@visit.
uk.com
�$ EARL'S COURT
Purpose-built hotel with private car
park. Centrally situated, within walking
distance of Earl's Court underground
station and exhibition centres. All
rooms with en suite facilities.
Bedrooms: 10 single, 5 double,
5 twin, 10 triple, 5 family
Bathrooms: 35 en suite
Bed & Breakfast: single £63.00-
£65.00, double £83.00-£85.00
Evening meal: 1900 (l.o. 2100)
Parking for: 10
Methods of payment: Mastercard/
Visa/Barclaycard/American Express/
Switch

Kensington Edwardian

40-44 Harrington Gardens, London
SW7 4LT
Tel: (020) 7370 0811

Fax: (020) 7373 5138
E-mail: edwardian@realco.co.uk
�$ GLOUCESTER ROAD
A 69-bedroomed Edwardian hotel
situated in one of the most
fashionable residential areas of
London.
Bedrooms: 15 single, 18 double,
26 twin, 7 triple, 3 family
Bathrooms: 69 en suite
Bed & Breakfast: single £89.00,
double £109.00
Methods of payment: Mastercard/
Visa/Barclaycard/American Express/
Diners/Switch

Kensington International Hotel ◆◆◆

4 Templeton Place, London SW5 9LZ
Tel: (020) 7370 4333
Fax: (020) 7244 7873
E-mail: hotel@kensington-
international-hotel.co.uk
�$ EARL'S COURT
Club-style hotel, tastefully decorated.
Bedrooms: 15 single, 17 double,
23 twin, 2 triple, 1 family
Bathrooms: 58 en suite
Bed & Breakfast: single £80.00-
£95.00, double £95.00-£115.00
Evening meal: 1800 (l.o. 2300)
Methods of payment: Mastercard/
Visa/Barclaycard/American Express/
JCB/Eurocard/Diners/Switch/Delta/
Eurocheque

London Town Hotel ◆◆◆

15 Penywern Road, Earls Court,
London SW5 9TT
Tel: (020) 7370 4356
Fax: (020) 7370 7923
E-mail: townhotel@compuserve.com
�$ EARL'S COURT
Situated within two minutes' walk of
Earl's Court underground with direct
connections to Heathrow, Victoria
and Piccadilly Circus. All rooms with
colour television and telephone.
Bedrooms: 9 single, 4 double,
13 twin, 6 triple
Bathrooms: 32 en suite
Bed & Breakfast: single £55.00-
£78.00, double £69.00-£98.00
Methods of payment: Mastercard/
Visa/American Express/JCB/
Eurocard/Switch/Delta/Eurocheque

Lord Jim Hotel ◆◆

23-25 Penywern Road, London
SW5 9TT
Tel: (020) 7370 6071/07957 167081
Fax: (020) 7373 8919
E-mail: taher_tayeb@compuserve.
com
�$ EARL'S COURT
An attractive, well-appointed and
moderately priced hotel. Located
centrally for easy access to
museums, the City and Earl's Court
and Olympia exhibition halls.
Bedrooms: 8 single, 6 double, 5 twin,
9 triple, 7 family
Bathrooms: 11 en suite, 3 shower
only, 6 shared
Bed & Breakfast: single £25.00-
£48.00, double £35.00-£59.00
Methods of payment: Mastercard/
Visa/Barclaycard/American Express/
Eurocard/Diners/Switch/Delta/
Eurocheque

Manor Hotel ◆◆

23 Nevern Place, London SW5 9NR
Tel: (020) 7370 6018
Fax: (020) 7244 6610
�$ EARL'S COURT
Centrally located hotel offering a
pleasant atmosphere. Car parking
available. Convenient for Heathrow.
Bedrooms: 6 single, 11 double,
10 triple
Bathrooms: 9 en suite, 2 shower
only, 5 shared
Bed & Breakfast: single £26.00-
£35.00, double £45.00-£55.00
Parking for: 4
Methods of payment: Mastercard/
Visa/Barclaycard/Eurocheque

Mayflower Hotel ◆◆

26-28 Trebovir Road, Earls Court,
London SW5 9NJ
Tel: (020) 7370 0991
Fax: (020) 7370 0994
E-mail: mayfhotel@aol.com
�$ EARL'S COURT
Clean, bright, independent, centrally
located hotel with easy access to
transport, major tourist attractions
and exhibition centres. Open all year.
Bedrooms: 6 single, 18 double,
15 twin, 7 triple, 2 family
Bathrooms: 46 en suite, 1 shared

hotels & b&bs

Bed & Breakfast: single £53.00-£69.00, double £59.00-£89.00
Methods of payment: Mastercard/Visa/Barclaycard/American Express/JCB/Eurocard/Diners/Switch/Delta/Eurocheque

The Millennium Bailey's London

140 Gloucester Road, London SW7 4QH
Tel: (020) 7373 6000
Fax: (020) 7370 3760
E-mail: baileys@mill-cop.com
➜ GLOUCESTER ROAD
Traditional Victorian property, built and opened as a hotel in 1876. Close to Knightsbridge, Kensington Palace and Gardens, the South Kensington museums, the Royal Albert Hall and Earl's Court and Olympia exhibition centres.
Bedrooms: 36 single, 137 double, 35 twin, 2 triple
Bathrooms: 210 en suite
Evening meal: 1730 (l.o. 2230)
Parking for: 75
Methods of payment: Mastercard/Visa/Barclaycard/American Express/JCB/Eurocard/Diners/Switch/Delta/Eurocheque

Millennium Gloucester London   ★★★★ Silver Award

4-18 Harrington Gardens, London SW7 4LH
Tel: (020) 7373 6030
Fax: (020) 7373 0409
E-mail: sales.gloucester@mill-cop.com
➜ GLOUCESTER ROAD
Newly refurbished, luxury hotel, situated in Kensington and Chelsea, with direct links to Heathrow and Gatwick airports and the City. Elegant stores of Knightsbridge and Kensington only minutes away.
Bedrooms: 11 single, 327 double, 259 twin, 7 triple, 6 family
Bathrooms: 610 en suite
Bed & Breakfast: single £225.00, double £225.00
Evening meal: 1800 (l.o. 2245)
Parking for: 110
Methods of payment: Mastercard/Visa/Barclaycard/American Express/JCB/Eurocard/Diners/Switch/Delta/Eurocheque

Montana Hotel   ★★

67-69 Gloucester Road, London SW7 4PG
Tel: (020) 7584 7654
Fax: (020) 7581 3109
➜ GLOUCESTER ROAD
Centrally located hotel. Convenient for Knightsbridge, Kensington and Earl's Court Exhibition Centre. Gloucester Road underground opposite provides direct links to Heathrow and West End.
Bedrooms: 10 single, 5 double, 21 twin, 15 triple
Bathrooms: 45 en suite, 6 shared
Bed & Breakfast: single £67.00, double £80.00
Evening meal: 1800 (l.o. 2330)
Methods of payment: Mastercard/Visa/Barclaycard/American Express/Eurocard/Diners/Eurocheque

Mowbray Court Hotel   ◆◆

28-32 Penywern Road, Earls Court, London SW5 9SU
Tel: (020) 7370 2316/(020) 7370 3690
Fax: (020) 7370 5693
E-mail: mowbraycrthot@hotmail.com
➜ EARL'S COURT
Tourist-class hotel near Earl's Court Exhibition Centre.
Bedrooms: 30 single, 15 double, 15 twin, 20 triple, 8 family
Bathrooms: 72 en suite, 8 shared
Bed only: single £46.00-£53.00, double £57.00-£68.00
Non-smoking establishment
Methods of payment: Mastercard/Visa/Barclaycard/American Express/JCB/Eurocard/Diners/Switch/Delta/Eurocheque

Nevern Hotel   ◆

29-31 Nevern Place, London SW5 9NP
Tel: (020) 7244 8366/(020) 7370 4827
Fax: (020) 7370 1541
➜ EARL'S COURT
Small hotel located in a quiet residential area. Convenient for Earls Court and Olympia, also within easy reach of the West End.
Bedrooms: 4 single, 6 double, 9 twin, 8 triple, 8 family
Bathrooms: 19 en suite, 7 shared

Methods of payment: Mastercard/Visa/Barclaycard/American Express/Eurocheque

Oliver Plaza Hotel   ◆◆

33 Trebovir Road, Earls Court, London SW5 9NF
Tel: (020) 7373 7183
Fax: (020) 7244 6021
E-mail: oliverplaza@capricornhotels.co.uk
➜ EARL'S COURT
A small hotel with the emphasis on efficiency of service and comfort for guests.
Bedrooms: 3 single, 13 double, 14 twin, 3 triple, 5 family
Bathrooms: 38 en suite
Bed & Breakfast: single £40.00-£45.00, double £40.00-£65.00
Parking for: 4
Methods of payment: Mastercard/Visa/Barclaycard/American Express/JCB/Eurocard/Diners/Switch/Delta/Eurocheque

Radisson Edwardian Vanderbilt Hotel

68-86 Cromwell Road, London SW7 5BT
Tel: (020) 7589 2424
Fax: (020) 7225 2293
➜ GLOUCESTER ROAD
This country-house-style hotel is located a short walk from Harrods and is easily recognisable by its classical Victorian facade.
Bedrooms: 81 single, 55 double, 86 twin, 1 triple
Bathrooms: 223 en suite
Evening meal: 1700 (l.o. 2200)
Methods of payment: Mastercard/Visa/Barclaycard/American Express/JCB/Eurocard/Diners/Switch/Delta/Eurocheque

Ramsees Hotel   ◆◆

32-36 Hogarth Road, Earls Court, London SW5 0PU
Tel: (020) 7370 1445
Fax: (020) 7244 6835
E-mail: ramsees@rasool.demon.co.uk
➜ EARL'S COURT
Located in Earls Court, within one minute's walk from Earl's Court underground station.

Rasool Court Hotel

Central location near Earl's Court Tube Station and 10 minutes from West End. All rooms with colour TVs, Sky Channels and direct dial telephones.

**Single from £33,
Double from £45,
Triple from £64.**

19/21 Penywern Road,
Earl's Court,
London, SW5 9TT
Tel: (020) 7373 8900 Fax: (020) 7244 6835
Email: rasool@rasool.demon.co.uk
Web. Address: www.rasoolcourthotel.com

Ramsees Hotel

**32/36 Hogarth Road, Earl's Court,
London, SW5 0PU
Tel: (020) 7370 1445
Fax: (020) 7244 6835
Email: ramsees@rasool.demon.co.uk
Web. Address: www.ramseeshotel.com**

For the best rates and location

One minute walk from Earl's Court Tube Station.
Open 24 hours, most rooms with private showers.
All rooms with colour TV, Sky Movies & Sport
Channels and telephone.

**Single from £33,
Double from £45,
Triple from £64**

LONDON HOTEL
BEST RATES!

WINDSOR HOUSE HOTEL, 12 PENYWERN RD, LONDON SW5 9ST
Tel: +44 (020) 7373 9087 Fax: +44 (020) 7385 2417
3/4/5 ROOMS: £12-£24 pppn
TWINS: £19-£32 pppn
SINGLES: £23-£42 pppn

**INCLUDES BIG BREAKFAST
USE OF KITCHEN. GARDEN
CENTRAL LONDON!**

Who has one of London's best bed & breakfast hotels?

(see back cover)

TROCHEE HOTEL

**21 Malcolm Road and 52 Ridgeway Place, Wimbledon,
London SW19 4AS. Tel: 020 8946 1579/3924 Fax: 020 8946 1579**
Bed and English Breakfast. Television, tea and coffee making facilities and
hairdryers in all bedrooms. En suite facilities available. Wimbledon British
Rail and Underground Station close by. Near Wimbledon Common and
tennis courts. Free parking available.

hotels & b&bs

Bedrooms: 13 single, 22 double, 11 twin, 15 triple
Bathrooms: 47 en suite, 8 shower only, 13 shared
Bed & Breakfast: single £34.00-£41.00, double £45.00-£52.00
Methods of payment: Mastercard/Visa/Barclaycard/American Express/JCB/Eurocard/Diners/Switch/Delta/Eurocheque

Rasool Court Hotel ◆◆

19-21 Penywern Road, Earls Court, London SW5 9TT
Tel: (020) 7373 8900/
(020) 7373 4893
Fax: (020) 7244 6835
E-mail: rasool@rasool.demon.co.uk
↔ EARL'S COURT
Situated near Earl's Court underground station, 20 minutes from the West End and Heathrow by train.
Bedrooms: 25 single, 16 double, 8 twin, 8 triple
Bathrooms: 35 en suite, 12 shower only, 4 shared
Bed & Breakfast: single £36.00-£42.00, double £48.00-£54.00
Methods of payment: Mastercard/Visa/Barclaycard/American Express/JCB/Eurocard/Diners/Switch/Delta/Eurocheque

Swallow International Hotel ★★★★

Cromwell Road, London SW5 0TH
Tel: (020) 7973 1000
Fax: (020) 7244 8194
E-mail: international@swallow-hotels.co.uk
↔ EARL'S COURT
Ideally situated in the heart of Kensington, close to Harrods and Knightsbridge. All 421 rooms are fully air-conditioned. Two restaurants, bar, leisure club and swimming pool also available.
Bedrooms: 28 single, 131 double, 226 twin, 25 triple, 11 family
Bathrooms: 421 en suite
Bed only: single £160.00-£170.00, double £170.00-£195.00
Evening meal: 1800 (l.o. 2345)
Parking for: 70

Methods of payment: Mastercard/Visa/Barclaycard/American Express/Eurocard/Diners/Switch/Delta/Eurocheque

Swiss House Hotel ◆◆◆

171 Old Brompton Road, London SW5 0AN
Tel: (020) 7373 2769/
(020) 7373 9383
Fax: (020) 7373 4983
E-mail: recep@swiss-hh.demon.co.uk
↔ GLOUCESTER ROAD
Comfortable, conveniently situated hotel near London museums, shopping and exhibition centres. Room service from 1200-2100.
Bedrooms: 5 single, 5 double, 2 twin, 4 triple
Bathrooms: 15 en suite, 1 shower only, 1 shared
Bed & Breakfast: single £50.00-£70.00, double £85.00-£105.00
Methods of payment: Mastercard/Visa/Barclaycard/American Express/Eurocard/Diners/Switch/Delta/Eurocheque

Windsor House ◆

12 Penywern Road, London SW5 9ST
Tel: (020) 7373 9087
Fax: (020) 7385 2417
↔ EARL'S COURT
Budget-priced bed and breakfast establishment in Earls Court. Easily accessible from airports and the motorway. The West End is minutes away by underground.
Bedrooms: 2 single, 4 double, 4 twin, 1 triple, 8 family
Bathrooms: 10 en suite, 8 shower only, 6 shared
Bed & Breakfast: single £32.00-£56.00, double £32.00-£56.00
Methods of payment: Eurocheque

York House Hotel ◆◆

27-28 Philbeach Gardens, London SW5 9EA
Tel: (020) 7373 7519/
(020) 7373 7579
Fax: (020) 7370 4641
E-mail: yorkhh@aol.com
↔ EARL'S COURT
Bed and breakfast hotel, located close to Earl's Court station, served

by Piccadilly Line, with direct links to Heathrow and West End.
Bedrooms: 16 single, 3 double, 3 twin, 2 triple, 3 family
Bathrooms: 3 en suite, 7 shared
Bed & Breakfast: single £33.00-£47.00, double £54.00-£73.00
Methods of payment: Mastercard/Visa/Barclaycard/American Express/JCB/Eurocard/Diners/Switch/Delta/Eurocheque

EC1
City of London

Thistle City Barbican

Central Street, Clerkenwell, London EC1V 8DS
Tel: (020) 7956 6000
Fax: (020) 7253 1005
E-mail: barbican@thistle.co.uk
↔/⇄ OLD STREET/KING'S CROSS
A modern hotel within easy walking distance of the Barbican Centre and the historic City of London. The hotel has conference rooms, restaurant, bar and coffee shop. Full leisure centre opened in September 2000.
Bedrooms: 65 single, 133 double, 247 twin, 18 triple, 2 family
Bathrooms: 465 en suite
Bed & Breakfast: single £105.00-£185.85, double £115.50-£198.45
Evening meal: 1800 (l.o. 2230)
Parking for: 12
Methods of payment: Mastercard/Visa/Barclaycard/American Express/JCB/Eurocard/Diners/Switch/Eurocheque

NW1
Marylebone/Euston

Americana Hotel ◆◆◆

172 Gloucester Place, Regent's Park, London NW1 6DS
Tel: (020) 7723 1452
Fax: (020) 7723 4641
E-mail: manager@americanahotel.demon.co.uk
↔ BAKER STREET
Quiet hotel ideally situated near to Baker Street and Madame Tussaud's. Clean, comfortable accommodation recently refurbished.

CB/Eurocard/Diners/Switch/Delta/
Eurocheque

Arena Hotel ◆◆◆

6 Forty Lane, Wembley, Middlesex
HA9 9EB
Tel: (020) 8908 0670/
(020) 8904 0019
Fax: (020) 8908 2007
E-mail: enquiry@arenahotel.fsnet.co.
uk
⊖ WEMBLEY PARK
Friendly, private hotel with a large
garden. Parking for 15 cars. Close to
bus stops and underground.
Convenient for Wembley Stadium,
Arena and Conference Centre and
within easy reach of the M1 and
North Circular.
Bedrooms: 2 single, 2 double, 3 twin,
3 triple, 3 family
Bathrooms: 13 en suite, 1 shared
Bed & Breakfast: single £45.00-
£49.00, double £51.00-£55.00
Parking for: 15
Methods of payment: Mastercard/
Visa/Barclaycard/American Express/
JCB/Eurocard/Diners/Switch/Delta/
Eurocheque

Ashdowne House ◆◆◆◆

4 Pownall Gardens, Hounslow,
Middlesex TW3 1YW
Tel: (020) 8572 0008
Fax: (020) 8570 1939
E-mail: mail@ashdownehouse.com
⊖ HOUNSLOW CENTRAL
Comfortable Victorian house with
elegant rooms, all en suite and non-
smoking. Conveniently situated for
travel to Heathrow and central
London.
Bedrooms: 2 single, 3 double, 2 twin
Bathrooms: 7 en suite
Bed & Breakfast: single £65.00,
double £79.00
Parking for: 4
Non-smoking establishment
Methods of payment: Mastercard/
Visa/Barclaycard/Delta/Eurocheque

Bridge Hotel

Western Avenue, Greenford,
Middlesex UB6 8ST
Tel: (020) 8566 6246
Fax: (020) 8566 6140
⊖/⇌ GREENFORD

The Bridge Hotel has 71 bedrooms,
each with hairdryer, trouser press
and satellite TV. Two bedrooms are
specifically designed for the
disabled. The lounge and bars have
the original wood panelling and
open fireplaces. Modem points in
bedrooms.
Bedrooms: 24 double, 44 twin,
3 family
Bathrooms: 71 en suite
Bed & Breakfast: single £58.00-
£92.00, double £68.00-£105.00
Evening meal: 1900 (l.o. 2145)
Parking for: 68
Methods of payment: Mastercard/
Visa/Barclaycard/American Express/
Diners/Switch

Channins Hounslow Hotel ★

41 Hounslow Road, Feltham,
Middlesex TW14 0AU
Tel: (020) 8890 2358
Fax: (020) 8751 6103
**⇌ FELTHAM, ⊖ HATTON
CROSS**
Hotel with 24 en suite rooms,
convenient for Heathrow and
Gatwick. Long-term parking
available. The hotel has restaurant
and bar facilities.
Bedrooms: 14 single, 5 double,
2 twin, 1 triple, 2 family
Bathrooms: 24 en suite
Bed & Breakfast: single £45.00-
£49.00, double £55.00-£62.00
Evening meal: 1830 (l.o. 2115)
Parking for: 31
Methods of payment: Mastercard/
Visa/Barclaycard/American Express/
Diners/Switch/Delta/Eurocheque

Cheshunt Marriott Hotel

Halfhide Lane, Turnford,
Hertfordshire EN10 6NG
Tel: (01992) 451245
Fax: (01992) 440120
⇌ CHESHUNT
The Cheshunt Marriott offers peace
and tranquility. Set in the beautiful
Hertfordshire countryside, the hotel
offers an ideal base for exploring the
area, or for a weekend retreat.
Bedrooms: 105 double, 38 twin
Bathrooms: 143 en suite
Bed & Breakfast: single £160.00,
double £160.00
Evening meal: 1830 (l.o. 2200)

Parking for: 200
Methods of payment: Mastercard/
Visa/Barclaycard/American Express/
Eurocard/Diners/Switch/Delta/
Eurocheque

Civic Guest House ◆◆

87-89 Lampton Road, Hounslow,
Middlesex TW3 4DP
Tel: (020) 8572 5107/
(020) 8570 1851
Fax: (020) 8814 0203
E-mail: enquiries@civicguesthouse.
freeserve.co.uk
⊖ HOUNSLOW CENTRAL
Warm and friendly guesthouse
conveniently located for Heathrow,
200 yards from Piccadilly Line
underground station. Twenty
minutes from central London.
Bedrooms: 6 single, 3 double,
11 twin, 7 triple, 1 family
Bathrooms: 13 en suite, 1 shower
only, 4 shared
Bed & Breakfast: single £45.00-
£50.00, double £58.00-£65.00
Parking for: 8
Methods of payment: Mastercard/
Visa/Barclaycard/American Express/
JCB/Eurocard/Switch/Delta/
Eurocheque

Cliveden

Taplow, Berkshire SL6 0JF
Tel: (01628) 668561
Fax: (01628) 661837
⇌ BURNHAM
One of the country's most famous
stately homes. Boasting a
spectacular setting and close
proximity to Heathrow Airport.
Bedrooms: 38 double
Bathrooms: 38 en suite
Bed & Breakfast: single £317.00-
£364.00, double £364.00-£394.00
Evening meal: (l.o. 2230)
Parking for: 100
Methods of payment: Mastercard/
Visa/Barclaycard/American Express/
JCB/Diners/Switch/Delta

Crescent Hotel

58-62 Welldon Crescent, Harrow,
Middlesex HA1 1QR
Tel: (020) 8863 5491/
(020) 8863 5163
Fax: (020) 8427 5965

hotels & b&bs

E-mail: jivraj@crsnthtl.demon.co.uk
♿/⚡ **HARROW-ON-THE-HILL**
Offering quality accommodation and a friendly atmosphere, within the heart of Harrow. Close to Wembley Conference Centre, the West End, Heathrow and motorways.
Bedrooms: 9 single, 3 double, 6 twin, 2 family
Bathrooms: 16 en suite, 4 shared
Bed & Breakfast: single £40.00-£50.00, double £55.00-£65.00
Parking for: 7
Methods of payment: Mastercard/Visa/Barclaycard/American Express/JCB/Eurocard/Diners/Switch/Delta/Eurocheque
⬜ ✿ ℂ ◖ 🛏

Crowne Plaza London Heathrow

Stockley Road, West Drayton, Middlesex, UB7 9NA
Tel: (01895) 445555
Fax: (01895) 445122
E-mail: cplhr@netscapeonline.com
⚡ **WEST DRAYTON**
Just ten minutes from Heathrow with Hoppa On Bus service to and from hotel to Terminals 1, 2, 3 at £2.50 each way. Thirty minutes from central London.
Bedrooms: 285 double, 173 twin
Bathrooms: 458 en suite
Bed & Breakfast: single £195.00, double £210.00
Evening meal: 1730 (l.o. 2230)
Parking for: 400
Methods of payment: Mastercard/Visa/Barclaycard/American Express/JCB/Eurocard/Diners/Switch/Delta/Eurocheque
⬜ ✿ ℂ ✂ 🖥 ◖ 🛏 ♦ 🍽 🎿 🚗

Elm Hotel ◆◆◆

1-7 Elm Road, Wembley, Middlesex HA9 7JA
Tel: (020) 8902 1764
Fax: (020) 8903 8365
E-mail: elm.hotel@virgin.net
♿/⚡ **WEMBLEY CENTRAL**
About 1,200 yards from Wembley Stadium, Arena and Conference Centre. Jet spa baths available.
Bedrooms: 7 single, 7 double, 11 twin, 6 triple, 3 family
Bathrooms: 30 en suite, 1 shared
Bed & Breakfast: single £50.00, double £67.00

Parking for: 7
Methods of payment: Mastercard/Visa/American Express/Eurocard/Switch/Delta/Eurocheque
⬜ ✿ ℂ 🛏 🏌 🍽 🚗

Forte Crest, Heathrow

Sipson Road, West Drayton, Middlesex UB7 0JU
Tel: (020) 8759 2323
Fax: (020) 8897 8659
⚡ **HEATHROW TERMINALS 1, 2, 3**
A large, modern hotel close to the sliproad from the M4 motorway to Heathrow, offering an excellent choice of restaurants, bars and conference facilities.
Bedrooms: 459 twin, 137 triple, 8 family
Bathrooms: 604 en suite
Bed & Breakfast: single £69.00-£179.00, double £79.00-£189.00
Evening meal: 1830 (l.o. 2300)
Parking for: 400
Methods of payment: Mastercard/Visa/Barclaycard/American Express/JCB/Diners/Switch/Delta/Eurocheque
⬜ ✿ ℂ ✂ 🖥 ◖ 🛏 🍽 🚗

Forte Travelodge

A24 Epsom Road, Morden, Surrey SM4 5PH
Tel: (020) 8640 8227/ 0800 850 950
Fax: (020) 8640 8227
⚡ **SAINT HELIER**
Prices are for room only. Meals are available at adjacent Harvester restaurant.
Bedrooms: 32 triple
Bathrooms: 32 en suite
Parking for: 40
Methods of payment: Mastercard/Visa/Barclaycard/American Express/Eurocard/Diners/Switch/Delta/Eurocheque
⬜ ✿ 🖩 ◖ 🏌 🚗

The George

High Street, Crawley, West Sussex RH10 1BS
Tel: (01293) 524215
Fax: (01293) 548565
⚡ **CRAWLEY**
Famous 17th-century inn combining old-world charm with modern amenities, including an up-to-date bedroom wing.

Bedrooms: 16 single, 21 double, 28 twin, 15 triple
Bathrooms: 80 en suite
Bed & Breakfast: single £95.00, double £104.00
Evening meal: 1900 (l.o. 2130)
Parking for: 95
Methods of payment: Mastercard/Visa/Barclaycard/American Express/Eurocard/Switch/Eurocheque
⬜ ✿ ℂ ✂ ◖ 🛏 🍽 🚗

Glendevon House Hotel ◆◆

80 Southborough Road, Bickley, Bromley BR1 2EN
Tel: (020) 8467 2183
Fax: (020) 8295 0701
⚡ **BICKLEY**
Family-run hotel with private car park, convenient for London and Kent. Caters for tourists and business travellers. All en suite rooms with tea and coffee making facilities and TV.
Bedrooms: 2 single, 3 double, 2 twin, 3 triple
Bathrooms: 10 en suite
Bed & Breakfast: single £34.00-£39.95, double £50.55-£54.50
Evening meal: 1900 (l.o. 2000)
Parking for: 7
Methods of payment: Mastercard/Visa/Barclaycard/Eurocard/Switch/Delta/Eurocheque
⬜ ✿ ℂ 🖩 ✂ 🛏 🏌 🚗

Heathrow Park Hotel

Bath Road, Longford, West Drayton, Middlesex UB7 0EQ
Tel: (020) 8759 2400
Fax: (020) 8759 5278
E-mail: heathrow.park@thistle.co.uk
⚡ **HEATHROW TERMINALS 1, 2, 3**
Modern hotel with conference and training facilities for up to 700 people. Easy access to M3, M4 and M25. Airport transfer bus £2.00.
Bedrooms: 135 double, 119 twin, 55 triple, 1 family
Bathrooms: 310 en suite
Bed & Breakfast: single £151.50, double £163.00
Evening meal: 1800 (l.o. 2330)
Parking for: 500
Methods of payment: Mastercard/Visa/Barclaycard/American Express/JCB/Diners/Switch/Delta/Eurocheque
⬜ ✿ ℂ ✂ ◖ 🏌 🛏 🍽 🎿 🚗

hotels & b&bs

Hilton Bracknell

Bagshot Road, Bracknell, Berkshire
RG12 0QJ
Tel: (01344) 424801
Fax: (01344) 487454
E-mail: reservations_bracknell@
hilton.com
⇄ BRACKNELL
Well situated in a thriving part of
Berkshire.
Bedrooms: 22 single, 95 double,
50 twin
Bathrooms: 167 en suite
Bed only: single £185.00, double
£195.00
Evening meal: 1900 (l.o. 2200)
Parking for: 180
Methods of payment: Mastercard/
Visa/Barclaycard/American Express/
Diners/Switch/Delta
⊡ ♤ ⌕ ⌅ ⊞ ◐ ⊟ ⌛ ⊠ ⇆

Hilton Croydon

Waddon Way, Purley Way, Croydon,
Surrey CR9 4HH
Tel: (020) 8680 3000
Fax: (020) 8681 6171
⇄ EAST CROYDON
A modern hotel with excellent
facilities including conference
rooms, two restaurants and a well-
equipped health club.
Bedrooms: 102 double, 66 twin
Bathrooms: 168 en suite
Bed & Breakfast: single £122.00-
£152.00, double £134.00-£164.00
Evening meal: 1900 (l.o. 2200)
Parking for: 185
Methods of payment: Mastercard/
Visa/Barclaycard/American Express/
JCB/Eurocard/Diners/Switch/Delta/
Eurocheque
⊡ ♤ ⌕ ⌅ ⊞ ◐ ⊟ ⌛ ⊠ ⇆

Hilton London Gatwick Airport

Gatwick Airport, Gatwick, West
Sussex, RH6 0LL
Tel: (01293) 518080
Fax: (01293) 528980
E-mail: hilton@gatwickairport.
freereserve.com
⇄ GATWICK
The only hotel linked by direct,
covered walkway to the South
Terminal and by rapid transit system
to the North Terminal.
Bedrooms: 357 double, 155 twin,
35 family

Bathrooms: 547 en suite
Bed & Breakfast: single £215.00-
£250.00, double £215.00-£250.00
Evening meal: 1900 (l.o. 2300)
Parking for: 120
Methods of payment: Mastercard/
Visa/American Express/Diners/
Switch/Delta/Eurocheque
⊡ ♤ ⌕ ⌅ ⊞ ◐ ⌛ ⊠ ⇆

Hilton London Heathrow Airport

Terminal 4, Heathrow Airport,
Middlesex TW6 3AF
Tel: (020) 8759 7755
Fax: (020) 8759 7579
E-mail: gm_heathrow@hilton.com
✈ HEATHROW TERMINAL 4
Large hotel with three restaurants,
cocktail lounge, leisure and
conference facilities. Linked to
Terminal 4 by a covered walkway.
Bedrooms: 231 double, 164 twin
Bathrooms: 395 en suite
Bed & Breakfast: single £110.00-
£260.00, double £110.00-£260.00
Evening meal: 1600 (l.o. 2300)
Parking for: 250
Methods of payment: Mastercard/
Visa/Barclaycard/American Express/
JCB/Diners/Switch
⊡ ♤ ⌕ ⌅ ⊞ ◐ ⊟ ⌛ ⊠ ⇆

Hilton National Cobham

Seven Hills Road South, Cobham,
Surrey KT11 1EW
Tel: (01932) 864471
Fax: (01932) 868017
⇄ COBHAM/WEYBRIDGE
Set in 27 acres of Surrey woodland,
close to the M25. Traditional hotel
with range of amenities.
Bedrooms: 108 double, 38 twin,
6 triple, 3 family
Bathrooms: 155 en suite
Bed only: single £160.00-£210.00,
double £160.00-£210.00
Evening meal: 1700 (l.o. 2200)
Parking for: 300
Methods of payment: Mastercard/
Visa/Barclaycard/American Express/
JCB/Eurocard/Diners/Switch/Delta/
Eurocheque
⊡ ♤ ⌕ ⌅ ⊞ ◐ ⌛ ⊠ ⇆

Hilton National Watford

Elton Way, Watford WD2 8HA
Tel: (01923) 235881
Fax: (01923) 220836

E-mail: wathnhngm@hilton.com
⇄ WATFORD JUNCTION
The hotel is just off the M1, 30
minutes from London and ten
minutes from the M25.
Bedrooms: 102 double, 89 twin,
6 triple
Bathrooms: 191 en suite
Bed & Breakfast: single £55.00-
£280.00, double £55.00-£280.00
Evening meal: 1900 (l.o. 2200)
Parking for: 350
Non-smoking establishment
Methods of payment: Mastercard/
Visa/Barclaycard/American Express/
Eurocard/Diners/Switch
⊡ ♤ ⌕ ⌅ ⊞ ◐ ⊟ ⌛ ⊠ ⇆

Hilton National Wembley

Empire Way, Wembley, Middlesex
HA9 8DS
Tel: (020) 8902 8839
Fax: (020) 8900 2201
E-mail: fom_wembley@hilton.com
✈ WEMBLEY PARK,
✈/⇄ WEMBLEY CENTRAL
Located within the Wembley complex,
this is the headquarters hotel for the
conference centre. Within easy
reach of major motorways. Free car
parking available.
Bedrooms: 93 double, 194 twin,
16 triple
Bathrooms: 301 en suite
Bed & Breakfast: single £100.00-
£180.00, double £100.00-£180.00
Evening meal: 1900 (l.o. 2200)
Parking for: 250
Methods of payment: Mastercard/
Visa/Barclaycard/American Express/
Diners/Switch/Delta/Eurocheque
⊡ ♤ ⌕ ⌅ ⊞ ◐ ⌛ ⊠ ⇆

Hotel Antoinette of Kingston ★★

Beaufort Road, Kingston upon
Thames, Surrey KT1 2TQ
Tel: (020) 8546 1044
Fax: (020) 8547 2595
E-mail: hotelantoinette@btinternet.
com
⇄ SURBITON
Well established, family-owned hotel,
providing comfortable
accommodation and an inviting
atmosphere. Brasserie restaurant
offering excellent cuisine.
Bedrooms: 25 single, 19 double,
24 twin, 5 triple, 26 family

hotels & b&bs

Bathrooms: 99 en suite
Bed & Breakfast: single £52.00-£60.00, double £62.00-£68.00
Evening meal: 1830 (l.o. 2115)
Parking for: 100
Methods of payment: Mastercard/Visa/Barclaycard/American Express/Switch/Delta/Eurocheque

Jarvis International Heathrow ★★★

Bath Road, Cranford, Middlesex TW5 9QE
Tel: (020) 8897 2121/(020) 8897 3079
Fax: (020) 8897 7014
E-mail: reservations@jarvis.co.uk
⊖ HOUNSLOW WEST
Modern hotel with its own delightful English garden. Convenient for Heathrow and central London and nine miles from Windsor. Close to M25 and M4.
Bedrooms: 1 single, 40 double, 42 twin
Bathrooms: 83 en suite
Evening meal: 1900 (l.o. 2215)
Parking for: 80
Methods of payment: Mastercard/Visa/Barclaycard/American Express/JCB/Eurocard/Diners/Switch/Delta/Eurocheque

Le Meridien Excelsior Heathrow

Bath Road, West Drayton, Middlesex UB7 0DU
Tel: 0870 400 8899
Fax: (020) 8759 3421
E-mail: rm1249@forte-hotels.com
⊖ HEATHROW TERMINALS 1, 2, 3, ⇌ HAYES
On the A4 Bath Road opposite the main entrance to Heathrow. Three restaurants to choose from, ranging from under £10 to over £20.
Bedrooms: 5 single, 526 double, 278 twin, 19 triple
Bathrooms: 828 en suite
Bed & Breakfast: single £83.00-£223.00, double £90.00-£223.00
Evening meal: 1815 (l.o. 2300)
Parking for: 540
Methods of payment: Mastercard/Visa/Barclaycard/American Express/JCB/Eurocard/Diners/Switch/Delta/Eurocheque

Le Meridien Gatwick Airport

North Terminal, Gatwick Airport, West Sussex RH6 0PH
Tel: 0870 400 8494
Fax: (01293) 567739
⇌ GATWICK AIRPORT
Modern hotel attached to North Terminal, Gatwick Airport.
Bedrooms: 309 double, 149 twin, 36 family
Bathrooms: 494 en suite, 5 shared
Bed & Breakfast: single £166.00-£195.00, double £176.00-£200.00
Evening meal: 1830 (l.o. 2300)
Parking for: 100
Methods of payment: Mastercard/Visa/Barclaycard/American Express/Eurocard/Diners/Switch/Delta/Eurocheque

The Mary Rose Hotel ★

40-50 High Street, St Mary Cray, Kent BR5 3NJ
Tel: (01689) 871917/(01689) 875369
Fax: (01689) 839445
⇌ ST MARY CRAY
Sixteenth century inn with modern hotel facilities, 25 minutes by train from Victoria. Chartwell, Leeds and Hever Castles are all within 45 minutes.
Bedrooms: 4 single, 11 double, 7 twin, 5 triple, 11 family
Bathrooms: 29 en suite, 2 shared
Bed only: single £34.50-£55.00, double £49.50-£55.00
Evening meal: 1900 (l.o. 2115)
Parking for: 50
Methods of payment: Mastercard/Visa/Barclaycard/American Express/Diners/Switch/Delta

Palms Hotel

Southend Arterial Road, Hornchurch, Essex RM11 3UJ
Tel: (01708) 346789
Fax: (01708) 341719
⇌ HAROLD WOOD
Modern hotel with good access to central London. Stylish restaurant and bar. Extensive conference facilities.
Bedrooms: 68 double, 68 twin, 1 triple
Bathrooms: 137 en suite
Bed & Breakfast: single £66.00-£125.00, double £76.00-£135.00

Evening meal: 1900 (l.o. 2200)
Parking for: 200
Methods of payment: Mastercard/Visa/Barclaycard/American Express/Diners/Switch/Delta/Eurocheque

Posthouse Heathrow

Bath Road, Hayes, Middlesex UB3 5AJ
Tel: 0870 400 9040
Fax: (020) 8564 9265
⊖ HEATHROW TERMINALS 1, 2, 3
Convenient for Heathrow. Linked to all Heathrow Terminals via Hoppa Bus Service. Free parking for residents on night of stay.
Bedrooms: 85 single, 53 double, 48 twin
Bathrooms: 186 en suite
Bed & Breakfast: single £66.50-£126.50, double £74.00-£134.00
Evening meal: 1700 (l.o. 2230)
Parking for: 100
Methods of payment: Mastercard/Visa/Barclaycard/American Express/JCB/Diners/Switch/Delta

Quinns Hotel ◆◆◆

48 Sheen Road, Richmond, Surrey TW9 1AW
Tel: (020) 8940 5444
Fax: (020) 8940 1828
⊖/⇌ RICHMOND
Ideally located for business or pleasure, within easy reach of central London, airports and local places of interest.
Bedrooms: 6 single, 24 double, 7 twin, 1 family
Bathrooms: 23 en suite, 6 shared
Bed & Breakfast: single £75.00-£105.00, double £85.00-£105.00
Parking for: 14
Methods of payment: Mastercard/Visa/Barclaycard/American Express/JCB/Diners/Switch/Delta/Eurocheque

Radisson Edwardian Hotel Heathrow

140 Bath Road, Hayes, Middlesex UB3 5AW
Tel: (020) 8759 6311
Fax: (020) 8759 4559
E-mail: resreh@radisson.com
⊖ HEATHROW TERMINALS 1, 2, 3

Award-winning hotel, with large atrium with pool and spa, opulent lounges and sumptuous restaurants.
Bedrooms: 3 single, 356 double, 86 twin, 14 triple
Bathrooms: 459 en suite
Bed & Breakfast: single £90.00-£180.00, double £110.00-£210.00
Evening meal: 1900 (l.o. 2230)
Parking for: 500
Methods of payment: Mastercard/Visa/Barclaycard/American Express/Eurocard/Switch/Delta/Eurocheque

The Renaissance London Heathrow Hotel

Bath Road, Hounslow, Middlesex TW6 2AQ
Tel: (020) 8897 6363
Fax: (020) 8897 1113
E-mail: heathrow@renaissance hotels.com
✈ **HOUNSLOW WEST**
Modern airport hotel with extensive conference, business and leisure facilities, restaurant, bar and health club.
Bedrooms: 325 double, 285 twin
Bathrooms: 610 en suite
Bed & Breakfast: single £80.00-£187.95, double £80.00-£290.90
Evening meal: 1800 (l.o. 2230)
Parking for: 680
Methods of payment: Mastercard/Visa/Barclaycard/American Express/JCB/Eurocard/Diners/Delta/Eurocheque

The Royal Berkshire Hotel

London Road, Sunninghill, Ascot, Berkshire SL5 0PP
Tel: (01344) 623322
Fax: (01344) 627100
Queen Anne country mansion set in mature parkland.
Bedrooms: 6 single, 42 double, 9 twin, 6 triple
Bathrooms: 63 en suite
Bed & Breakfast: single £110.00-£210.50, double £175.00-£235.50
Evening meal: 1930 (l.o. 2130)
Parking for: 250
Methods of payment: Mastercard/Visa/Barclaycard/American Express/JCB/Eurocard/Diners/Switch

Selsdon Park

★★★★ Silver Award
Addington Road, Sanderstead, South Croydon, Surrey CR2 8YA
Tel: (020) 8657 8811
Fax: (020) 8651 6171
E-mail: caroline.chardon@principal hotels.co.uk
⇌ **EAST CROYDON**
Historic country house hotel with sporting and leisure facilities, including golf course. Thirty minutes from London and Gatwick.
Bedrooms: 49 single, 84 double, 62 twin, 4 family
Bathrooms: 199 en suite
Bed only: single £110.00-£130.00, double £145.00-£165.00
Evening meal: 1930 (l.o. 2200)
Parking for: 265
Methods of payment: Mastercard/Visa/Barclaycard/American Express/Eurocard/Diners/Switch/Delta/Eurocheque

Shalimar Hotel

◆◆◆
215-221 Staines Road, Hounslow, Middlesex TW3 3JJ
Tel: (020) 8572 2816/0500 238239
Fax: (020) 8569 6789
✈ **HOUNSLOW CENTRAL**
Family-run hotel close to Heathrow. Hounslow High Street, underground station and bus stop are all nearby.
Bedrooms: 14 single, 7 double, 14 twin, 5 triple
Bathrooms: 30 en suite, 1 shared
Bed & Breakfast: single £55.00, double £65.00
Parking for: 10
Methods of payment: Mastercard/Visa/Barclaycard/American Express/JCB/Eurocard/Diners/Switch/Delta/Eurocheque

Sheraton Heathrow Hotel

Colnbrook Bypass, West Drayton, Middlesex UB7 0HJ
Tel: (020) 8759 2424
Fax: (020) 8759 2091
E-mail: sales_heathrow@sheraton.com
✈ **HEATHROW TERMINALS 1, 2, 3**
A modern, comfortable hotel with an ideal location for Heathrow Airport

and London. Smart rooms available for business travellers. Windsor, Henley and Maidenhead nearby.
Bedrooms: 209 double, 181 twin, 10 triple, 24 family
Bathrooms: 424 en suite
Bed & Breakfast: single £127.25-£199.25, double £141.50-£213.50
Evening meal: 1900 (l.o. 2330)
Parking for: 280
Methods of payment: Mastercard/Visa/Barclaycard/American Express/JCB/Eurocard/Diners

Sheraton Skyline Hotel and Conference Centre

Bath Road, Hayes, Middlesex UB3 5BP
Tel: (020) 8759 2535
Fax: (020) 8750 9150
✈ **HEATHROW TERMINALS 1, 2, 3**
Located on the main Bath Road (A4) at Heathrow. Modern three-storey building with tropical garden feature.
Bedrooms: 163 double, 177 twin, 12 triple
Bathrooms: 352 en suite
Bed only: single £90.00-£210.00
Evening meal: 1600 (l.o. 2300)
Parking for: 300
Methods of payment: Mastercard/Visa/Barclaycard/American Express/JCB/Eurocard/Diners/Delta/Eurocheque

The Ship Hotel

Monument Green, Weybridge, Surrey KT13 8BQ
Tel: (01932) 848364
Fax: (01932) 857153
E-mail: info@peelhotel.com
⇌ **WEYBRIDGE**
Grade II Listed building which combines modern, comfortable facilities with traditional exterior. Excellent service and standards.
Bedrooms: 9 single, 10 double, 20 twin
Bathrooms: 39 en suite
Bed & Breakfast: single £128.40-£144.45, double £155.15-£165.85
Evening meal: 1930 (l.o. 2145)
Parking for: 50
Methods of payment: Mastercard/Visa/Barclaycard/American Express/Diners/Switch/Delta/Eurocheque

group and youth

Tel: (020) 7833 9400
Fax: (020) 7833 9677
E-mail: info@ashleehouse.co.uk
⊖/⇄ KING'S CROSS
Contact: Ms A Dolan
Ashlee House is two minutes' walk from King's Cross station, ideally located for visiting the British Museum, the British Library and Camden markets.
Caters for: Males, Females, Individuals, Groups
Bedrooms: 4 double/twin, 8 family
Total no of bedspaces: 180
Bathrooms: 24 public showers
Open over Christmas
Months open: February/March/ April/May/June/August/September/ October/November/December
⛄🛏🖥☎🛍⛱

Astor's Museum Inn

27 Montague Street, Bloomsbury, London WC1B 5BH
Tel: (020) 7580 5360
Fax: (020) 7636 7948
E-mail: astorhostels@msn.com
⊖ RUSSELL SQUARE
Contact: Astor Hostels, 2-6 Inverness Terrace, London W2 3HY
Contact Tel: (020) 7229 7866
Contact Fax: (020) 7229 1283
The Museum Inn is located next to the British Museum and within walking distance of Soho, Covent Garden and Oxford Street.
Caters for: Males, Females, Individuals, Groups
Bedrooms: 2 double/twin, 1 triple, 4 family
Total no of bedspaces: 70
Bathrooms: 7 public showers
Bed & Breakfast: single £14.00-£20.00, double £28.00-£40.00
Open all year
Open over Christmas
🛏🖥☎🛍

Cartwright Hall

36 Cartwright Gardens, London WC1H 9BZ
Tel: (020) 7388 3757
Fax: (020) 7388 2552
E-mail: carthalls@aol.com
⊖/⇄ KING'S CROSS,
⊖ RUSSELL SQUARE
Contact: Mr E Sefain
Centrally located accommodation at affordable prices, near train stations

and tourist attractions. With reception, bar, restaurant, laundrette and a television and games room.
Minimum age unaccompanied: 15
Caters for: Males, Females, Individuals, Groups
Bedrooms: 126 single, 35 double/twin, 5 triple, 10 family
Total no of bedspaces: 400
Bathrooms: 7 en suite, 40 public showers
Bed & Breakfast: single £26.00-£35.00, double £38.00-£50.00
Open all year
Open over Christmas
⛄🛏🖥☎🛍⛱

The Florida State University London Study Centre

100-103 Great Russell Street, London WC1B 3LA
Tel: (020) 7813 3223
Fax: (020) 7813 3270
E-mail: info@acorn-london.co.uk
⊖ TOTTENHAM COURT ROAD
Contact: Mr I Watkins, Sutherland House, 70-78 West Hendon Broadway, Edgware Road, London NW9 7BT
Contact Tel: (020) 8202 3311
Contact Fax: (020) 8202 6797
Self-contained, comfortably furnished, fully equipped apartments, classrooms, offices, computer lab and lecture theatre. Minimum stay three nights.
Caters for: Males, Females, Individuals, Groups
Bedrooms: 4 single, 31 double/twin, 14 triple, 7 family
Total no of bedspaces: 136
Bathrooms: 36 public showers
Bed only: single £31.50
Open all year
Open over Christmas
⛄🛏🖥☎🛍⛱

Generator

Compton Place, off 37 Tavistock Place, London WC1H 9SD
Tel: (020) 7388 7666/
(020) 7388 7655
Fax: (020) 7388 7644
E-mail: info@the-generator.co.uk
⊖ RUSSELL SQUARE
Contact: Miss L Duffy
Budget accommodation with an exciting futuristic design theme. Extensive communal areas including

bar, games room, Internet room and tourist information centre.
Minimum age: 10
Caters for: Males, Females, Individuals, Groups
Bedrooms: 37 double/twin, 58 triple, 89 family
Total no of bedspaces: 833
Bathrooms: 70 public showers
Bed & Breakfast: single £36.50-£39.00, double £46.00-£54.00
Open all year
Open over Christmas
⛄🛏🖥☎🛍⛱

John Adams Hall (Institute of Education)

15-23 Endsleigh Street, London WC1H 0DP
Tel: (020) 7387 4086/
0870 357 0007
Fax: (020) 7383 0164
E-mail: jah@ioe.ac.uk
⊖/⇄ EUSTON
Contact: Mr M Lam-Hing
John Adams Hall is an assembly of elegant Georgian houses, offering comfortable budget accommodation.
Caters for: Males, Females, Individuals, Groups
Bedrooms: 127 single, 22 double/twin
Total no of bedspaces: 171
Bathrooms: 2 en suite, 26 public showers
Bed & Breakfast: single £22.00-£24.00, double £38.00-£42.00
Months open: March/April/May/ June/July/August/September
⛄🛏🖥☎🛍⛱

LSE Residence High Holborn

High Holborn Residence, 178 High Holborn, London WC1V 7AA
Tel: (020) 7379 5589
Fax: (020) 7379 5640
E-mail: high.holborn@lse.ac.uk
⊖ HOLBORN
Contact: Ms S Jons
Modern, self-catering flats situated in the heart of London.
Caters for: Males, Females, Individuals, Groups
Bedrooms: 310 single, 94 double/twin, 4 triple
Total no of bedspaces: 496

Stay in a London home

from only £16 to £40
*per person per night with breakfast **

Enhance your London experience by staying in a real London home. Our 200 homes are all within 20 minutes of Piccadilly by underground, and you will have your own house key.

Bed and breakfast is from £16 a night. Rooms in the centre with bath-rooms ensuite are from £25 - £40.

Tel: +44 (0)20 8949 4455 or +44 (0)20 8541 0044. Fax: +44 (0)20 8549 5492.
Email: lhs@netcomuk.co.uk

Credit cards accepted   **URL: lhslondon.co.uk**   *Minimum 3 nights.*

London Homestead Services, Coombe Wood Road, Kingston-upon-Thames, Surrey KT2 7JY

group and youth

Bathrooms: 20 en suite, 114 public showers
Bed & Breakfast: single £28.00-£35.00, double £46.00-£70.00
Months open: July/August/September
♿🚪🖥️📶♨️🅿️🔔

Passfield Hall

1-9 Endsleigh Place, London WC1H 0PW
Tel: (020) 7387 7743/ (020) 7387 3584
Fax: (020) 7387 0419
E-mail: passfield@lse.ac.uk
⊖/⇄ EUSTON
A conversion of Georgian houses in a quiet, central location. Well served by both train and underground stations.
Caters for: Males, Females, Individuals, Groups
Bedrooms: 100 single, 34 double/twin, 10 triple
Total no of bedspaces: 198
Bathrooms: 36 public showers
Months open: March/April/May/ July/August/September
♿🚪🖥️📶♨️🅿️

W2
Paddington/Bayswater

Astor's Hyde Park Hostel

2-6 Inverness Terrace, London W2 3HY
Tel: (020) 7229 5101
Fax: (020) 7229 3170
E-mail: astorhostels@msn.com
⊖ QUEENSWAY
Contact Tel: (020) 7229 7866
Contact Fax: (020) 7229 1283
With an excellent location directly opposite Hyde Park and within walking distance of Notting Hill Gate, Portobello Road Market and Queensway. Close to all forms of public transport.
Caters for: Males, Females, Individuals, Groups
Bedrooms: 4 double/twin, 18 family
Total no of bedspaces: 210
Bathrooms: 30 public showers
Bed & Breakfast: single £12.50-£21.00, double £25.00-£42.00
Open all year
Open over Christmas
🚪🖥️📶♨️🅿️🔔

Astor's Leinster Inn

7-12 Leinster Square, London W2 4PR
Tel: (020) 7229 9641
Fax: (020) 7221 5255
E-mail: astorhostels@msn.com
⊖ BAYSWATER/QUEENSWAY
Contact: Mr R Rennie
Fun, young hostel, located in the vibrant Bayswater and Notting Hill Gate area. Walking distance from Portobello Road Market and Hyde Park. Accommodation for groups and individuals.
Caters for: Males, Females, Individuals, Groups
Bedrooms: 15 single, 40 double/twin, 20 triple, 36 family
Total no of bedspaces: 339
Bathrooms: 325 public showers
Bed & Breakfast: single £14.50-£30.00, double £29.00-£60.00
Open all year
Open over Christmas
🚪🖥️📶♨️🅿️🔔⛏️

Astor's Quest Hotel

45 Queensborough Terrace, Bayswater, London W2 3SY
Tel: (020) 7229 7782
Fax: (020) 7727 8106
E-mail: astorhostels@msn.com
⊖ QUEENSWAY/BAYSWATER
Contact Tel: (020) 7229 7866
A fun and friendly hostel located close to Hyde Park and Kensington Palace, with lots of restaurants, cafes and pubs in the area.
Caters for: Males, Females, Individuals, Groups
Bedrooms: 2 double/twin, 6 family
Total no of bedspaces: 90
Bathrooms: 4 en suite, 7 public showers
Bed & Breakfast: single £14.00-£20.00, double £28.00-£40.00
Open all year
Open over Christmas
🚪🖥️♨️🅿️🔔

Leinster

46 Leinster Gardens, London W2 3AT
Tel: (020) 7723 7803
Fax: (020) 7262 3794
⊖ BAYSWATER
Contact: Mr T Perkins, Head of Personnel and Residential Services, The London Hostels Association, 54 Eccleston Square, London SW1V 1PG

Contact Tel: (020) 7828 3263
Contact Fax: (020) 7834 7146
Contact E-mail: bookings@london hostels.co.uk
Budget accommodation near Paddington. Three-course evening meal included.
Caters for: Males, Females, Individuals, Groups
Bedrooms: 14 single, 32 double/twin
Total no of bedspaces: 198
Bathrooms: 15 public showers
Bed only: single £15.50-£19.50, double £31.00-£39.00
Open all year
Open over Christmas
🚪🖥️♨️🅿️

Lords Hotel

20-22 Leinster Square, London W2 4PR
Tel: (020) 7229 8877
Fax: (020) 7229 8377
E-mail: lords@netcomuk.co.uk
⊖ BAYSWATER/QUEENSWAY
Contact: Mr N G Ladas
Bed and breakfast accommodation in the heart of London. Television in rooms. Most rooms with private facilities.
Minimum age unaccompanied: 10
Caters for: Males, Females, Individuals, Groups
Bedrooms: 9 single, 27 double/twin, 11 triple, 17 family
Total no of bedspaces: 175
Bathrooms: 61 en suite, 7 public showers
Bed & Breakfast: single £30.00-£45.00, double £44.00-£65.00
Open all year
Open over Christmas
♿🚪🖥️♨️⛏️

New Atlantic Hotel

1 Queen's Gardens, London W2 3BB
Tel: (020) 7262 4471
Fax: (020) 7706 8548
E-mail: newatlantichotel@vienna-group.co.uk
⊖/⇄ PADDINGTON
Contact: Ms N Pickering
Budget hotel in Bayswater, ideal for youth groups.
Minimum age: 2
Caters for: Males, Females, Individuals, Groups
Bedrooms: 37 single, 99 double/twin, 11 triple, 37 family

group and youth

Total no of bedspaces: 462
Bathrooms: 94 en suite, 34 public showers
Bed & Breakfast: single £49.00-£55.00, double £65.00-£72.00
Open all year
🛏 🖾 ☎ ⚓ ♨

New Mansion

38 Lancaster Gate, London W2 3AT
Tel: (020) 7723 4421
Fax: (020) 7262 3797
🚇 **LANCASTER GATE**
Contact: Mr T Perkins, The London Hostels Association, 54 Eccleston Square, London SW1V 1PG
Contact Tel: (020) 7828 3263
Contact Fax: (020) 7834 7146
Contact E-mail: bookings@london hostels.co.uk
Single, double and dormitory rooms available. Price for dormitories includes bed, breakfast and a three-course evening meal.
Caters for: Males, Females, Individuals, Groups
Bedrooms: 18 single, 38 double/twin
Total no of bedspaces: 89
Bathrooms: 15 public showers
Bed & Breakfast: single £18.50-£22.50, double £37.00-£45.00
Open all year
Open over Christmas
🖵 🖾 🚿 ☎ 🖴

The Porchester Hotel

33 Princes Square, London W2 4NJ
Tel: (020) 7221 2101
Fax: (020) 7727 9976
E-mail: porchesterhotel@vienna-group.co.uk
🚇 **BAYSWATER**
Contact: Mrs B Charles
Ideal for youth groups, The Porchester has its own passenger lift and offers rooms with private facilities. The hotel offers affordable accommodation.
Caters for: Males, Females, Individuals, Groups
Bedrooms: 6 single, 17 double/twin, 11 triple, 21 family
Total no of bedspaces: 175
Bathrooms: 31 en suite, 10 public showers
Bed & Breakfast: single £44.00, double £59.00-£69.00
Open all year
Open over Christmas
🛏 🖵 🖾 🚿 ☎ 🖴 ♨

Railton

10 Craven Hill, London W2 3DT
Tel: (020) 7723 5643
🚇/🚆 **PADDINGTON**
Contact: Mr T Perkins, Head of Personnel and Residential Services, The London Hostels Association, 54 Eccleston Square, London SW1V 1PG
Contact Tel: (020) 7828 3263
Contact Fax: (020) 7834 7146
Contact E-mail: bookings@london hostels.co.uk
Self-catering hostel.
Caters for: Males, Females, Individuals, Groups
Bedrooms: 14 single, 40 double/twin
Total no of bedspaces: 142
Bathrooms: 9 public showers
Bed only: single £15.50-£19.50, double £31.00-£39.00
Open all year
Open over Christmas
🖵 🖾 🚿 ☎ 🖴

Sandeman Allen

40 Inverness Terrace, London W2 3JB
Tel: (020) 7727 2719
Fax: (020) 7229 2526
🚇 **BAYSWATER/QUEENSWAY**
Contact: Mr T Perkins, Head of Personnel and Residential Services, The London Hostels Association, 54 Eccleston Square, London SW1V 1PG
Contact Tel: (020) 7828 3263
Contact Fax: (020) 7834 7146
Contact E-mail: bookings@london hostels.co.uk
Budget accommodation in Paddington. Three-course evening meal included.
Caters for: Males, Females, Individuals, Groups
Bedrooms: 29 single, 36 double/twin
Total no of bedspaces: 122
Bathrooms: 15 public showers
Bed & Breakfast: single £18.50-£22.50, double £37.00-£45.00
Open all year
Open over Christmas
🖵 🖾 🚿 ☎ 🖴

SW5/7
Chelsea/Earls Court/South Kensington

Baden-Powell House 🚶

65-67 Queen's Gate, South Kensington, London SW7 5JS
Tel: (020) 7584 7031
Fax: (020) 7590 6902
E-mail: admin.bphhostel@scout.org.uk
🚇 **GLOUCESTER ROAD**
Contact: Mr J Kilpatrick
Baden-Powell House is a hostel and conference centre, close to many museums, offering good value and service.
Caters for: Males, Females, Individuals, Groups
Bedrooms: 6 single, 8 double/twin, 3 triple, 8 family
Total no of bedspaces: 180
Bathrooms: 34 en suite, 3 public showers
Bed & Breakfast: single £65.00, double £80.00
Open all year
Parking for: 9
🛏 🚗 🖵 🖾 🚿 ☎ 🖴 ♨

Belvedere

6 Grenville Place, London SW7 4RT
Tel: (020) 7373 5701
Fax: (020) 7370 7556
🚇 **GLOUCESTER ROAD**
Contact: Mr T Perkins, Head of Personnel & Residential Services, The London Hostels Association, 54 Eccleston Square, London SW1V 1PG
Contact Tel: (020) 7828 3263
Contact Fax: (020) 7834 7146
Contact E-mail: bookings@london hostels.co.uk
A self-catering hostel.
Caters for: Males, Females, Individuals, Groups
Bedrooms: 23 single, 52 double/twin
Total no of bedspaces: 271
Bathrooms: 17 public showers
Bed only: single £15.50-£19.50, double £31.00-£39.00
Open all year
Open over Christmas
🖵 🖾 🚿 🖴

Culture Link International Student Residence

161 Old Brompton Road, Kensington, London SW5 0LJ
Tel: (020) 7373 6061
Fax: (020) 7373 7021
🚇 **GLOUCESTER ROAD**
Contact: Ms M Flemisch
Student residence in Kensington.
Minimum age: 2
Minimum age unaccompanied: 14

'Eryr gwyllt ar war gelltydd,
Nid ymgêl pan ddêl ei ddydd.'
'Marwnad Syr Owain ap Gwilym',
William Llŷn

'... a pha fodd bynnag yr enwodd y dyn bob peth
byw, hynny fu ei enw ef.'
Genesis 2:19

'But above all Kafka is the writer of middles. Of
elaborations, of contradictions, of
prevarications, of digressions.'
Michael Hofmann

'What has Kafka taught you about the
possibilities of literature?'
The Times Literary Supplement,
31 Mai 2024

The man comes around
Johnny Cash

Diffygio

Yr oedd yn y bỳs sdop wedi diffygio'n llwyr. Ar ôl y pla newydd. Bỳs ar ôl bỳs yn mynd heibio a heb y nerth i godi o'r fainc haearn. Pob bỳs yn arafu, ond pan welai'r gyrrwr nad oedd neb am ddod ar y bỳs cyflymodd ac yn ei flaen yr aeth.

Yr oedd cyfnodau fel hyn o ddiffygio yn digwydd o bryd i bryd.

Cofiodd adeg y Pla Du.

Yr hyn a elwid y Rhyfel Mawr. Yr holl fwd cleiog. Y llygod mawr.

Ond nid oedd angen mynd drwy'r holl restrau. Roedd gormod ohonynt. Y ganrif ddiwethaf, y gwaethaf un.

Cofio ambell i enw.

Carol (60).

Carl (12).

Ond yr oedd wedi mwynhau, os gweddus dweud, yn ystod ambell seibiant annisgwyl, ddinas Hanoi.

Ogla'r bwyd stryd.

'Nenwedig y porc.

Enw

Unwaith yn unig y mentrodd i mewn i un o'r adeiladau rhyfedd hynny, rheiny y clywodd rhywun yn defnyddio'r enw 'eglwysi' amdanynt, yn bennaf fel y medrai gael golwg ar sgil-gynnyrch ei swyddogaeth. Nid oedd wedi 'dirnad' erioed o'r blaen fod ei 'Hei-Ho Ffarwél' yn cynhyrchu'r trymder a'r ysbryd affwysol a deimlai yn yr adeilad.

A'r dagrau.

Ond yma hefyd y canfyddodd ei enw. Pan glywodd rhywun yn holi: 'Pa le mae dy golyn?' rhywsut teimlodd fod pawb yn edrych arno, ac mai ef oedd y Colin hwnnw.

Cynt meddyliodd mai Biwrocrat oedd ei enw. Ond hwyrach mai ei snâm oedd hynny? Colin Biwrocrat?

Yn ddiweddarach yn y bỳs sdop lledodd rwbath tebyg i gywilydd dros Colin. Teimlad nad oedd wedi ei gael o'r blaen.

Dywedwyd wrtho un tro mai peth perygl oedd i rywun gael enw.

Ar ei ben ei hun fel hyn yn y bỳs sdop penderfynodd y byddai'n anfon sìc nôt atyn nhw, Y Fiwrocratiaeth, yfory. Rhyw ddeng niwrnod o hoe.

'Ancsaiyti.'

Dyna a ddywedai'r nodyn.

Sìc Nôt

Yn benisel yr oedd Colin yn ôl yn y bỳs sdop. Gwyddai mai dybl decyr fyddai'r bỳs nesaf, ac y câi ef eistedd yn y top yn y sêt gefn. Roedd wedi mwynhau hynny erioed. A heddiw byddai hynny'n gysur; cysur ar ôl i'w sìc nôt gael ei wrthod.

'Sìc nót!' dywedwyd wrtho.

'Biwrocratiaeth,' sibrydodd Colin dan ei wynt.

'Dach chi ddim yn sylweddoli,' mynegwyd, 'fod teulu Hana Ephraim (89) yn awyddus i gael bob dim drosodd o fewn yr wythnos nesaf neu mi fyddan nhw'n colli pres y crŵs i'r Med? Mae petha'n annioddefol i Tegid Moore (42). A chwarae teg i Llion Ballantyne (67). Loti (5) hefyd.' Dangoswyd awyren dros yr Iwerydd iddo a 'Joban fawr, honna.'

Gwyrth

Gorfu i Colin hoblan yr holl ffordd o dŷ Eluned Cabot-Symms.

A dyma fo yn y bỳs sdop yn pendroni sut ar wyneb y ddaear y medrai o esgyn fyth eto o'r pafin i'r bỳs.

Troi ei ffêr ddaru o ar y sdeps sy'n arwain at ddrws ffrynt Bethesda'r Fro, cartref Eluned Cabot-Symms. Ni allai symud gam ymhellach i fyny'r grisiau, heb sôn am fedru cyrraedd erchwyn ei gwely mewn pryd.

Nid yw hyn yn ddigon da, dywedwyd yn fiwrocrataidd wrtho, ei ffêr wedi chwyddo'n enbyd, ac yntau'n trio hopian a hoblan am yn ail i gyrraedd hafan y bỳs sdop.

Yn y cyfamser, yr oedd Eluned Cabot-Symms yn sipian cwpanaid o de ar ei heistedd yn ei gwely, clustogau'r holl dŷ y tu ôl iddi, ei lliw wedi dychwelyd, pawb yn dweud iddi ddŵad o le pell, rhai'n sôn am wyrth.

A dyna yw gwyrth mae'n debyg, Colin yn hwyr, neu Colin yn hoblan.

Adlewyrchiad

Yn ddiweddar yr oedd Colin wrth fynd o gwmpas y lle wedi bod yn clustfeinio ar ambell sgwrs ymhle yr honnai hwn a'r llall eu bod yn *adlewyrchu* ar y pwnc a'r pwnc – mae'n amlwg fod yr adlewyrchiadau hyn yng Nghymru'n ddigon i ddallu unrhyw un – rhai, ac yr oedd hyn wrth fodd Colin, yn adlewyrchu ar ddifodiant. Yn ei ddiniweidrwydd meddyliodd Colin mai gweld eu lluniau yn y pynciau hyn yr oeddynt, fel mewn drych. Yr oedd wedi cynhyrfu'n lân ac mewn cryn benbleth wrth geisio dychmygu y rhai hyn yn gweld eu lluniau mewn difodiant. Dyna'r peth olaf – i'w roi o fela – a ddigwyddai mewn difodiant, ie ddim?

Wrth fyfyrio fel hyn a hithau'n nosi y tu allan a'r tu mewn i'r bỳs sdop, y ddau ddyn yn ôl yn y car du'n cael smôc a phanad o fflasg, gwelodd Colin am y tro cyntaf ei adlewyrchiad ar y persbecs.

Gwelodd ei wyneb ei hun.

Cynt, eraill yn unig oedd yn cael ei weld. Ei weld am lai nag 'eiliad'. Cyn diffodd.

Ond gwelodd ei hun. Sibrydodd i'w adlewyrchiad 'Hei-Ho Ffarwél', fel petai o ei hun hefyd yn dymuno'r diffodd. Ond ni eill wneud hynny iddo'i hun, gwyddai'n iawn.

Rhyfeddodd pa mor ieuanc ydoedd. Wedyn heneiddiodd. Daeth yn ganol oed. Un munud yn ddyn, y munud nesaf yn wraig. Yn hogyn bach. Yn hogan fach. Newidiodd lliw ei groen. A siâp ei lygaid. Moelodd. Aeth ei wallt drwy liwiau'r enfys. Brithodd. Gwynnodd. Moelodd yn ôl. Ar lesni ei lygaid yr oedd hapusrwydd. Ar eu gwyrddni, dristwch. Gwyddai ei fod yn ddall.

Pawb ydoedd.

Clywodd y dyrnu ar y persbecs.

Y ddau foi, Hector a Gordon 'Lucy', ar wŷs y Bois o'r Fiwrocratiaeth: 'Sgynnon ni'm trw' dydd.'

Ond mae gin i, meddyliodd Colin.

Hwylustod Gramadegol

Mae'n rhaid fod Colin wedi 'syrthio i gysgu' – hwylustod gramadegol yw'r ymadrodd yma i ddisgrifio mewn dull cyfarwydd, hawdd i'w ddeall, yr hyn nad yw'n digwydd i Colin o gwbl. Ond pan 'ddeffrodd' – eto, i ddefnyddio gair sy'n lledegluro heb y sdrach o orfod esbonio yr hyn sy'n anesboniadwy – canfu Colin fod y car du wedi mynd.

Mae'n debyg fod Y Fiwrocratiaeth wedi 'maddau' iddo, neu o leiaf wedi sylweddoli na all Colin fyth newid ei swyddogaeth, er ambell i brotest o'i du a dymuno arall. Colin yw Colin. Ydyw yr hyn ydyw.

Gwyddai'r Fiwrocratiaeth hynny. Gwyddai Colin hynny.

Hynny mae'n debyg oedd y rheswm dros ymadawiad y car du. I be' oedd angen Y Sgwrs? Ni allai Colin ddengid rhag ei 'dynged' – gair arall handi; a gwyddoch beth a feddylir heb orfanylu.

Felly ar ei arffed yr oedd y rhestr o enwau ac oedrannau ar gyfer heddiw. Edrychodd Colin arni a'i hagor yn y man.

Nid oedd ond un enw: Eiddon (17). Yr hogyn yr oedd Colin wedi cogio bach peidio ei weld ar y bỳs y dydd o'r blaen.

Gorchymyn, cosb a maddeuant oddi wrth Y Fiwrocratiaeth yng nghlwm wrth un enw: Eiddon (17).

Yn y munud bydd Colin yn dal y bỳs ac fe wyddai y bydd Eiddon (17) arno.

Heddiw fe'i gwelai.

Tynnu'r llun wedyn oherwydd yr angen am dystiolaeth ffotograffig erbyn 2 y pnawn, a'i anfon yn ei ddull ei hun i'r offis.

Jobsys Hawdd

Yn blygeiniol daeth y car du heibio'r bỳs sdop lle'r oedd Colin, a sdopio. Agorodd y ffenasd ddu a daeth wyneb Hector Dafis i'r fei.

'Ty'ma,' meddai wrth Colin.

Nid oedd gan Colin, wedi iddo 'ddarganfod' – gair handi, gyda llaw – ei fod yn barhaol yn y stad gyd-rhwng unrhyw reswm dros wrthod y cais.

'Y Bois,' meddai Hector, 'am i mi ddeud wel-dỳn wrthat ti. Ond mi oedd y llun yrrast ti o'r hogyn Eiddon (17) 'na'n blỳr i gyd. Crynu oeddat ti, washi? Hwda, ma hwn i ti.'

Estynnodd restr newydd i Colin. A Colin ar fin ei chipio tynnodd Hector hi'n ôl, wedyn ei chynnig eto a'i thynnu drachefn yn ôl wrth i Colin estyn eto amdani; a'r 'nôl a blaen gwirion hwn deirgwaith arall hyd nes y penderfynodd Colin beidio â chwarae'r gêm.

'Ma 'di monni, Gordon 'Lucy',' meddai Hector. ''Ma ti yli, washi.'

Yn y bỳs sdop yn eistedd ar y set haearn darllenodd Colin yr enwau:

* Y Teulu Ifansys: Bob (40), Joslyn (39), Ceidio (19), Sabel (16)
# Happy Jordan (20) a Summer (5)

Pur anaml yr ychwanegwyd unrhyw nodiadau cyfarwyddol ar waelod y rhestr – câi Colin ddewis ei ddulliau ei hun – ond yr oedd y tro hwn. Gyferbyn â'r * yr oedd: 'Mecanical ffeiliyr ar yr ariciwleited lorri sy'n i hitio nhw tu allan i Clatter.' T.E.

Ac wrth yr #: 'Dreifar meddw; y pafin tu allan i giatiau'r parc.' J.C.

LLUNIAU FEL ARFER. DIM-DIM! – BLŶR.

'Dirnadodd' Colin fod Y Fiwrocratiaeth yn ei wthio fwyfwy er mwyn iddo wneud iawn am ei simsanrwydd blaenorol. Nid oedd am gael jobsys hawdd mewn ysbytai a chartrefi hen bobl neu Mart Bryncir hyd yn oed, ambell ffarmwr canol oed ar ganol ffrai-yp.

'Irish linen,' meddai'r ci, yn gweld y rhyfeddod ar wyneb Colin.

Llieiniau byrddau claerwyn wedi eu startjo.

Dynesodd Colin at un gistfedd er mwyn cael gweld yn iawn. Ar y lliain yr oedd doilis. Stand enfawr platiau tri llawr ar y canol yn llawn o sandwijis, cacennau bychain del, busgets, bara brith, jami dojyrs, wagn wîls. Pob math o jelis.

'Rowntree's,' ebe'r ci.

Blymonjis pinc fel pwrsus bychod wyneb i waered, yn gryndodau melys drostynt. Ac instant whips bytyrsgotj.

'Ar nacw ma'r seifyris,' meddai'r ci, yn dangos cistfedd arall yn llawn ar ei lliain bwrdd o sosej rôls, fóla fóns, ham a tyng, rôl mops, picls, picylili, picyld yniyns, picyld egs, gyrcins, salad crîm... a bryd hynny y sylwodd Colin ar yr ugeiniau a oedd yn bwyta'n hapus, hamddenol. Un hen wreigan, y cryndod yn ei llaw, ei cheg ar un ochr a'r glafoeri, yn gwneud llanast o frechdan ham, ond yn ddedwydd ddigon.

'Mae'r platia a'r resd o'r tjeina yn Roial Doltyn,' esboniodd y ci.

Clywodd Colin o'r tu ôl i'r coed ryw sŵn canu 'Pen Blwydd Hapus', tair gwraig yn dyfod i'r fei efo cacen anferth ac arni ddau gant naw deg ac un cannwyll ynghyn. Dechreuodd pawb arall ganu a neidiodd Meirwen – wel, ei chodi, deud y gwir, gan ddau hen Fethusala – i ben cistfedd a oedd yn gyforiog o flodau ac Arctig Rôls.

'Wt ti am weld yr hogia'n trwsio'r car – hen Ffordyn – ben pella 'cw?' holodd y ci Colin.

Ond nid oedd ynddo unrhyw awydd i weld hynny. 'Teimlodd' Colin ei fod wedi cael ei – a dyma air hwylus yn dŵad rŵan – 'amddifadu' o rwbath.

Gwelodd hogyn a hogan yn eu harddegau yn dengid yn slei law yn llaw o'r parti rownd ochr yr eglwys.

Deuai sŵn meri-go-rownd o rywle yn y cefnau tu ôl i'r holl fieri.

Gwaith cyfyng iawn oedd gweithio i'r Fiwrocratiaeth. Nid

oedd dihangfa ar esgyll Ffansi. Nid oedd wedi meddwl holi erioed beth oedd yn digwydd wedi'r Hei-Ho Ffarwél – os unrhyw beth.

Yn ôl yma yn y bỳs sdop, sylweddolodd Colin mai'r un peth oedd bywyd cyn ac ar ôl pob Hei-Ho.

Diwrnod Rhydd

Gwisgai Colin iwnifform yn unol â'i swyddogaeth ddyddiol, a than orchymyn Y Fiwrocratiaeth, ar wahân i'r un Diwrnod Rhydd misol pan oedd ganddo'r hawl i wisgo unrhyw beth a fynnai. A chan mai 'dyn' ffrogiau yn y bôn oedd Colin gwisgai felly ffrog bob Diwrnod Rhydd.

Gwell esbonio'r Diwrnod Rhydd.

(Ond cyn gwneud hynny, diddorol fyddai cofnodi i Colin weld ar y dybl decyr o'r bỳs sdop ben bora heddiw Mari'r Fantell Wen a Letỳs Prei yn cydeistedd: bỳs Sdiniog oedd o ma raid; er mai mantell goch oedd gan Mari amdani gan mai dydd Llun yw hi ac nid y Saboth.)

Felly y Diwrnod Rhydd, am hynny yr oedden ni'n sôn, 'nde.

Y mae'r Fiwrocratiaeth yn hoff iawn o ddefnyddio gair fel 'rhydd' – 'dewis' yw un arall – i greu ym meddyliau ei gweision yr 'ymdeimlad' o annibyniaeth barn a meddwl a gweithred. Ond y mae popeth, wrth gwrs, wedi ei reoli a'i drefnu rhag-blaen.

Yr ydych yn 'rhydd' yn unig tu mewn i'r trefniant rhag-blaen hwn, ac yn 'teimlo' yn yr un cywair eich bod wedi gwneud 'dewis'. Y 'teimlo' hwnnw yw'r peth. Felly 'teimladau' yw 'rhydd' a 'dewis' fel ei gilydd, nid gweithredoedd neu benderfyniadau.

Mae Colin wedi hen weld drwy hyn. A byddai'n well ganddo petai'r Diwrnod Rhydd yn cael ei ddiddymu'n llwyr. Ond dyna fo, mae yntau hefyd yn chwarae'r gêm fel pawb arall tu mewn i'r Fiwrocratiaeth.

Yn ei ffrog polca dot du a gwyn yn y bỳs sdop a sawl bỳs wedi mynd heibio eisoes oherwydd na allai Colin benderfynu ar 'Sbectaciwlars' heddiw. A dyna un o amodau – yr unig amod fel y gŵyr Colin bellach – y Diwrnod Rhydd: ni chaniateir Hei-Ho Ffarwél cyffredin megis strôc neu hartan, rhaid wrth 'Sbectaciwlars'. Wyth enghraifft ar gyfer pob Diwrnod Rhydd.

Y tro blaenorol, chwe 'Sbectaciwlar' yn unig a gyflwynodd. Cafodd gerydd a rhybudd. Y tro cynt, tri yn unig. Cafodd gerydd a rhybudd. Buan y deallodd mai mympwy oedd wyth. Ac nad oedd y cerydd na'r rhybudd yn golygu affliw o ddim byd. Sut oedd o i'w geryddu? A rhybudd o beth? Ei ddiswyddo? Gwyddai'r Fiwrocratiaeth fel y gwyddai yntau mai hyn oedd ei swyddogaeth ac na ellid yn wahanol. Nid oedd yn 'rhydd'. Nid oedd ganddo 'ddewis'. Mwy nag unrhyw un arall. Hyd yn oed penaethiaid Y Fiwrocratiaeth, pwy bynnag oeddynt – roedd rhyw 'Clive' gwyddai. Ac ers iddo ddirnad hyn, roedd Colin yn ddistaw bach wrth ei fodd yn saernïo'r 'Sbectaciwlars'.

Un o bennaf ddiléits y 'Sbectaciwlars' oedd creu 'cyflafan'.

A bỳs ar ôl bỳs yn mynd heibio, cynllunio 'cyflafan' yr oedd Colin...

Ar fore mor boeth teimlodd Peredur ap Huw nad peth doeth oedd cadw'r can petrol yng nghist y car, felly penderfynodd fynd ag o i'w swyddfa yn yr ysgol ymhle yr oedd ef yn brifathro.

Eisteddodd wrth ei ddesg yn rowlio pensil 'nôl a blaen â blaen ei fys. 'Staedtler HB' medrai ddarllen ar y bensil, a chan nad oedd yn un gron ond yn un â phum ochr, nid oedd yn rowlio'n esmwyth. Nid oedd dim byd yn esmwyth.

'Mewn!' meddai pan glywodd gnoc ar ei ddrws.

''Mond isio deud 'thach chi, Syr, fod deng ffenasd 'di ca'l clec dros y wicend eto,' ebe Payne Butterfield, y gofalwr, yn piciad ei ben rownd ymyl y drws.

Yn yr hen ddyddiau byddai Peredur wedi gwneud y cysylltiad rhwng enw cyntaf y gofalwr a'r gwydr shwrwd ar lawr y dosbarthiadau.

Clywodd sŵn y plant ar hyd y coridor y ben bore hwn ac wythnos newydd ar fin dechrau eto. Adnabu lais athrawon. Ei le yntau oedd bod ar y coridor yn cyfarch, yn gwenu, yn 'Ara' deg fanna, Ifan Huw'.

Cnoc arall ar ei ddrws.

'Mewn!'

'Ti'n ocê?' holodd Donna Presley, hithau fel Payne Butterfield yn picio'i phen rownd ymyl y drws. ''Mond tjecio!'

A winciodd arno.

Wedi iddo arllwys y petrol o'r can hyd-ddo i gyd a'i gynnau, agorodd y drws a cherddodd yn wenfflam i'r coridor.

Ceinwen Balls (41)

Rhith neu beidio – fel'na mae petha; be' wyddon ni? – yr oedd Colin a'i restr yn ei law y tro hwn yn aros am y bỳs.

A daeth y dybl decyr ffyddlon.

Capal Batus Bara Caws oedd yr Iwcylyptus yn wreiddiol. Wedyn argraffdy am gyfnod byr. Un o 'ystafelloedd' cudd MI5 yn ystod yr arwysgiad. Bron yn furddyn wedi hynny. Yn nyddiau cynnar S4C, a'r arian yn lliffo'n ffastiach na'r Seiont, pencadlys Cwmni Teledu Sgeris ydoedd – hwy wnaeth y rhaglen blant *Dei y Deinasor* a'r ddrama ddogfen *Sgandals* W.J. A rŵan, yr Iwcylyptus – clwb Chwiorydd Bling – eu cyfieithiad hwy o 'Drag Queens'.

Yma mae Colin o flaen y drws yn darllen y postyr:

HENO
9:00
Y CHWIORYDD BLING –
ARTURA JENI,
FFANI GALÔR,
JINI-MÊ TODD,
CEINWEN BALLS,
COCKSURE MARGOT,
MISS CLIT WESTWOOD.

A sdicyr ar ei draws fel sash biwti cwin: WEDI GWERTHU ALLAN. Mae'n rhaid mai bryd hynny y croesodd y peth 'feddwl' – mae'r gair hwylus hwn wedi ei esbonio droeon o'r blaen – Colin. Y mae deilema. Yr enw ar dop ei restr ef oedd Ceinwen Balls (41). Enw llwyfan yw Ceinwen Balls – chwaer bling. Tu ôl i Ceinwen y mae Carwyn? Neu efallai, Glyn? Neu Tegid? Hubert? Amlyn? Amig? Nid oedd Y Fiwrocratiaeth wedi amgyffred hyn o gwbl. Wrth bwy felly yr oedd Colin i ddweud 'Hei-Ho Ffarwél'? Wedi'r cyfan y mae popeth i'r Fiwrocratiaeth yn unplyg, syml, heb unrhyw gymhlethdod. Norm sydd yna nid gwahaniaethau, a'r norm hwnnw wedi ei gonsurio o ddim byd a'i awdurdodi'n rheol a rheolau. A chan fod Y Fiwrocratiaeth mor dwp â hyn, penderfynodd Colin y byddai yntau hefyd yn dynwared yr un twpdra a gwneud dim.

Penderfynodd hefyd y byddai'n troi i fyny heno i'r perfformiadau ac y deuai fel Colleen yn un o ffrogiau ei Ddiwrnod Rhydd (gweler y stori 'Diwrnod Rhydd' am esboniad o hyn). Yr un sicwins aur, gwta, dynn debyg.

A phan ddaw heno, fel hyn y bydd petha: yr Iwcylyptus dan ei sang, Colleen yn eu plith. Yr holl le yn debyg i ffenasd siop gemydd. Y Chwiorydd Bling ar y llwyfan. Rhywun yn meddwl iddo glywed ogla mwg ond yn ei anwybyddu. Yr oedd y tannau wedi eu cynnau yn yr allanfeydd.

Llosgwyd Ceinwen Balls (41) a dau gant naw deg ac wyth arall.

Yn ôl yn y bỳs sdop 'deallodd' Colleen – a mynnodd gadw'r enw am ychydig – mai Diwrnod Rhydd fu hwn, ond na ddywedwyd hynny wrthi. A chafwyd un o'r sbectaciwlars.

Nid yw'r Fiwrocratiaeth fyth yn dwp.

Alffa Romeo

Un waith yn unig y bu i Colin weld Y Fiwrocratiaeth, neu ran ohoni, agwedd arni, cip sydyn – go iawn neu mewn breuddwyd – ond rhyw hangar o le ydoedd. Oddi allan yn goriwgeited iyrn du bitj, siâp hanner cylch, ond oddi mewn ni byddai'r ymadrodd 'ymestyn am byth' yn gwneud cyfiawnder â'i 'enfawredd'. Yno wrth ddesgiau unffurf yr oedd y dynionach unffurf.

Mae'n debyg iddo 'gofio' hyn – yn null Colin o 'gofio' – pan ddaeth i'w feddwl yr holl lofruddiaethau yr oedd o wedi ymwneud â hwy drwy'r canrifoedd. Ond sut yn hollol yr oedd o wedi 'ymwneud' â rheiny? Rhywun yn Hei-Hoio rhywun arall mewn ffyrdd 'annymunol'. Ble'r oedd o'n ffitio i mewn i hyn i gyd? (Deuai petha fel hyn i'w 'feddwl' weithiau yn blygeiniol yn y bỳs sdop wrth iddo aros am y rhestr. Anawsterau a phroblemau ei swyddogaeth. Anawsterau 'gwybod' a 'disgrifio'.)

Mae'n rhaid fod Y Fiwrocratiaeth wedi darllen ei 'feddwl' oherwydd pan ddaeth y rhestr yn y ffordd y deuai'r rhestr y dyddiau hyn, yno yr oedd:

'Wenceslas' Evans (67)

Dyn Salfeishyn Armi oedd 'Wenceslas' Evans. Mae'n debyg iddo gael ei lysenw oherwydd ei hoff dymor oedd y Nadolig, ac ef, efo'r band tu allan i Nelson's, yn arwain y carolau. Ond bu i'r Meijyr 'Wenceslas' Evans syrthio. Yn lle troi niferoedd lawer oddi wrth y botel, trodd ef ei hun at y botel. Enghraifft loyw ac eithafol, efallai, o garu gelyn. Ond dyna fo, mae pobl sydd wedi syrthio yn llawer rheitiach petha na'r rhai sydd wedi cadw'r llwybr cul. Ond nid yng ngolwg y rhelyw wrth gwrs; yn eu golwg hwy collodd 'Wenceslas' Evans bopeth. Ond gan mai'r ddiod oedd ei bopeth, a chyn belled fod y gwirodydd – waeth p'run –

yn dewach na'i waed, ni fyddai'r Meijyr (a pharhaodd i alw ei hun yn hynny) yn ymwybodol o golli unrhyw beth. Yr oedd o'n hapus. Rwbath a anghofir am y rhai sy'n licio cyffur: am gyfnodau hirion iawn maen nhw'n hapus ryfeddol.

Yn y sefyllfa hapus hon y canfu Colin y Meijyr 'Wenceslas' Evans ar ei ben ôl, ei goesau ar led mewn lle parcio gwag ar ail lawr y mylti-stori, a dim ond rhyw ddyrnaid o geir eraill o gwmpas, yn drachtio Martini.

Trît oedd y Martini. Fel sy'n digwydd yn anaml iawn, iawn, ond sy'n digwydd weithiau yn y pedwar amser fel y bo i'r Meijyr, y dyn crefyddol ag ydyw o hyd, ei ddirnad fel gwyrth. A phwy sydd i wadu hynny gan fod gwyrth cystal esboniad unrhyw ddiwrnod ar hap a damwain â chyd-ddigwyddiad? Cafodd hyd i waled tu ôl i fainc yn y Sowth o'Ffrans. Ynddi roedd hanner canpunt bron iawn. Duw a'i rhoddodd iddo. A dyma esbonio y Martini. Mae gan Dduw chwaeth, ac ni fynn gadw ei alcoholiaid mewn seidr rhad a phlonc am byth.

Ni wyddai Colin beth i'w wneud. Yr oedd yn rhaid iddo wneud rwbath. Yr oedd yr enw 'Wenceslas' Evans ar ei restr.

Ond daeth y car.

Alffa Romeo piws. Parciwyd y car yn y lle parcio o flaen y Meijyr. Parcio twt ryfeddol. Diffoddwyd yr injan dawel. O'r car daeth gwraig ifanc hynod drwsiadus. Aeth yn ôl i mewn i'r car a'i danio. Yn araf symudodd y car i gyfeiriad y Meijyr 'Wenceslas'. Edrychodd ef mewn hapusrwydd arno'n dyfod i'w gyfeiriad a chodi ei law. Aeth y car dros ei goesau, gwasgu ei frest i'r paneli concrit, a hollti ei ben. Rifyrsiodd y wraig y car am yn ôl yn araf a gadawodd y mylti-stori'n hamddenol iawn i barcio'n rhywle arall mae'n debyg. Yn wyrthiol yr oedd y botel Martini yn gyfa o hyd.

Gwelodd Colin hyn i gyd.

Mae'n rhaid fod a wnelo ef â hyn?

Taflu Pêl

Weithiau bydd Y Fiwrocratiaeth yn 'dewis' – mae'r ddadl athronyddol ynglŷn â'i medr hi i gyflawni gwir 'ddewis' yn parhau'n fywiog o hyd. Gweler y gyfrol: *Choice as Omnipotence*, Alexander Bucephalus (Cambridge, 1992) – gohirio anfon y rhestr ben bore tan ganol pnawn, ac yn ddi-feth y pryd hynny, hogyn ifanc ar ei feic a ddaw â hi, gyda'r geiriau di-amrywiaeth: 'Syr, hon i chi gin y Mustyrs.'

Felly y digwyddodd heddiw.

Yma mae Colin bellach y tu allan i ddrws ffrynt:

> Y Bytholwyrdd
> Cartref i'r Ieuanc sy'n Mynd i Oed.

Yn edrych arno drwy baen gwydr y drws yr oedd un o'r ieuenctid. Fel sawl geneth ieuanc arall – o leiaf yn nealltwriaeth y Bytholwyrdd – yr oedd doli yn ei llaw. Barbie anweddus o noeth a thenau. Y tu ôl iddi yn practisio carate ag ystumiau lled sydyn yr oedd Action Man. Helmet sosban ar ei ben.

Ymrithiodd Colin drwy'r pren a'r gwydr, cerdded ar hyd y coridor llawn lliwiau (*pastel shades*) nes cyrraedd y feithrinfa lle'r oedd llawer o'r ieuenctid. Dau neu dri ohonynt yn cerdded rownd a rownd mewn cylchoedd yn dynwared ceir rasio araf. Dwy gyrl-geidaidd eu natur yn ymarfer gwahanol fathau o glymau â hancesi poced. Un yn dysgu yfed orenj jiws gwan drwy droi ei bicyr pinc wyneb i waered a rhyfeddu at y dafnau bychain a ddeuai o'r pig melyn. Un arall yn dysgu darllen drwy ddal y papur newydd ben i lawr. Un hogyn bach wedi tynnu ei drowsus i ddangos ei glwt. Un hogan fach yn edrych arni ei hun mewn drych crwn bychan a'i gefn blodeuog. Edrych ac edrych. Edrych. Yr oedd teledu tawel yn edrych arnynt i gyd, a'r ddau y

Rhwng dau dywyn torrodd ar draws dau ddyn.

'Sori, fedra i'm siarad Susnag.'

Tu ôl i dywyn arall aflonyddodd ar ddwy ddynes yn ymarfer.

'Sori, fedra i'm siarad Susnag.'

Clywodd rhywun yn bytheirio mewn Birminghamaneg.

'Sori, fedra i'm siarad Susnag.'

O'r gofod daeth llong ofod goch a tharo Colin ar ei 'dalcen'.

'Sori, fedra i'm siarad Susnag.'

A chododd yr hogyn bach ei ffrisbi a'i anelu drachefn i gyfeiriad Colin, ond aeth heibio'i glust efo wwhwsh.

'Sori, fedra i'm siarad Susnag.'

Ym mhen pella'r traeth yr oedd stondin yn gwerthu crysau amryliw ac ar bob un y geiriau:

sori fedraim siarad susnag

– Colin

Roedd y tonnau'n dawel; yn feddal fwyn fel acen merched Llŷn.

Yn Ein Plith

Ni wyddai Hiwi MacMillan (62) lle i droi. Ni wyddai lle yr oedd. Un munud roedd o'n siarad efo Clayton Mott. Gwelai ei hun yn dweud:

"'

"'

Gwelai symudiadau ei wefusau. Y dyfynodau fel bachau yn dal affliw o ddim.

Edrychodd o'i gwmpas a dirnadodd sawl sgwrs yn mynd ymlaen:

"'   "'
"'   "'
"'   "'
"'   "'
"' "'

Y dyfynodau fel pryfed. Eu symudiadau chwim.

"' "'
"'   "'
"' "'
"'   "'

Haid ohonynt. Tryblith ohonynt.

Yn cau amdano. Agorodd ei wefusau.

Llanwasant "'"""""""""""""""""""""""""""""" ei geg.

Blodau

Euthum drwy'r Brŵs.

Dyma fo: Hollyhocks.

A'r enw Cymraeg ydy: Malws y Gerddi.

Dyna'r enw a hoffais fwyaf.

Gwneuthum hyn oherwydd i mi glywed y stori hon am Ivy Tilsley.

Ers pan oedd hi'n ddim o beth yr oedd Ivy wedi teimlo yn anfoddog yn ei chnawd ei hun. Efallai fod cyfarchiad ben bore, bob bore, ei mam wedi bod yn rhannol gyfrifol am yr anfodlonrwydd hwn, neu, yn wir, wedi cychwyn petha. 'Helô, blodyn.'

A beth oedd hi fod i'w wneud â cherydd dyddiol ei hathrawes?

'Ivy, dwi bron â dringo'r wal efo chi.'

A thrît pnawniau Sul: ffrŵt salad Del Monte efo... Carnation Milk.

A bob Dolig: bocs o Roses.

Cyfarchiad wedyn gan y jentylman drws nesa – pan nad oedd neb o gwmpas ond y hi – 'Helô, primrose darling.'

'Nôl i'r Dolig, ei thad yn mynnu: dydy hi ddim yn Ddolig heb hyacinth – wrth ddŵad â'r blodyn tebyg i frwsh llnau potal lefrith neu ban lafytori o dywyllwch y cwpwrdd dan grisiau. Wedyn mynd yn ôl i'r tywyllwch gan ailymddangos drachefn efo 'Un sbesial i chdi, Ivy'.

Hyn i gyd wedi arwain at y ben bore hwnnw – yn wir, yr oriau mân – pan ddaeth iddi'r alwad:

'Ty'd ata i i'r ardd.'

A hi â aeth.

Bu'r chwilio'n ddyfal am ddyddiau. Heddlu. Teulu. Ffrindiau. Pobl leol. Pobl o bell. Pobl od. Cŵn. Hofrenyddion. Camerâu.

Aethpwyd mor bell â chodi lloriau un tŷ.

Yn y man, tyfodd Malws y Gerddi.

A chan eu bod yn greaduriaid mor dal, medrent weld dros bob dim a gweld ymhell.

Eu blodau'n fyrddiwn llygaid.

Stori Blant

Dysgodd Colin ymadrodd newydd. Clywodd ef sawl tro bellach, ac fel sy'n digwydd bob amser (sylwer ar blant bach), amsugnir y geiriau a'r ymadroddion yn raddol i'r crebwyll. Weithiau fe'u defnyddir yn gywir, dro arall yn ddigrif o anghywir. (Cofiaf am y dyn gyflwynodd ei hun i'w gynulleidfa drwy ddweud 'Pysgodyn oedd fy nhad'.) Felly yn y bỳs sdop y bore hwn yr oedd Colin yn 'gwningen hapus' – oherwydd dyna'r ymadrodd. Ambell waith clywsai nad oedd rhywun yn 'gwningen hapus', dro arall 'cwningen hapus' ydoedd 'pawb'.

Un tro, gwelodd Colin 'gwningen hapus' mewn cae yn bwyta gwair. Tybed mai'r bwyta gwair oedd yn gyfrifol am 'gwningen hapus'? Ond daeth clec a syrthiodd y gwningen ar ei hochr. Fe'i codwyd gerfydd ei choesau ôl. (Nid oedd gan Colin gysylltiad â'r adran anifeiliaid yn Y Fiwrocratiaeth.) Oedd hi'n dal yn 'gwningen hapus'?

Y bore hwn yn y bỳs sdop yr oedd dwy 'gwningen hapus' yn aros am y bỳs. Gwyddai Colin hynny oherwydd i'r naill ddweud wrth y llall: ''Dan ni'n ddwy gwningen hapus bora 'ma. Waeth ni ddeud y gwir ddim. Does 'na'm byd gwell na chladdu'n gwŷr.'

Mewn te parti – te parti yr efeilliaid Cara a Mara Middleton – gorfu i Colin Hei-Hoio Ffarwél Aneirin Tendrill (39) oedd wedi ei wisgo mewn siwt 'cwningen hapus' ac yn gwneud triciau. Aneirin yn gorwedd ar y llawr a'r plant yn chwerthin yn afreolus ar ben y tric. Y mamau'n rhyw amau nad tric oedd hwn, gan arwain y plant allan yn ddi-ffýs fesul un a dau i dderbyn y *party bags*.

Pan dynnwyd Aneirin Tendrill (39) o'r siwt yn ddiweddarach gan y merchaid ambiwlans, canfyddwyd nad ef oedd yno ond yn hytrach Jamie 'Esquire' fel roedd o'n cael ei alw. Yr oedd Aneirin wedi ei ddarbwyllo i gymryd ei le: 'Wêl neb abilities?" At the time I didn't understand what he was asking, but now I know that he was trying to help me recognize my true abilities the way he had. In order words, he was asking what is my true hustle.

I can go on and on about acceptable, expectable and respectable hustles, because business and hustle are both about manipulation. Sales, marketing, and advertising are media mind games and programming; It's all hustles. In business this is the key to gain customers and profit. No matter what business you're in, you have to manipulate your services or goods thought media to build room for profit.

The media can be your ally or enemy. If you're a consumer it can make you aware, educate you to buy, or scar the hell out of you. If you're a business person/hustler, it can promote you, inform you, and make you money. Everyone is controlled and hypnotized by the media, so it is within your best interest to understand how it works. For more on this subject of media. Refer to my online article, "the matrix of media @marcellusscott.com/matrixofmedia"

As an entrepreneur, I sell talent, products, service time, information, etc. It's all about selling resources. You can be a legal or illegal hustler the choice is yours; however, each one can lead to achievement or despair.

True hustle is also a state of motivation. It's the will to take advantage of opportunities, and there are too many opportunities in life not to take advantage of them. I guess this is why I became a career entrepreneur; I instinctively take advantage of things that can improve my life. It's surprising to me that a lot of people see those same opportunities and don't take advantage of them. They don't have any obstacles in their way, but they never take action on any of the things they say they want to do. Talk sells for cheap and most people buy it for themselves!

At the age of 24, I started a roadside assistance company and a few years later I started two publishing companies, where I published two magazines and a TV show. I also launched two graphic design businesses and worked with some of the smartest and most intelligent people in my area. I have achieved a lot over the years, but at the same time I have also lost money. I've done all the hard work, but this has only gotten me close to my dreams, but not to the completion of them. At least that is what I thought. I would always seem to succeed and then feel a level of failure. This is because I had one small problem; I didn't understand my purpose.

Let's start from the beginning because that is where true hustle begins. Everyone has a talent, which is their purpose or in other words, "the hustle". Most people notice their talents as children, but unfortunately if it does not agree with their parents' morals and ethics they immediately want to stop them. They feel it is inappropriate to voice what they think is right or wrong. It's very important not to hinder children, but observe and allow them to hone in on their talents.

I believe that the purpose in being attentive to children's skills is to guide them appropriately. There are always facts, opinions, and balance in all things. This means, negative or positive action can lead to success and/ or failure among people. By learning this, I understand that success is about true effort toward all talents. Success can be granted to any focus skilled effort, with the acceptance of consequence of actions taken.

Most of my life has been structured around business and hustle to make money. I've always had a passion for writing, teaching, and inspiring people. I like to listen and learn from people that think conventionally and unconventionally about success. It helps me to see different sides of what most people believe and feel about life.

I have witnessed many people who have done things they felt was negative and it led to their failure, while with others it led to their success. I use to think like most people that success was defined by the amount of good deeds or money that I have accumulated. Now I define success as the accumulation of what makes me happy. Success for me is having what I need, which in turn gives me the things that I want. I've found enjoyment from learning, which gave me the ability to write this book.

The completion of this book is the level of proven success for me, which is part of my purpose. I don't claim to have the absolute answer to everyone's success because in all honesty, I don't know the answer. Like most, all I know is what I have been told. I can only reveal recorded information left by others to help people that seek success, find it for themselves.

There is a difference between getting motivated and staying motivated. As we all know, life can be very difficult with today's issues, so we must continue to motivate ourselves to continue. This is why In some environments aggressive hustle causes a level of crime that give the illusion of a successful future. This is what has created a misrepresentation of the term hustle.

Hustling is not solely related to crime. It's important to understand that what someone feels can be achieved illegally, can also be achieved legally. It's possible by being just as aggressive legally with your goal as you are with eating, seeing, hearing and drinking. All five senses need to be focused on what you want.

Subject 1
Ambition

When it comes to hustle and ambition, people are employers or employees, leaders or followers, producers or consumers, controllers or controlled. All these things are needed to give the individual purpose. For example, to be an employer, you need employees. To be a leader, you have to have followers, and to control you must have things to control. This is part of our common environmental life cycle.

As I explained in my introduction, people are either achieving their goals morally or immorally and negatively or positively. From experience, most ambitious people use 7 mental tools to support their actions.

1. Knowledge - Information & Experience. Acquiring the knowledge you need to give you the power to achieve what you want.

2. Belief- Confidence & Reliability. Having confidence in you abilities and know that they are the key to your success or failure.

3. Focus - Concentration, Attention, Preparation in single order

4. Motivation - Inspiration & Action. Always take action toward achieving what you want, even if you don't currently have all the resources. Just get started and learn and build as you go.

5. Sacrifice - Giving up something to achieve something more or less

6. Patience - The act of endurance under difficult circumstances

7. Persistence -Resilience, Endurance, & Commitment. Never give up, no matter what happens. You only fail if you give up.

For More On Info. www. marcellusscott.com

Ambitious State of Mine

I Believe:

• All people respect ambition

• No one can judge others without being judged.

•.No one knows any one outcome without knowing their future

• Beliefs and perception is reality.

• Nothing is yours solely (There is always a linkage to others)

• Things aren't always as they seem (Situations are unpredictable)

• There are different points of view to any one story

• Whatever you may feel is bad, could be worst

• Everything has room for improvement

• All things can make a difference "Everything Matters"

• Success is achieved by continuous energetic intent

Life ambitions seem to fall under two categories, working for self or others. It's important to understand that if you work a job or working for yourself you have to put the same effort into both practices. Most people feel that business is all about working for self. Well that is somewhat true, but it's not that simple. In reality, you don't work for yourself; you work for your customers.

When working for an employer, it's similar except you're working for your employer's customers. You might think because you're the owner you pay yourself what you want, but in reality, you pay yourself based on what your overhead cost and profit margin can permit. Another misconception is that you can go to work or stay home when you want. In order to do this, someone has to be working for you when you're not. Someone has to manage the business, no matter if it's your business or your employer's.

and supply themselves with all their needs, so they rely on others to do it for them. This is how to become an effective product.

If you create products or services for the majority, you will sell to the majority. I have talked with many entrepreneurs about their products and services, and they all have different standards for themselves. I believe it is more about creating standards for others, because they're the ones that are buying.

Lesson 13
Be A Middle Man

There is money in circulation at all times in all levels of your life. All you have to do is get in the middle of it. Roughly, 90% of products and services that are sold are placed in positions between sell transactions. Your talent is a product or service that you can sell. If you have a problem selling your own talent, then sell someone else's.

For example, there are ways to get products of others to sell to get started and these methods are known as sales affiliations, MLM (multi-level marketing), brokers, referral agents or independent contractors. The company gives you access to their list products, and you sell them to get a percentage of the profit for handling the transaction or sale. This is an effective way to start a career or business with investing less money.

The key to success with this type of venture is to present what you're selling to everyone you come in contact with. This is based on a science called the law of averages. It's a known fact that most people will buy almost anything, if you can give them a good that is good enough to buy. It's all about good persuasion skills. It is important to understand that you can sell your talent this way also. The law of averages says that if you ask 10 to 20 people to accept something, 1 out of 10 will accept what you are offering or selling.

For More On Info. www. marcellusscott.com

18

For example, if you in an area of 10,000 people, if you collect $1 from 1000 of those people, that would earn you $1,000. Then multiply this process x 10, which would give you $10,000. Start thinking to yourself; what are some ways to get $5 $10, or even $100 using this same process? It's called a money cycle. It's taking place around as you now, through production, marketing, distribution and sales. The key is to have a good idea to be placed in the middle of the circulation.

Lesson 14
Follow The Big Fish

If you need money and everyone around you is lacking in that area, then go where the money is. For example, if you stand around a swimming pool, more than likely you're going to get wet. If you want to catch big fish, you go to the deeper part of the lake where the big fish are. To find the people with

money, start by searching the internet and in the newspaper for special events with people who will support your interests.

There is an abundance of people with large sums of money and they are looking for people with ideas to invest their money in. They won't know about you if you don't go into their environment. It's also very important to be prepared for anything. Be ready to sell yourself at will by being sharp and ready to present your mission and goal in the most simplest and creative ways. Always have business cards available and always take one from all the people you meet. Follow up on those connections regularly, because you never know who could one day be an asset to you.

For More On Info. www. marcellusscott.com

Lesson 15
Redefine Failure

Avoid failure, by reevaluate it. See failure as only feedback, and don't let it change your focus. We all have wanted one thing but got something different. We've all have gotten poor result on a test, or put together the right plan only to see everything go left. It's important to use the words "outcome" and "results." Always see the productive results by looking at what you've learned. There a learn process in all actions. If you have learned you have not fail.

Lesson 16
Don't Cancel On Your Dreams

You will have people telling you what you can't do, or what will not work. Do not let anyone tell you that you cannot do something. If you have a dream, live it. If you have the desire, act on it. If you have an idea, bring it to life.

> People Can Be Like Walls, Which Mean You
> Can Walk Around Them or Climb Over Them

People tend to make negative and opinionated comments about your dreams because of their previous experiences, envy, jealousy, insecurities, or lack of understanding about your goals. It's important to understand that whether positive or negative, it's only an opinion. It's your opinion that matters the most. The negative opinions are often a reflection of someone's failure to achieve their own success. Because of pre-conceived notions of situations that somewhat relate to yours, they feel justified to feel that you will share the same fate as they did. What didn't work for them doesn't mean the same will not work for you. At the same time, if someone else had a positive experience, it doesn't mean that you're going to have the same positive experience. There are different strokes for different folks.

I call these people "Dream Killers." These could be family, friends, or anyone that tries to hinder you because of their views based on their personal views of your dreams. Dream killers will feel proud of killing your dreams, all the while not knowing what the future holds. Sometimes they don't have negative intent toward you; it's just that they don't understand your dreams. It's important to  understand that the only way others can understand your dreams, is if they can see your mental vision.

Giving someone the view inside of your mind is not an easy task for most; so expect to be misunderstood sometimes. My message is very clear. It's okay for someone to give you an opinion and constructive criticism, but that doesn't give you a reason to stop. It should give you more of a reason to continue.

If someone thought enough of you to say something to you, it means that they noticed you. That also means you are interesting to someone. If you are interesting to one person, you are interesting to many others. People don't entertain non-interest. So take any negative comments as feedback and know that you're making an impact in peoples' lives and "KEEP IT MOVING."

For More On Info. www. marcellusscott.com

Lesson 17
Attract Your Dreams

When you think of being attractive, you think of being physically beautiful or handsome. Well that's one way to look at it; but do you feel attractive as you look? For some people attractiveness starts outside but for some people it starts inside. One thing is for certain; both attract certain types of people, places, and things. Being attractive starts with energy, and the type of energy you give out and take in. This gives you a certain type of attractive spirit. To be ambitious, it is very important to have an attractive spirit to attract what you want.

There is a mental science known as, "The Law of Attraction." It is the belief "like attracts like." That by focusing on positive or negative thoughts, you can bring about positive or negative results. This belief is based upon the idea that people and their thoughts are both made from pure energy. It's the belief that the same type of energy attracts each other. In some cases, I personally believe this is correct. When I researched the science of magnetic energy it made logical sense.

The body is made up on elements electricity and magnets called electromagnetic energy. They regulate physical and mental body functions. Also, everything around you that you want has metal in them

Important Business Facts:
A New Business Is Like A Baby
It Need:

- Name & Ownership
- Belief & Financial Support
- Focus & Dedication
- Time & Patience To Grow

Business & Baby Comparison:

The difference between business and child success and failure
- The ability to take action (motivation and ambition)
- Getting the right financing (money)
- Getting good suppliers (nutritious food)
- Getting the right customers (community support)
- Finding the right staff (parental involvement)

Most businesses and children fail because of:
- Stress & Labor
- Lack Of Financial Support
- Lack Of Knowledge
- Poor Management

What failing business owners and parents has In common:
- They're Indispensable & Irreplaceable
- The business or child cannot do without them
- Nothing can happen without them
- Everything happens because of them

For More On Info. www. marcellusscott.com

34

Business Start Up

Step 1. Think of An Idea

A business is only as successful as the idea of the person running it. It's logical for you to do what you have a passion for. You need to have love for what you do or be familiar with it based on your experience with the subject. Passion, experience, and repetition in work performed leads to excellence.

Step 2. Create A Name

• Something you can explain easily
• Something with purpose
• Something you will be proud of
• Make it short as possible and internet domain friendly by being easy to find and remember

Step 3. Decide On Your Overall Objective

• It's purpose
• Decide what you want your business to give you and do for you?
• How does the thought of business make you feel right now?
• How do you want your business to make you feel?
• How do you want your customers to feel about your business?

Step 4. Setup Rules And Discipline

The Way You Set Standards Is By Using Consistency.

• Gather information that models your business
• Always take a look at other businesses that are similar to your own
• Shop the competition
• Avoid copying or being too close in the local service area in order to avoid business inflation in your community.
• Innovate your business, but be effective with the standard

For More On Info. www. marcellusscott.com

Step 5. Get A Stable Working Environment And Equipment.
Here are the basic business tools to get started.

• Computer or Digital Table for work production
• Cell phone - Mobile for communication
• Internet - For information, sales, and networking
• Work Station area at home or office - For workforce organization

Step 6. Change Your Environment
If you want to change your life, it should be in an environment that is different from what you are used to. If possible, you want the change your living conditions to match your business objectives and goals. It starts with the company of friends and family you keep. Try to surround yourself with productive family, friends, and loved ones that support your goals.

Step 7. Create A Network
Make a record of resources. A list of all people, skills, and tools you have access to at the present time. Some may not be important at the present time, but could be of some importance in the near future. They could be the difference between your success and failure.

• Networking With People That Can Help You
• Attend Related Seminars & Conventions
• Join Online Business Social Networks
• Follow Up With All Contacts Major and Minor

Step 8. Get A Business License
• Get A DBA is an abbreviation for "doing business as"
• Get A City, State, & Federal Tax Number
• City, Parish, Tax Permit & Ordinance
  These above Items can be gotten at your city government offices in your area.
• Get A EIN - Employee ID Number – For filing employee taxes
  This number can be received by contacting the IRS @ irs.gov

Step 9. Get A Lawyer & An Accountant

Always get protection for your money and investments. It's better to be safe than sorry, especially if you have a lot to protect. When it comes to money and time invested, always have people on your side that can protect and control your money. A lawyer and accountant are always involve with money, because they deal with contracts and numbers. So protect yourself at all times by getting these two very important assets.

Step 10. Create Business Paraphernalia

Business cards, postcards, media kit etc. for business network and promotion.

Step 11. Open A Bank Account

No matter how much money you have, you need to open and maintain a bank account for business financial transactions and records.

Step 12. Setup A Web Presence

Having a web site or social media page can help you connect with others and establish relationships with associates that you may not see every day. It gives you that extra edge in business, and makes it easier to reach your audience. It is a central location for your business products and services. It is your business area and view to the international world.

Step 13. Start Building Credit

For Future Business Ventures or Expansion
• Obtain a starter loan from a bank
• Get a secure or unsecured credit card
• Get a retail charge account
• Get a DUN Number (This is a credit reporting agency for businesses)

Step 14. Create A Time, Money & Management System
• Keeps records of all transactions
• Always pay yourself
• Don't procrastinate work
• Separate personal and business transactions
• Record all business activity. Keed all receipt and purchases

Step 15. Choose A Business Entity
(The type Of following business structure)

• **Sole Proprietorship -** You and your business are the same entity.

• **Partnership -** Having business partners in with your business.

• **INC** - Corporations "S" Corporations: You and your business are different entity. You are separated from all business liabilities. (your business carries all liabilities)

• **LLC** - Limited Liability Companies: You and your business are different entity, but you are not totally separated from all business liabilities. (Your business carries some liabilities. because of this you have certain tax breaks, credits, and benefits)

(Your Business Name), INC or
(Your Business Name), LLC

It's Smart To Incorporate Your Business

In most cases, it protects you personally from lawsuits. You and your business operates as separated entities. When your business become a corporation, you personally become an employee of your company, and you work for your companies invested interest. Your business has a board of directors that also have invested interest. It becomes solely business and not personal on all levels. "At least in principles."

For More On Info. www. marcellusscott.com

What Is A Non Profit Business?

A company that does private, public or community services to communities for free. For Private research or public welfare

What is the difference in
Profit Business & Non- Profit Business

• They are the same, but profit business shows earning, and non-profit organizations do not show earnings, "when filing taxes.""

• The rules on how they file tax record and received money are different

• They are about making money and serving people. Profit businesses call their money received "sell earnings." Non- profit businesses call their money received "operating capital," in the form of grants, contributions, sponsorships, & donations.

• Nonprofit businesses have tax-exempt status under tax codes. They must pay taxes on net earnings with these following codes:

Basic Tax Exemption Section Codes

Charitable organizations   501(c) (3)
Social welfare organizations   501(c) (4)
Agricultural/horticultural organizations 501(c) (5)
Labor organizations 501(c) (5)
Business leagues (trade associations 501(c) (6)
Social Clubs   501(c) (7).
Fraternal Societies Internal Revenue Code 501(c) (8) and 501(c) (10).
Employee Benefit Associations 501(c) (4), 501(c) (9) and 501(c) (17)

These organizations are call non-profits; however, they do make profits

How Does Non-Profit Businesses Make Profit?

• By providing public or community service to citizens under the previous list of tax codes, for fundraises, grants, contribution, foundations, sponsorships, & donations.

These tax codes are the codes used when non-profit businesses file for tax exemption each year. It's also the code the non-profit give to businesses that give the non-profit business funding listed above. It is the same code that is needed by the business to get tax benefits from the government when they file taxes each year, such as write offs.

• Even though the business is so called "non-profit" The board of directors are paid for personal service rendered for administrating fundraises, grants management, funds foundations contribution, sponsors, & donations..

Important Hustle:
"The Administrators Makes The Profit"
In the name of public or community services

Why Non-Profit Business Do Not Pay Taxes?
Because taxes are only paid from profit businesses.

The hustle is, there are no profits recorded when filing taxes for non-profits service for the business. "All money collected is spent on the directors for business operations and administrative services." Only the board of director pays taxes for personal service rendered, because the directors are the ones that is making profit. "Get It!"

For More On Info. www. marcellusscott.com

How To Start
A Non Profit Business

Step 1. Follow the steps I explained earlier on page 35 - 38.
On step 15 for a business Entity Choose an INC or LLC

Step 2. Apply For Non-Profit Mailing Permit
The U.S government provides reduced postage rates to non-profits on bulk mailings. U.S. postal service and ask for publication 417

Step 3. Fulfill Charitable Solicitation Law Requirements
Few local jurisdictions regulate organizations that solicit funds within that state, county, or city. This allows you to publicly raise money through fundraising.

Step 4. Create Community Cause Materials
Create an informational sheet that known as press kit that explains your organization and cause and why you need donations. Also explain what the donations will be used for and what some of the future goals are for your organization. Distribute flyers, contact local newspapers, submit a press release, Email all of your friends and family members explaining that you are trying to raise money and get donations. Tell them to pass the word on to their friends and family.

Step 5. Get Tax Exemption
WARNING: I'm not an experienced Lawyer or Accountant, but I do understand the Tax Exemption Process. Getting tax exemption involves "A lot of Paper Work." It can be a long filtrating process for some. I recommend you get an experienced professional to do this for you. Search the internet for tax lawyers.

Closing

I make no claims that these steps are absolute, but can be used as an intermediate stage of effective mind development. I believe that human success levels are too versatile to make an absolute science in this early stage in human evolution and development. It can only be studied, observed and applied within reason.

The idea behind my methods is "start using your natural abilities". It works by using the described subjects. By gaining control of your mental and economic knowledge, you will automatically program your future thoughts. Your behavior will then change which can control your life. All we have are opportunities for success and we relive these opportunities every day and they control different behavior patterns.

I believe we all have a talent locked deep inside our mind since childhood that has created different skills. These skills cause us to think, speak, and act creatively in different ways. They cause us to take actions that have caused different results in life. I truly believe that if you take action you will change the way you look at success. In doing so, the true hustle inside you will be truly shown."

This book is not about me changing anyone because I personally can't change everyone. I can only bring awareness in order for individuals to change themselves.

The Beginning…

BOOK DESCRIPTION

Are you like the many other recent high school graduates wondering what degree to pursue in College? Or maybe you've already graduated but are asking the question: what do Public Health graduates do?! Do you want to enter the medical field but aren't necessarily interested in courses like Chemistry and Biology? Are you thinking.... what does it even MEAN to major in Public Health?

If you answered yes to any of these questions, then this book is for you...

50 Things To Know About Getting A Bachelor's Degree in Public Health Policy by Mary Kim offers an approach to understanding the pros (and cons!) of a not so well-known (yet extremely useful) major in college. Most books on Public Health Major's tell you to enter the world of research, become an Epidemiologist or even apply to the Center of Disease Control and Prevention! Although there's nothing wrong with that, there really is so much more to a Public Health Major when looking outside the box-opportunity is endless. Based on knowledge from a recent college graduate majoring in Public Health, I bring to you, in total transparency, why (or maybe

even why not!) you should choose Public Health as your major.

In these pages you'll discover that a Public Health Major has endless amount of job opportunity upon job completion and not all are necessarily a given when thinking about Public Health. This book will help you fully understand what Public Health Major's do post-college!

By the time you finish this book, you will know all the benefits and not so-benefits of majoring in Public Health! So grab YOUR copy today. You'll be glad you did.

TABLE OF CONTENTS

16. Contribution To Breakthroughs
17. Immediate Employment
18. Opportunity To Be A Global Leader
19. Cultural Experiences
20. Happiness

(Courses Of A Public Health Major)

21. Applicable To Life
22. Not As Difficult As STEM
23. Research And Practicum
24. Great Opportunity For Professor Relationships
25. Online Opportunities
26. Ability To Double Major/Or Minor
27. Opportunity To Study Abroad
28. Finish Your Degree In Four, SOMETIMES Three, Years
29. Summer Course Opportunity
30. Different Course Routes

(How To: Complete A Public Health Major In 4 Years – OR 3)

31. Utilize Professor/Teaching Assistants Office Hours
32. Ask ALL Of The Questions
33. Utilize Summer Sessions
34. Connect With Classmates
35. Stay In Contact With Your Advisor
36. Manage Your Time

so much opportunity for Public Health working professionals to climb the ladder and end up in positions of leadership overseeing different departments/facilities!

12. TRAVEL EXPERIENCE

One of my favorites! Public Health is a necessary quality needed all around the world. Working in a position focusing on Public Health opens the doors for many different opportunities to travel the world and experience different wonders while helping other countries!

13. OPPORTUNITY TO HELP OTHERS

Now this is a given. Public Health fundamentally works on making the world (and communities) a healthier place. Health does not only equate to the level of physical health, but Public Health also focuses on divisions within communities that are less advantaged, food deserts, and so much more! The profession of Public Health, no matter what specific job title, always works on figuring out ways to help others live a happier and healthier life!

14. SALARY

After graduating with a degree, nobody, and I repeat NOBODY, wants to come out into the real world just to be given the short end of the stick with a salary that helps them barely scrap by. Many of the professions that Public Health majors are able to pursue offer salaries above the national average. Years in college are hard so why not aim to obtain a degree that ensures financial comfortability upon graduation!

15. EDUCATIONAL OPPORTUNITIES

Public Health is an extremely knowledgeable degree! Oftentimes, many individuals with Public Health professions aim to assume roles in universities or higher education. Having a Public Health degree can be great if you are interested in teaching others about real world issues that are occurring and to bring to light different disparities that affect people's everyday life and health!

16. CONTRIBUTION TO BREAKTHROUGHS

It would be an understatement to say that Public Health professionals contribute to simply changing communities and improving health around the world. These professionals contribute to the world's biggest breakthroughs! Vaccines are among the most advanced innovations that has benefited the health of the world entirely, and Public Health professionals have played a huge role in that

17. IMMEDIATE EMPLOYMENT

Another benefit that goes hand in hand to the promising salary that many Public Health Professionals receive upon graduation is immediate employment. Public Health is such a demanding need all around the world! As a result of the demanding need, there are job opportunities everywhere that are looking to fill Public Health related positions!

18. OPPORTUNITY TO BE A GLOBAL LEADER

Public Health is such an applicable major that this is a factor that many individuals take into account when choosing leaders all around the world. Being a Global Leader could entail travelling to other countries to inform others on health measures that could be benefit their community. Whatever you choose to do with your Public Health major, you will be leading a path to better the health of the world!

19. CULTURAL EXPERIENCES

As you will have the opportunity to travel around the world with a Public Health major, you will also be exposed to so many other cultures. In that, you will gain experiences of a lifetime as you will get the opportunity to change the world and see just how many different cultures there are that we are not always aware of! Once immersed in these different cultures, you'll get the experience to be a part of a community and experience these cultures fully

20. HAPPINESS

It's always important to choose a profession that makes you happy! Although we hear this constantly, it's sometimes hard to gauge what profession will actually make you happy. Statistically speaking, however, many Public Health Professionals report high levels of happiness and satisfaction with their jobs!

(COURSES OF A PUBLIC HEALTH MAJOR)

21. APPLICABLE TO LIFE

Many majors in college often times require courses to be taken that are a bit unrelatable to real life scenarios. Public Health majors are able to take courses that are applicable to life in the sense that you get to take courses about health disparity around the world and real issues. A Public Health major is extremely beneficial to a career as the courses really teach you a number of things about the world that you otherwise would not have known!

it's going to the gym, taking a walk, hanging out with friends or even just pampering yourself and getting your nails done! Taking the time of that day to do things that you enjoy doing will ensure that you succeed in college. You'll have more energy and avoid burnout syndrome

(SOME OTHER RANDOM PUBLIC HEALTH MAJOR ADVICE/TIPS)

41. REMEMBER THAT EVERYTHING TAKES TIME

College can be extremely daunting, but always remember to go at your own pace! College students graduate, on average, within 5 years. College is a challenging course of education and everyone is understanding of that. Be easy on yourself and while you should work hard and give it your best, take your time!

42. STYLE OF LEARNING

There will always be controversy on if taking notes on a notebook is better versus a laptop/tabloid, but at the end of the day, it really just depends on your preferred learning style! Don't let other people's preferences dictate how you take notes. If you try taking your notes by hand on a notebook and realize that that's your best learning style- go for it! If vice versa and you prefer your tabloid or laptop- do it! You won't know unless you try both and see which you prefer so take a go at it and figure out which works best for you

43. NOTE TAKING JOBS

There are so many jobs that you can do in college to earn some extra money that are just a bit random (you could say). A super interesting job that many of colleges offer are Student Disability Note Provider positions. Essentially, all that you have to do, is submit an image or online document of your notes at the end of lecture so that the Student Disability Association can provide them to another student who may be in need. You will be taking notes in lecture anyhow so why not try and just make some extra cash from it! You'll have to apply for this "position" and send in an example of previous notes from a past class that you have taken, but it really isn't too difficult to land a gig like this!

44. JOIN CLUBS

I'm sure you hear this time and time again…. but joining clubs associated to your major can really help you in the long run as having people on the same course (and route) as you can help you figure your way around easier. New things will always be different and sometimes even hard, but you don't have to go through it alone! There are many days where the college organizes a week where clubs all set up booths and you are given the opportunity to just stroll by and see which catch your eye!

45. UTILIZE THE CAREER CENTER

Not many students do this as, honestly, not many students know about it, but every college has a career center. Career centers are great for a multitude of reasons, a couple being improving your resume and your interviewing skills. College is your steppingstone into the real world! It's important to nurture your strengths and 'strengthen' your weaknesses to prepare you to be the best that you can be when you enter the real world! In the career center, there are many students like yourself that help others and are extremely relatable as they too are going through the same journey as yourself

46. MEDICAL JOB FAIRS

With a Public Health major, there is no doubt in mind that the job opportunity in the medical world is endless! That's primarily why I actually chose to major in Public Health, because I wanted to be in the medical world, but without the whole "medical" part of things. There are job fairs offered by colleges, but what many don't know is that there are specific medical job fairs in which I would strongly urge individuals interested in pursuing a public health major to attend! This can be a great opportunity for you to stand out as many other students will be going as a biology major or a chemistry major, but your unique Public Health major will make you stand out!

47. INTERNSHIP

Internships are a given when in college as they really help students figure out what path that they want to pursue and which path they don't want to pursue. You don't have to have ANY experience going into it, and while looking for an internship may seem tough at hand, there is so much opportunity out there for people that would just do the digging! A little tip when it comes to internships, you can even look online for places of interest hiring part-time workers. Then when it comes down to the interview, you can let them know of your position and the experience that you are wanting as a college student!

48. FRESHMEN DORM

This may seem like a random tip, but once you are experiencing your first dorm, then I'm sure you'll understand! I didn't fully understand the importance of creating relationships with freshmen dorm hallmates, but this goes a long way throughout your college experience. Hallmates are great study buddies and, typically, if you can study for a core class together in the very beginning of your college years,

*This book is dedicated to my clients
– past, present and future.*

*It's been a journey together yielding
thousands of improved careers and increased incomes.*

*The concise tried, tested and proven guidance distilled in
these pages comes with my gratitude.*

*Thanks to you all, I know these 3 steps will serve anyone
who applies them to their interviews.*

Contents

- Could you enhance your language and descriptions to make it more unique and more interesting?

- Could you add more facts and figures to clarify your story and enhance your credentials?

I suggest the answer is **"Yes"** to all of the above. What do you think you could improve?

In short, that Hiring Manager is working hard to do *their* job. By making it easier for them to identify you as a high calibre candidate, you are making *their* life easier and *your* chances of success significantly better.

Clearly good interview technique is no substitute for true talent, but my point is that good interview technique enables the talent to stand out and get hired!

The rest of this *'Essential Guide'* outlines some proven upgrades you can use **today** – in the next hour - to start to improve the impact and effectiveness of your interview skills.

Finally, I just want to add a personal *"Good Luck"* – from me to you.

If you've picked up this guide it probably means you are facing some challenges right now.

The good news is that you are clearly looking to the future and taking action. If you implement the interview upgrades in this report I'm certain that you'll agree, your performance will be in *'better shape'* to represent you and take on your interview competitors.

Good luck out there and contact me (or my team) if you want any more help in accelerating your job search or boosting your salary in the year ahead.

Every success,

Sam Waterfall

Founding Director

Interview Doctor®

PS – Due to my international speaker and consulting schedule I can only take on 4-5 new personal Clients per month.

But do **email our office – info@interviewdoctor.com**

One of my team will be able to confirm my availability for you. I'd love to work with you – and it really works: We recently added £16,400 to one candidate's salary.

Overview - Just 3 Steps To Land The Job

1. **Prepare**

2. **Perform**

3. **Follow Up**

Good news for you! You will be pleased to know that succeeding at interview *'isn't rocket science'* as they say. It's really quite straightforward. A few simple steps of preparation can set you up for a confident performance and they joy of the employer saying ***"You're hired!"***

If you follow the steps outlined in this guide you will come across better than 85% of other job candidates – regardless of whether they have more experience. You will give yourself the very best chance of not only getting the job, but getting the best salary on offer too.

There are hundreds of books written about interviews and they cover every aspect in detail. **The value in this guide is in its brevity**. It is short enough for you to read the night before an interview, and as a Kindle eBook, you can take with you in your portfolio on the day.

This content is tried, tested and proven. Use it. It will accelerate your job search significantly.

Step 2: Perform

*"I've learned that people will forget what you said,
people will forget what you did,
but people will never forget how you made them
feel."*
Maya Angelou

Put on a show!

Your meeting is a performance. You are putting on a show. You are not playing anyone else, you are playing yourself and you are the Star of the Show – so shine!

Treat everyone as if they are the most important person in the world

Earl Nightingale advised us to treat everyone we meet as if they are the most important person in the world. You never know who you might be holding the door for on your way in. That person could be the Head of Department, the CEO, or even your interviewer! Now wouldn't that be a first impression? Also realise that many interviewers will ask the receptionist what their impression was.

You don't need to be sycophantic or over-the-top. That will count against you. The point here is that you are putting on your show. Be a 'class act'... with everyone. Because everyone counts!

Put yourself in your interviewer's shoes

If you were doing their job, who would you be looking for to fill this job? What characteristics would you want to see?

You see, you already know what you'd want...

This, coupled with the details from the job description, let you know *exactly* what you need to demonstrate and how you need to perform.

First impressions are nearly everything!

Like it or not, looking the part is absolutely critical. The impression you create in the first few seconds will likely determine what the interviewer thinks of you. Research shows that people form an opinion about someone within 6 seconds of meeting. The next minutes / hours are largely spent justifying that impression. So make that first impression count for you and not against you! Show the enthusiasm. Be friendly. Act with class. Act with poise.

The handshake

A key part of the first impression you make. It's so important. A firm, positive handshake is best and it should always be accompanied with eye contact. This builds instant rapport and trust.

NB: Look away in a handshake and your interviewer will not bond in the same way with you and may feel you are disinterested or nervous.

TIP: Wash your hands in warm water while you are waiting to go in. Dry them well. This will avoid you having cold, damp or clammy hands - which is never a good start!

Eye contact

This is arguably the most important point of all. Good eye contact builds trust. Don't stare. That's scary! You should be looking to be in eye contact about 80% of the time. This gives you the chance to look away as you think and consider questions. Reverting to the eye contact really shows strong interpersonal skills and confidence.

TIP: If you feel uncomfortable doing this, it can help if you focus on the part of the person's nose just between their eyes. They won't know any different but it can make it easier for you.

Be what you say you are

Have you ever heard someone who looks shy and retiring try to tell you how excited and enthusiastic they are? It just doesn't work. Be yourself, but be positive, happy and upbeat. Smile! It is genuinely contagious!

Realise that **your interview is a chance to answer the employer's 3 critical questions:**

CAN you do the job?

WILL you do the job?

Will you FIT in?

This means you need to demonstrate **capability** and **relevant experience**; **motivation**; **social** and **interpersonal skills**.

Show you **CAN** do the job with evidence of your qualifications and work history.

Show you **WILL** do the job with evidence of your long-term interest in the field and motivation to work for this organisation in this location etc.

Show you will **FIT** in with evidence of success in similar situations, ability to work with others and by demonstrating your social skills and gravitas throughout your interview.

Dealing with Fear / Nervousness / Butterflies

Whole books have been written about fear. Boil fear down though, and you come to two thoughts:

Firstly, "**F.E.A.R – False Evidence Appearing Real**," according to my early Mentor, Dan Moore: Your mind can work for you or against you. Often a situation can be looked at in a positive or negative way. If we dwell on the negative we can incline our behaviours and emotions towards it.

Secondly, **hesitate and the fear grows**. Take action and you vanquish the fear. Ask yourself what is the worst thing that could happen? Usually, that's not really so bad.

Remember - a degree of nervousness is a good thing – this is your body's natural adrenal reaction which will help you respond quickly, remain attentive and perform at your best throughout the interview. Beyond this, nervousness is usually caused by just one thing: **Failure to prepare**. If you follow the steps outlined earlier in this guide you really should have nothing to feel overly nervous about.

Use the interviewer's name

In his all time bestselling book *'How to Win Friends and Influence People'*, Dale Carnegie wrote that a person's name may be the sweetest sound in the world to them. Find out your interviewer's name and use it. Not in every sentence, but just every now and then. (And if you have time, buy and read that book, it's a classic.)

TIP: Try this with your friends or in conversation with a Bank Clerk next time you are in town. They all have badges on, but virtually no one takes time to bother to

Expert Services to Accelerate Your Job Search

Contact us today to secure professional support to help you get the job you want.

Email info@interviewdoctor.com

Free CV Review

Send your CV to us via email and book a free of charge 15 minutes review meeting with one of our friendly CV experts. This is often all you need to fix the key elements of your CV which are currently holding you back.

Expert CV Phone Coaching (1x 60mins by phone)

Our most popular service. Sometimes 15 mins is not enough and many of our clients really benefit from taking a little longer on the phone with our CV experts. Working with you, we will point out what needs changing and explain how to do it. Specialist advice... and all from the comfort of your own home. UK clients call our London office. International clients usually prefer to use Skype for coaching calls.

Cover Letter Services

To ensure the very best first impression, most of our CV clients opt to include a professionally written cover letter to accompany their new CV. We will add our proven, door-opening words to give you the very best chance of success.

Application Form Services

If your chosen employer requires your application to be on their form we can help in this requirement too. Whether you want a critical edit of your first draft or you would like us to complete the form from scratch, we can rapidly create a competitive form to meet your needs.

Professional CV Writing

Our Guaranteed Service:

"Your Best CV Ever – or it's Free"

We will take time with you in advance to understand your requirements and take a complete career history before crafting your bespoke CV – no templates a 100% personal and professional document to get you to interview.

LinkedIn Profile Writing Services

An incredibly popular service selected by almost all of our clients. These days all potential employees have their online presence checked by potential employers. Luckily Google loves LinkedIn which means that often a candidate's LinkedIn profile is the first impression they create online. LinkedIn is the web's number 1 business social networking site with over 100 million members.

What you get:

- A professionally written online profile

- Search engine optimisation for your LinkedIn profile

- Our proven strategies for using LinkedIn to find your next job

Interview Preparation Coaching

Our Interview Preparation Coaching clients fit a number of descriptions. Maybe you have reached interview several times but can't quite land the job? Maybe you haven't interviewed for many years?

Either way, we work with you to ensure you are fully prepared. You'll know:

- How to answer the 4 most common interview questions

- How to deal with the 'impossible' interview questions

- How to spot the trick questions – and deal with them too

- What you should do to really impress an interviewer

- What you should say and what you must never say

- How to deal with nerves and give the best performance on the day

Salary Negotiation Coaching

Without a doubt, the service which provides the best return on your investment. It's possible with the right knowledge and confident approach to add 5% to 25% or more to your new salary. The key is to know what to say, what not to say and when. We recently helped one Marketer add £16,400 extra to his salary.

What you'll get:

- Advanced negotiation coaching to give you a simple plan to follow

- Clarity on what to say and when

- Understanding what you must not say and why

- Proven techniques which can add on extra value and benefits to your new package

Book now by email at info@interviewdoctor.com and ask about Discounted Pricing for readers of 'HIRED! The Essential Guide To Interview Success'.

Further Help And Advice

I hope you liked *'HIRED! The Essential Guide To Interview Success'* and have put its tried, tested and proven ideas to use in your job search?

Sometimes readers of this book find they would like some more help to prepare for a critical job interview. Of course, we do more than write books and guides here. We are available to help you with your job application from writing your CV to preparing for your interview and negotiating your best possible starting salary.

Contact Interview Doctor®

Email the office between 8.30am and 6pm on weekdays and we will be delighted to assist you in setting up your free 15 minutes CV Review or helping you to accelerate your job search with our Interview Success Coaching services.

Our international clients usually contact us via Skype (Skype ID = interviewdoctor)

Email us at info@interviewdoctor.com

Follow Interview Doctor® on Twitter @interview_dr

Call our London office on 020 7096 2089

From outside the UK call +44 20 7096 2089

been greatly outnumbered but had prevailed, despatching the creatures that had been terrorising the island of Haiti for several months. Fortunately they had been of a low order demonic force probably conjured by an island practitioner of voodoo, so despite their overwhelming numbers they were poorly matched against the warrior angels. As their breathing slowed to normal, they took in each other's injuries. It seemed Mal had got off the lightest despite the fact that he had endured the heaviest fighting of them all, but he was quick, much quicker at dodging the whipping tails and sharp teeth of the demons. Paschar had an ugly wound across his right shoulder. Mal strode across to him to examine the injury, "Better let Raphael look at that." He said as Paschar twisted his head attempting to look over his shoulder at his wound which was still bleeding and taking on a greenish puffy appearance. "Looks like you've been infected by some poisonous venom." Malchediel added.

Paschar shuddered, "By the saints, I hate those filthy creatures. Ugh!"

Malchediel laughed, "You'll live… you just can't bear the thought of being infected by one of them." Mal's wings had by now retracted back into his skin and he began to straighten several of Paschar's bent and twisted feathers so that his wings could also retract.

"I saw you go down." Nemamiah called across to Paschar, "You're lucky it was only a few bent feathers."

"Yeah," laughed Malchediel, "A broken wing could have put you out of action for a while, and how would we have managed fighting the forces of evil without you?"

Paschar flexed his shoulders and began to retract his rearranged wings back into his body before answering with a grin, "How indeed? Just ask yourself Mal, did I take that demon thunderbolt to save you from injury?" he raised his eyebrows in a questioning manner

Malchediels' grin died on his face. "I didn't realise that." He said.

"He's kidding." Nemamiah called out good humouredly. "You were nowhere near when he was injured."

Malchediel turned towards Paschar who shrugged, "Had you going for a while there didn't I?"

None of them had noticed that their return was being watched from one of the towers. Raguel, their overseer stood at the open window frowning at the light hearted banter going on below him as the four warrior angels turned to walk towards the building. His concern was mainly focussed on Malchediel. Wherever he happened to be and whoever he was with, inappropriate behaviour was sure to be detected. He was popular with his fellow angels but Raguel deplored his light-hearted attitude to life. He had a streak of arrogance about him which was only tempered by his carefree and friendly way with his contemporaries. It really wasn't to be tolerated. He took his position as defender and protector of the mortals far too lightly...it had to stop and Raguel knew exactly how he was going to deal with it

"Malchediel!" he called from the window just as the four warriors were about to enter the gatehouse, "I need to speak to you now. Please come up to see me."

The laughter died immediately as the three comrades looked towards Malchediel in puzzlement. He shrugged and left them standing just inside the doorway as he made his way to the stairs leading up to Raguel's quarters.

"Mal!" called Nemamiah. Malchediel turned as his friend tossed his shirt that he had taken from the coat peg inside the entrance. "Perhaps you need to be suitably dressed before going in to see him."

Malchediel grinned as he caught the shirt. "Thanks that would have been something else for him to grumble about." He pulled the garment over his head and with some trepidation began to climb the stairs. He reached Raguel's door but before he could knock Raguel called out, "Come in Malchediel." He entered the sparsely furnished room to find his overseer poring over several papers on the table before him. He didn't look up immediately but kept Malchediel waiting at the other side of his desk. Mal knew this was a ploy intended to make him aware of his inferior status. The corners of Mal's mouth turned up at the implied insult just as Raguel looked up at him.

"You find something amusing?" he asked coldly.

"Not at all. I was just anticipating the good news you are about to impart Raguel."

For a moment Raguel looked disconcerted then his frown deepened as he realised that Malchediel had wrong-footed him. This was just the sort of attitude that he was going to stamp out. He would not have a subordinate treat him with so little respect. "Let us hope you will still have something to smile about when you hear the 'good news' Warrior." Mal's lips tightened. He knew he had gone too far this time. Raguel only dropped his charges' names replacing them with the term, 'Warrior' when he was extremely displeased. Malchediel clasped his hands behind his back and stood up straight focussing on a point above Raguel's head. He waited.

"I have a mission for you."

Mal's eyes dropped to Raguel's face, "Just me?" he asked. "What about the others?"

"This doesn't involve the others. I have a task that I want you to fulfil alone." He sat back in his chair regarding Malchediel, his fingers steepling under his chin.

This doesn't bode well. Thought Mal, *He's enjoying it too much.* He waited. Eventually Raguel went on, "There is a child on earth that needs protecting. I have decided to send you." He said.

"But that's the duty of a Guardian." Mal blurted out. "I'm a Warrior. I don't protect."

"You do what I tell you to do." Raguel said icily.

For a moment both Angels glared at one another, then Mal asked, "Why me? Why are you punishing me? I am the best warrior you have and you know it. I'm not a Guardian Angel. I never have been. I fight evil; it's what I'm best at." He knew he was babbling but he was desperate, he didn't want to babysit some mortal child. How demeaning was that?

Now Raguel smiled. He had the upper hand at last. "You will prepare yourself immediately Warrior." He pushed a sheaf of papers across the desk towards Malchediel. "These are the details of your mission." He met Mal's eyes and for a second he paused. "You will need to take care Malchediel. We have already lost two Guardians on this mission; it is not without its dangers. Something is going on with this child. She needs special care." He paused for a moment before adding, "She is one of us. Don't let her or me down Malchediel."

'One of us!' What did that mean? Mal turned a puzzled face to his overseer. The mission at first so repellent suddenly took on a new interest. "I'm to protect another Angel?" he asked.

"Not exactly," was the reply, "She's a Nephilim."

Mal looked astounded. "A Nephilim...then surely she should be able to protect herself? Why the need for our help?"

Raguel didn't answer at once. After a pause he sighed. "She doesn't know she is a Nephilim. She has never felt the need to call upon her special powers; indeed she doesn't even know she has any." He stood up indicating that he felt the interview was over. "Read the report Malchediel...it explains everything you need to know." He regarded the warrior angel before adding, "Remember what I have told you...two guardian angels have disappeared trying to protect this girl. By your own admission you are the best warrior we have." At last he smiled. "Let us see if you can prove it."

Chapter One

Amy had no idea as she opened the shop that morning that she would meet someone who would change her life forever. It was Wednesday and as she only opened the shop from Wednesday to Saturday, so for her, this was the start of the week. The rest of the week she kept for painting the landscapes and seascapes that she sold in the shop. She was never going to make a fortune from her artistic endeavours but she made enough to keep body and soul together and a little left over for an occasional treat like a pub meal or a trip into Truro to scour the shelves of Waterstones. It was early September and the main street of Falmouth was noticeably quiet. The holiday season was winding down now that the new school term had started. The remaining tourists were quite obviously older childless couples but fortunately they were more likely to browse through the canvases that were on display in the shop and occasionally make a purchase to take back home as a reminder of their holiday in Cornwall. The shop had been open for about an hour and she was busying herself with attaching hanging wires to the back of half a dozen small canvases for hanging on the back wall. Reaching for a handful of the small tacks on the work bench she dropped some onto the floor. Cursing her clumsiness she knelt down to retrieve them. Some had rolled under the table that served as a counter and she had to inch forward on hands and knees to gather them up. As she reached forward she came face to face with a pair of legs clad in cut-off cargo pants. She hadn't heard the bell on the door indicating someone entering the shop and in her surprise at finding that she wasn't alone, she shot up hitting her head sharply with a resounding crack on the underside of the table. She pulled back and looked above the table top rubbing her sore head. Standing opposite her was a tall stranger.

"Helston, Lizard, Gunwalloe...got it!" he said and with that he opened the door and left leaving her slightly bemused. She fingered the charm resting against her skin thinking about his comment regarding its dubious portent. She shrugged and with a sigh turned towards the little kitchenette at the back of the shop to make herself a cup of tea.

The rest of the week passed quietly. She made a further two sales but for nothing like the one hundred and twenty five pounds that Malchediel had paid for his canvas. When she thought about it she felt a little guilty but she was never going to see him again and he had seemed content with his purchase so she dismissed all thoughts of him.

The weather was still holding well and the forecast was good until the following Tuesday so she decided to spend Sunday at Gunwalloe producing a new view of the cove to replace the one sold. She arrived a little after nine o'clock to a deserted beach. She walked past the little beach café now closed for the season carrying all the paraphernalia that she would need. Easel, paints, small folding stool, Tupperware box of sandwiches and a flask of tea. She strolled along the beach until she found a suitable spot to set up her easel. She turned it this way and that looking up with each re-positioning of it to check the view. The choice of vista was paramount and she always spent considerable time choosing the right aspect. She moved backwards so that she was under an overhang of rocks at the back of the beach nodding to herself when she felt she had achieved the best view possible. The sky was a beautiful pale blue, totally cloudless and the sun's warmth was already causing tiny beads of perspiration to appear across her nose and cheeks. She stood for a moment eyes closed listening to the rush and drag of the waves. She tilted her head to one side listening for any other sounds. The distant call of one of the Herring Gulls but nothing else. She was totally alone. She stretched her arms above her head and let them fall to her sides shaking out the tension through her fingertips, and then she opened her eyes and surveyed the scene she was going to capture in watercolours.

After about an hour she had finished pencilling in the scene and was about to start painting. She linked her fingers together and turning her palms away from her, stretched her arms straight in-front of herself. It was a little ritual she always went through before she started painting. Releasing her grip she gently shook out her fingers bending to start applying a colourwash. Suddenly there was a crashing, dragging noise from behind her. Almost as if in slow motion she turned behind but saw nothing but the rock face of the twenty foot bank at her back. Her eyes travelled up to where the noise was coming from and hesitated for a fraction of a second before she realised that a rock fall was cascading down towards her. Realising that she was directly beneath the dry rock strewn avalanche she hurled herself forwards crashing into the easel. As the easel fell flat onto the sand, her paints scattered in all directions. Her knee caught painfully against the edge of the small side table which she had pushed into the sand to hold her brushes and paints. She stumbled forwards two or three strides realising that she was going to fall before she would be clear of the tumbling rocks and stones. As she instinctively raised her arms to cover her head she heard a rushing of wind. She closed her eyes waiting for the first of the rubble to hit her but suddenly she felt herself being lifted up. The air was whipping past her face as her feet left the ground. She was being held by strong arms against someone's body. She twisted around trying to see who it was.

"Stop struggling!" came a male voice, "You're safe ...hold still." Her head was against his chest just below his chin and they were flying...God! They were flying. She couldn't see his face but she saw his hair... golden blonde streaming away behind him in the rush of air around them. He was bare-chested and she could smell his sun-warmed skin and he had wings...Bloody hell! He had wings...and they were beating behind him. She was feeling light-headed. Don't faint, don't faint she kept telling herself. There is a rational explanation for this. The wind against them was slowing and she had a sensation of falling but she was still in his arms so she held herself still. The beating of his wings changed. They were sweeping forwards rapidly and she could tell that they were slowing down. Within seconds she felt the thud of his feet hitting the sand. Easing his arm from beneath her legs he set her gently down but as soon as her feet felt the sand, her legs buckled and he had to hold her up. She was leaning against him breathing erratically, confused and scared. Without letting go of her he asked, "Are you okay?"

Without moving away from him she nodded numbly. His arms slid from around her back to hold her arms just above her elbows. "Can you stand now?"

Again she nodded.

"Can you speak?" he asked and she heard the note of amusement in his voice. She straightened up as his hands dropped to his sides. Malchediel looked down at her. She stepped backwards and met his eyes, those startlingly blue eyes that now held a hint of humour. She let her eyes travel up over his shoulders at the amazing cream wings that seemed to be sprouting from his shoulders. She took another hasty step back, her face blanching. "What the hell are you?" she whispered.

He turned his head, looking over his shoulder at the wings which had now stopped beating and were hanging motionless gleaming in the morning sunlight.

"Let me see," he said lifting his closed hand. "Wings..." He lifted one finger as if counting, "Extremely good-looking..." another finger, "Angelic countenance..." a third finger. "Why I must be an Angel." He finished.

She looked from his three raised fingers to his grinning face. "Jesus Christ!" she breathed.

"Tsk, tsk! Didn't your father ever tell you that it was bad to blaspheme?" He said with mock severity. She swallowed trying to make some sense of this weirdness.

"You can thank me if you like." He said turning to look back up the beach to where all her artistic implements lay scattered, some of them buried beneath the rubble. The dust was still settling as he surveyed the debris. She really couldn't take in the damage done to her equipment. She was staring at his wings. They were definitely sprouting from his back. There was no sign of a harness or straps or anything which could be holding them there.

"There are no such things as Angels." She said, her voice barely above a whisper. He turned back to her frowning. Lifting his right arm he placed his forefinger and index finger against the pulse on his wrist and waited. "Yep…" he said after a second or two, "I have to disagree with you. I certainly do exist."

"But you didn't have wings the last time we met."

"Your sense of observation is very acute Amy. You're right…watch." He flexed his shoulders and instantly his wings began to retract as she watched. Where they were going she had no idea. They were one hell of a size. They had to be. He must be almost six feet tall and they had been strong enough to lift not only him but her as well. "You can close your mouth now by the way Amy." He said smiling at her expression. Her lips snapped to as she walked behind him to examine the small openings where the wings had been a moment before. As she watched even those closed over leaving his back as smooth as ever. She completed her three hundred and sixty degree walk around him coming back to face him.

"Where have you come from?" she asked.

"Ohh, Amy I would have thought that was obvious."

"Alright…What are you doing here?"

"Now you're asking the right questions. Come on let's sort out your equipment first." He said as he began to walk back up the beach to where her easel lay on the sand. She hesitated for a moment or two before following him up the beach. His legs were long and well- proportioned and she had to scoot to catch up with him.

"How did you do that?" she called to him from behind,

"the wings thing. Where did they go?"

He gave a soft laugh. "I packed them away. They're useful at times but they can get in the way when you're grounded."

"But where did they go? I mean they were big and there's no sign of them now."

"Amy, I'm an angel. I can do things that mortals can only dream of." He had reached the spot where minutes before she had been painting. With hands on hips he surveyed the damage done to her equipment. The easel was undamaged lying flat on the sand. Her little stool was almost buried under a mound of loose rocks and shale and looked to be bent beyond repair. Most of the avalanche had been made up of small rocks and stones but there were a couple of sizeable boulders which had partially buried themselves into the dry powdery sand. Her tray of paints which had been lying open on the side table was covered in debris and dust and he reached for them to shake them off. She stood slightly behind him still fixated on his back which now looked quite normal, no marks, no bulges nothing in fact to show where his wings may have gone. He turned to her holding out the tray. She took a hasty step back from him.

"What?" he asked frowning at her.

"I can't believe what just happened." She shot at him, "You ask 'What?' as though this is a daily occurrence to you. My God! I could have been badly injured or even killed if you hadn't turned up. How the hell did you know I was even here?" Her eyes narrowed, "Have you been following me?" she asked, suspicion suddenly dawning on her.

He placed the paints back on the table before looking into her eyes. "I think it's time I explained my purpose here Amy." He said. "But first I need to check something out." He turned back to the rock face and as she watched he reached for a hand hold and began to steadily climb upwards. He dislodged clumps of loose shale as he heaved himself up until he reached the top of the rocky outcrop. Without looking back at her he disappeared from view appearing to be scanning the ground only moved in to live with girls for one reason. "Um...I don't suppose you know how long you will be staying, do you?"

"Ohh Amy we haven't even gone inside yet and you want to get rid of me." He said turning a hurt expression on her. She began to deny such a motive before becoming aware of his mischievous smile. He laughed as she coloured realising that he was again pulling her leg. "Do all Angels behave the way you do?" she asked in exasperation. "I thought they were supposed to be kind, inoffensive beings. There's a streak of devilment in you."

Still smiling he murmured, "I think Raguel would probably agree with you on that. As to how long I'll be around...that depends on how quickly we can sort out just what is going on here." He looked past her to the front door of the cottage, "Shall we go in?"

He forestalled her attempt to unload the boot suggesting that they first go inside so that he could check the cottage out. "Do you think that someone may be inside then?"" she asked in a low voice. He tilted his head to one side and appeared to be listening then he shook his head, "I don't think there is anyone inside at the moment but there is that same odour that I detected back at the beach. Someone or rather something has been here recently." He looked up at an open upstairs window and frowned. "Is that where you sleep?" he asked. When she nodded he grimaced. "Do you sleep with your window open?"

"Usually, yes."

"From now on keep it closed at night," he paused, "unless I'm in there with you...which thinking about it may be a good idea. If we can entice whatever is lurking around here inside we'll have a better chance of finding out who is behind all of this." He turned heading for the front door and she held back on the retort she was going to make regarding his sharing her bedroom. She would cross that bridge when she came to it. She fumbled in her pocket for the key but watched in astonishment as he touched the Yale lock with his fingers. Inexplicably the lock clicked as though a key had turned the locking barrel. Without looking at her he pushed the door open and stepped inside. "Were you a house breaker in a former life?" she muttered following him inside. He was standing in the hallway appearing to be listening for any sound from within. Still with his back to her he answered. "There was no former life. I've only ever been an Angel."

"I'll check my insurance policy later. There has to be a clause excluding Angelic housebreaking...One of those 'Acts of God' exclusions perhaps."

"Amy...if there was anyone here, your constant babbling would have alerted them by now."

"Fine!" she muttered, "You carry on casing the joint. I'll put the kettle on." She walked past him into the little kitchen. He stared after her as a smile spread across his face. He wondered if all mortals were as feisty as her. In the kitchen Amy too was smiling to herself as she filled the kettle at the sink. She was beginning to enjoy the verbal banter that was going on between them and after what had happened at the beach earlier, she did feel safer having him around. She turned back towards the hallway calling, "I suppose you do eat and drink." There was no reply and she walked to the doorway to ask him again. The hall was empty. She heard a sound in the living room. Looking in she saw him standing at the French doors. As she watched he ran his fingers all around the frame. "What on earth are you doing?" she asked.

He looked over his shoulder at her. "I'm sealing all the openings. If any demonic forces attempt to enter they'll get quite a surprise."

"Are you going to do that at every window and door in the building?"

"Uh-hu" he said working on the window next to the doors. Straightening up, he turned to face her. She was standing in the doorway with her arms folded across her chest watching him. She let out a long sigh. "A week ago," she said almost to herself, "I was living a normal life then you turn up and my world is turned upside down."

"I'm not the cause of all this Amy. It had already started happening. I've been sent to sort it all out." They stood facing one another.

Eventually she nodded. "I'm   sorry...it's   all   very unnerving. If you hadn't turned up I would have put today's mishap down to an unfortunate accident. It's difficult for me to come to terms with your theory of evil intent and demonic forces. This is the twenty first century. Angels, Fallen or otherwise should just be a myth."

"If I hadn't been around today, you could have been seriously injured Amy. We need to find out why you are being targeted like this. It's not as though you are unique, there are thousands of Nephilim out there. How safe are they I wonder?"

She couldn't have been more shocked if he had thrown a bucket of cold water over her. "There are more like me?" she asked in astonishment.

"Well probably not quite like you." He grinned, "But there are many Angel offspring walking this earth. The difference is they know what they are."

"Then how come this isn't common knowledge?" she exclaimed.

"If you read your Bible you would know about them. The thing is most people think like you. Angels and Demons are just the stuff of myth. As for Nephilim I imagine not many people have ever heard of the term, although you can Google it." He said the corner of his mouth quirking upward.

An   Angel   with   knowledge   of   computing terms...whatever next she thought. The kettle began to boil and she suddenly remembered what she had come to ask him. "I'm making some tea... I was wondering... do you eat and drink?"

"I don't need to, but I have in the past tried food and drink. I have a particular liking for honey. Do you have some?"

"Are you serious?" she laughed. "When did you develop a liking for honey?"

"Ohh, a few millennia ago we were alerted to a sighting

of Beelzebub in Mesopotamia. It was while on that mission that I was introduced to wild honey by the local people. I've found it irresistible ever since."

Her eyes were as big as saucers. "You are kidding." She breathed.

"About Beelzebub...yes I am, but it was in Mesopotamia that I first tasted honey." He laughed.

With a raised eyebrow she turned back to the kitchen. "Bread and honey coming up."

As she made a pot of tea and spread a thick layer of honey on crusty bread for him she wondered what her father would have made of todays' happenings. How strange that he never mentioned their Nephilim background during her childhood years. According to Malchediel, all Nephilim had special powers but she had never been aware of anything out of the ordinary in either her father or herself and she began to think that perhaps the Angel was mistaken. She unpacked the Tupperware container of sandwiches that she had taken to the beach – no point in wasting them. It was well past lunch time and she was feeling hungry. As she carried the tray into the living room Malchediel was coming back downstairs. "All the windows upstairs except yours are now sealed Amy...we won't be caught unawares if anything tries to get in tonight."

"Are you seriously expecting something to happen then?"

"We'll see. It will have been noticed by now that you're not wearing the talisman any longer and that you escaped the little rock-fall unscathed. Whatever or whoever is behind this will have to show his face soon."

Amy placed the tray onto the coffee table and without turning to him asked quietly, "How much at risk do you think I am? Do you think it wants to kill me or just scare me?"

He was standing behind her. He couldn't see her face just the curve of her cheek, her hair falling forward as she bent over the tray of food. He could hear the fear in the slight tremor in her voice. "That's what I intend to find out Amy." He reached forward and touched her shoulder giving it a gentle squeeze, "Nothing is going to happen to you, I promise. I've never failed a mission yet. Once we know what all this is about we'll better be able to deal with it." She met his eyes and smiled. He was very confident of his capabilities and that confidence was contagious. She lifted one of the plates and handed it to him. His eyes lit up as he lifted a corner of bread to survey the honey. "Ohhh Amy, fantastic! It must be at least two centuries since I last tasted honey." It was a couple of seconds before they both burst out laughing.

As they ate a late lunch Amy plied the Angel with questions. He informed her that there were Nephilim all over the planet living normal lives alongside human beings. They were aware of their differences but never drew attention to themselves and so blended into society with little difficulty. On rare occasions a few were called upon to assist the Angelic host in ridding the planet of malevolent forces that found their way into human society.

"Malevolent forces? How do they find their way here? I mean where do they come from and do they have bodies or do they shimmer like ghosts?" Amy asked, her sandwich momentarily forgotten. "How do the Angels deal with them? What do they look like and how come I've never seen them?"

"One question at a time Amy!" he laughed. "Sometimes an anomaly opens up between this dimension and the one that you call hell allowing evil to escape. This can manifest itself as a form of low-life demon…nasty smelling creatures like the one that I believe caused the rock-fall at the beach earlier. More seriously, Fallen Angels can slip through and they are much more dangerous to humans. They are powerful and they have millennia of anger and resentment locked inside them. They have been banished from their former home and they want revenge. They know that the optimum way to get back at their Maker is to target His big experiment…humans. As to why you have never seen demons or Angels in the past I'm assuming it's because they have left you alone. Your father was very careful move really quickly or making people see you as something you're not. There are so many possibilities. It's something that you're parents notice when you are young and they nurture that particular skill so that by the time you reach adulthood you are quite adept at whatever it is you can do."

She drove on in silence for a while thinking on what he had said eventually commenting more to herself than to him. "Perhaps I'll never know and never be able to use whatever I was endowed with."

He was acutely aware of the disappointment in her voice. "I can't see that happening Amy. It will come. When the time is right you will know about it."

Once Amy had unlocked the door to the shop Malchediel eased past her and checked inside. She waited just inside the doorway as he walked around the interior opening the door at the back into the little kitchen area before coming back to her. "Everything seems to be normal. I can't detect any Angelic or demon presence. She took off her jacket and hung it on a coat-hanger at the back of the kitchen door before turning to face him across the shop interior. "Will you be adopting 'invisibility mode' whilst we're here?" she asked.

"If that's what you want?"

"It might be the best thing...just in case someone comes in that I know. It will save explanations about who you are." He nodded and as she watched he closed his eyes. She caught her breath as the complete outline of his body shimmered for a few seconds then stilled again. He opened his eyes, "Done." He said. She shook her head in wonderment. He looked the same as he always had. There was no faint outline surrounding him, no ghostly glow. She couldn't see through him. To her he looked completely normal. Beautiful, knee-weakingly gorgeous but otherwise ...normal. She realised she was staring and looked away quickly.

"What are you going to do here today? Is it something I can help you with?" he asked.

"What? Um…oh…I thought I would do a general tidy-up. I need to check how much canvas I have left. I may need to put an order in for more." She was a little flustered by how strongly she was physically attracted to him. It was hard to keep in mind just what he was. She knew that there could never be any sort of relationship between them but boy oh boy she could dream couldn't she? They worked together for almost an hour pulling out all the canvas material from under the stairwell and stacking it in order of size. Malchediel had just carried the pile of canvas to the counter when the little door-bell tinkled announcing the entrance of someone. Malchediel moved quickly to the front of the shop as Amy stood up looking to see who it was.

"Hello," said Stephen, "You don't normally come in on a Monday…is everything okay?" Amy dusted off her trousers with the palms of her hands. "Hello Stephen." She said brightly, aware of Malchediel standing watching them. "I needed to go through my stock and have a general tidy-up. Today seemed as good a time as any." Stephen nodded at her explanation but she noticed that there was a frown on his face. He moved towards her placing himself between her and Malchediel and with his back to the Angel he mouthed silently to Amy, 'Who's that?' indicating behind him with his eyes. Amy's mouth dropped open. "You can see him!" she cried in astonishment. Stephen looked quickly behind him taking in Malchediels equally astonished expression. "Yeah…" he said in some confusion. Amy and Mal's eyes met across the shop.

"By all the saints!" said the Angel, "Another Nephilim!"

Chapter Three

For a moment there was total silence and then all three began speaking at once.

"Stephen? A Nephilim? Are you sure?" Amy threw at Malchediel

"What did you say? What do you know about Nephilim?" Stephen wanted to know. He had wheeled around and was now facing Malchediel who was regarding him in disbelief.

"No-one told me there were two Nephilim here." Mal said.

"Whoa, whoa!" said Amy. She looked at Stephen, "Is that true Steve? Are you a Nephilim...a half Angel?"

Stephen looked warily at Malchediel then back at Amy. "I thought you didn't know anything about our race." He said blankly. "Dad said we weren't to mention it to you. How did you find out about it?"

Amy dragged her hand across her forehead in an attempt to clear the confusion in her brain. "WHAT! You knew about me...you knew about me and said nothing. How long have you known?" She was rubbing at her temples with her fingers. At this point Malchediel stepped forwards causing Stephen to back up away from him, his eyes wary.

"It's alright Steve. This is Malchediel...you're not going to believe this but..."

"Hold on Amy." Malchediel cut in. "Use your powers boy...check out my aura."

Stephen glanced quickly at Amy who nodded slightly then turned his gaze on the Angel. After a few seconds he staggered backwards coming up against the counter sharply. "Hellfire!" he exclaimed shock in his eyes.

Malchediel shook his head in mock dismay. "You mortals do love to blaspheme don't you?"

Stephen turned his shocked expression on Amy, "An Angel...Christ he's an Angel."

"Tsk, Tsk." Malchediel grinned leaning backwards against the desk. "I think we have some explaining to do Amy."

Half an hour later Stephen was in full command of the facts. Malchediel had left Amy to do most of the explaining only adding odd pieces of information like how he knew a demon had been behind yesterdays' attack on Amy at the beach. Amy was amazed at how readily Stephen was accepting Malchediel's presence indeed he told Amy that he was glad she was now under his protection.

"I can't believe that in all the years you have known me you never once let slip that we weren't normal human beings." she threw at him.

"That wasn't my choice Amy." He answered. "Your Dad made it quite clear to my family and me that you weren't to know about your heritage. After the way your Mum died he made my Mum and Dad promise never to mention your Nephilim background. As I grew up I was included in that promise."

Amy frowned picking up on what he had said, "Hang on...what do you mean? 'The way my Mum died.' She was killed in a road accident wasn't she?"

Stephen glanced quickly towards Malchediel who gave a barely noticeable nod encouraging him to go on. Amy saw Stephens throat move as he swallowed. She guessed that he was about to tell her something that he would rather not. "The inquest on your Mum's death ruled that it was an accident...hit and run. The driver was never found. Given that your Mum was an active Demon Hunter it was seen in Nephilim circles that she had been eliminated."

"What! What are you saying?" Amy turned from Stephen to Malchediel who held her gaze for a moment before looking down at his feet. In that moment she knew that what

Stephen had said was probably true, and all her upbringing had been a lie. Her fist went to her mouth to stifle a sob.

Stephen looked towards Malchediel, his face a mask of wretchedness. He and his family knew many Nephilim across the country and the mystery surrounding Amy's mother's death was well known in those circles. It was only Amy that had been excluded from these facts. Now the task of acquainting Amy with the notion that her mother had been murdered had fallen to him and he was wishing he were any place other than standing watching her anguish. "I'm sorry Amy." His words fell like stones in the quiet room. Her face was hidden in her hands. Stephen looked again to Malchediel in a silent plea for assistance. He had little experience with tearful girls. Malchediel took the hint and crossed the room to take Amy gently in his arms. With her face pressed against the front of his shirt she fought back the tears. He waited. Eventually she pulled away from him wiping her eyes with the heels of her hands. She flicked a glance at Stephen who had been standing awkwardly watching the two of them. "I don't know anything about this world Steve...your world...my world I suppose now."

"It was the way your Dad wanted it Amy. He was terrified that if you knew about your background it would put you in danger."

She made a sound a mixture of derision and a mirthless laugh, "And of course in my ignorance I am completely safe."

"He did what he thought was right Amy, and you did grow up in relative safety." Malchediel put in. "Unfortunately finding the talisman has alerted someone to your whereabouts again. We need to find out why you are being stalked." He turned his attention to Stephen. "Was Amy's father involved in Demon hunting activities?"

"I don't think so. Dad never mentioned anything about that, only that Melissa, Amy's Mum was an active fighter." He glanced at his wrist watch then turning back to Amy said, "Look...I need to get back to the shop. I told Joe I'd only be a few minutes. I just wondered why you were in on a Monday. Do

"If and when? Ohh Amy you're showing your lack of faith in me again." Malchediel feigned a look of injured pride then broke into a broad grin. "I'll do what-ever is necessary to keep you safe." He finished. Despite her pique at his demeaning snub of Stephen Amy found herself returning his grin. Before anyone had a chance to speak again Malchediel eased himself out of his armchair. "Alex...Stephen, thank you for coming to see us. We have learned a lot from what you have told us." He glanced at the wall clock above the television. "It's late...I'm sure you're all tired so unless there is anything else you can think of that I should know perhaps we should all say goodnight." Alex was up on his feet in a trice, "Yes, yes you are right. I can't think of anything else that may be helpful but if you need any other information let Stephen know and I'll help if I can." He leaned across the space between them to shake Malchediel's hand. "It's been an honour meeting you." He said clasping the Angel's hand between both of his own. Stephen stood by; a hard edge to his mouth making Amy aware that he was still smarting from Malchediel's earlier snub. She smiled at him attempting to lighten his mood. "Let me show you both out." She murmured. Malchediel stayed where he was as she led the way to the front door. Alex, after saying goodnight to her went around his car and got in. Stephen stood facing her, "How are things going with him?" he asked in a whisper indicating with a tilt of his head the lit interior of the cottage. Amy was glad of the surrounding darkness as they stood in the tiny front porch. He wasn't able to see the slight uplift of her mouth. He didn't like Malchediel, that much was clear. His first feeling of awe upon meeting an Angel for the first time had now given way to blank hostility. She couldn't blame him, Malchediel's arrogant attitude towards him was offensive and Stephen unfortunately lacked the maturity to handle the situation in any way other than silent resentment.

"Between you and me I didn't like him at first. He came across as arrogant but I think that's just his way. When you get to know him better he's okay. He saved me from serious injury at the beach so I can forgive him his patronizing quirky sense of humour."

"Hmmph." Was the response. "Well as long as he keeps you safe I can put up with him I suppose." He leaned forwards to give her a peck on the cheek. "Will you be in the shop tomorrow?" he asked.

"Not sure." She answered surprised by the quickly planted kiss. "I was going to finish off a painting that I had started but I'm reluctant to go back to Gunwalloe beach at the moment. I'll decide how I feel tomorrow. They stood for a moment or two facing one another before Stephen said, "Okay I'll drop by tomorrow lunch time in case you decide to open up. Reaching for her hand he gave it a squeeze before turning towards his father's car. "Goodnight Amy." he called softly over his shoulder as he climbed in. Her response went unheard as Alex Goodrich started up the engine. She waited until they had pulled away before returning inside the cottage, closing the door behind her. Malchediel was standing with his back to the fireplace his hands in the back pockets of his jeans. As she entered the living room she took in his lean relaxed stance. The table lamp to his left lit only that side of his body highlighting the silky golden curls framing his face leaving his right side in soft shadow. He turned to look at her as she approached. With the light now fully on his face she almost caught her breath at the perfection of his features. How strange she thought, such dazzling flawlessness should have resulted in his looking almost feminine but far from it; his lean muscular body oozed masculinity. In an instant she again became aware of how very attracted she was to him. To cover her confusion at this sudden realisation she went straight on the offensive. "What was all that about with Stephen?" she asked bluntly. She noticed his body stiffen slightly at the mention of Stephen's name.

"What do you mean?"

"You practically shot him down in flames when he asked if there was anything he could do to help."

"I only said that I had it covered. I don't need the help

of a teenage Nephilim." He answered curtly. She didn't answer immediately; stung by his reaction then her cheeks began to burn. "He's twenty." She retorted, "Not a teenager."

He stood looking at her for a moment. Why was she angrily defending this boy? "I'm sorry…" he said as the silence between them lengthened, "Am I missing something here? Is there some sort of relationship going on between the two of you?"

"No! No…" she blustered, "I just got the impression that for some reason or other you really don't like him."
They were standing a few feet apart eyes locked on one another. "I noticed that he was sitting very close to you." He said at last. "I got the impression that it made you uncomfortable. Perhaps I misread the situation." Suddenly the pieces fell into place. Was he jealous she wondered? The tension she was feeling inside, eased. She sent a thought to him. *There is nothing between Stephen and myself…and yes I was a little uncomfortable by his closeness tonight…did it make you jealous Mal?* What was she doing? Should she be talking to an Angel in this way? He remained looking at her and she began to wonder if her thought had reached him or not. Then a smile slowly spread across his face.

Jealous? Was the one questioning word that popped into her head. It was at that point she decided to let the matter drop.
As she cleared away the coffee cups that they had been drinking from earlier Malchediel repeated the ritual of checking all the windows again leaving just her bedroom unsealed. At bedtime he again gave her time to shower and don her pyjamas before joining her in her bedroom. Once she had turned off the bedside lamp he again removed the sweater he had been wearing and settled himself in the armchair. "I feel very guilty about sleeping while you have to sit up awake all night." came her low voice into the darkness. She heard the armchair creak as he repositioned himself and he laughed softly. *I'll try to think of a way you can repay me while you sleep.* His answering

thought sent a shiver of excitement through her but she was careful not to transmit thoughts of her feelings to him.

She lay awake for some time listening to the occasional distant hoot of an owl, her mind going over all that she had learned about her mother. It was several minutes before she spoke. "My mother must have been a very brave woman to do what she did. I can't imagine doing anything like that." She paused and when he didn't immediately answer she went on, "Perhaps I took after my dad, after all it was his influence that I grew up with."

"I think you'll find that when the time comes you will be every bit as courageous as your mother." He commented. "It's in your blood."

The room settled back into a comfortable silence and it wasn't long before Amy succumbed to sleep. It was with a sudden jolt that she was bought back to wakefulness. For a second or two she didn't know what had caused the tightening around her mouth but then she realised that Malchediel was kneeling at her side with his hand over her mouth, his own mouth level with her ear. "Shhh." He whispered his warm breath fanning her cheek. *There's something outside Amy. Stay where you are. Don't make a sound. I'll be back,* she heard his projected thought inside her head. Her eyes were wide open now and she could see that he had unfurled his wings. Soundlessly he eased himself off the bed and padded across the room. As she watched, her eyes now accustomed to the moonlight through the blinds she saw him pass effortlessly through the wall beside the window. Her mouth fell open in disbelief but she lay still as he had instructed, listening. Suddenly there was a loud eerie howl and the sounds of a struggle from the garden beyond. Forgetting Malchediel's command to stay where she was, she scrambled out of bed and ran to the window. She yanked the blind up peering out into the moonlit garden. What she saw made every hair on her body bristle in terror.

Chapter Four

There were three figures that she could see by the light of the waxing moon on the lawn below. Malchediel, she could see clearly - his wings outstretched. The second figure that was facing him was a good two feet shorter but stockily built with arms that seemed to hang down almost to its shins. From her vantage point it looked like some grotesque malformed baby. What had terrified her though was the third figure, as ugly as its companion and hovering at Malchediel's back, crouched in a menacing way as if about to leap upon him at any second. At the precise moment that her brain comprehended the situation she knew that Malchediel was unaware of the threat behind him. His wings were possibly the most vulnerable part of his body and should the creature – for surely it couldn't be human – fasten itself onto them the damage it would do could be irreparable. All Mal's attention was focussed on the threat in front of him. To bang on the window would have caused him to look up distracting him from both creatures. She sent an instantaneous thought to him, *BEHIND YOU!* No sooner had the thought left her mind than Malchediel without taking his eyes off the creature threatening him from the front, reached behind him with his right hand, fingers splayed. There was a bright blinding flash that seemed to emanate from his very palm. The light hit the lurking monstrosity like a laser. As she watched the dwarf-like creature seemed to expand stretching like an inflated balloon until it exploded in a shower of blackened flesh, hair and gore. The beam of light faded and disappeared as did all of the creature's remains, fragmenting then fading into nothingness. It was as though it had never existed. Malchediel gave a shout of triumph never taking his eyes from the other monster which raised its head heaven-ward emitting a howl of rage and anguish. By the light of the moon Amy could see teeth, rows of them all sharp. It raised its arms. She could only count three fingers on the end of each leathery hand but the claws on each were bayonet sharp. Malchediel appeared to be beckoning opened the door saying, "I'll drive…get in the other side."

"You can't drive, you haven't got a licence."

"I'm an Angel." He smiled, "There's nothing I can't do. Get in the other side."

"Have you ever driven a car before?" she asked.

"No. Is it any harder than flying?" he asked with a grin.

As their eyes met he turned serious, "Look at your hands Amy. You're shaking. Let me drive us home…you can relax. That whole episode has unnerved you hasn't it?" She held out her hands. Looking down at them she saw that he was right they were shaking. "I hope we don't get stopped. With no licence we're both in trouble." She answered but she turned to make her way around to the passenger side of the car not wanting to press the matter. She felt that the events of the afternoon were catching up on her and she was relieved at his suggestion to take charge of the driving. As it happened she couldn't believe that he had never driven a car before. By the time they reached Helston she was completely at ease with the way he was handling the car. He had kept up a steady stream of mundane conversation which she recognised for what it was…his attempt to help her relax. She knew that they would eventually have to discuss Asmodeus' threat to both their lives but for now she preferred to listen to him telling her little anecdotes about his celestial life. She found it entertaining to hear about his frequent 'run-ins' with Raguel. He rarely spoke about himself and she was getting an insight into his personal life.   "You must really be the bane of his life. I feel quite sorry for the poor man."

"Oh-ho… you don't need to feel sorry for him. He enjoys being miserable. If I and the others were pleasant to him he'd have nothing to grumble about." She was watching him as he spoke and she started chuckling. He turned briefly to her and smiled. As he turned back to the road she felt a strange fluttering in the pit of her stomach. She didn't want to analyse the reason for that. She looked down at her hands resting in her lap…they weren't trembling any more.

When they reached home they found Stephen waiting for them, his mini parked on the verge at the front of the cottage. Amy supressed a smile when Malchediel drily commented, "Stevie-boy checking up on us? Does he think I'm going to abduct you?"

"Be nice." She murmured as they pulled up behind his car. Stephen climbed out and came around to Amy's passenger door to open it for her ignoring Malchediel who commented above the car roof, "Hope you haven't been waiting too long."

Amy scowled at him before smiling towards Stephen. "Hi...we went for a walk down at the Lizard." She hesitated unsure how he would react if she were to tell him about their encounter with Asmodeus. Stephen leaned across and kissed her lightly on the cheek. This was becoming a habit. He had never shown such affection before Malchediel had arrived on the scene and it was clear that it was his way of pressing the point that he considered himself more than just a friend to her. She wasn't completely comfortable with his presumptive show of affection and she wished the pair of them would stop using her to score points off one-another. "Dad has been doing some investigative work." He said without preamble, "and I came straight over to tell you what he found out. It's about your Mum."

At the mention of her mother Amy felt a tingle of excitement pass through her. She knew so little about the woman whose only image came from a few photographs that her father had kept in an album stored in a dresser drawer. "Come on in." she said leading the way to the front door. "We've got something to tell you as well." She added over her shoulder.

In the kitchen she made tea for the three of them as Stephen launched into the story of how his father, since their earlier meeting, had been searching through long-forgotten paperwork in an attempt to find some information that he vaguely remembered regarding an organisation that Melissa

Bernstein had belonged to in her youth. After several days he had found a dog-eared membership card. Stephen reached into his jacket pocket and produced the card for Amy's inspection. Taking it from him she looked at the writing on the front. It gave her mother's name as Melissa Monkshood together with a six digit number at the bottom right hand corner. The heading at the top comprised of just four letters in bold print. **N.F.F.O.** and a telephone number. "N.F.F.O? What does that stand for?" Amy asked.

Malchediel answered for her, "Nephilim Fighting Force Officer."

"Huh! Sounds like some sort of teen wannabe organisation." She said in disbelief.

"Oh don't underestimate them Amy." Malchediel spoke with feeling taking the card from her to examine. "These weren't a bunch of amateurs playing war games. They were regarded by many Angels as a fearless fighting unit. They fought alongside Warrior Angels for centuries. We parted ways back in the sixteenth century. We felt that they were becoming too expansive in their choice of targets."

Amy frowned at him.

"They were beginning to eliminate anyone they felt was guilty of wrong-doing. It was a time of extreme religious upheaval. We're talking the Spanish Inquisition, heretical trials, witchcraft and such like and they were setting themselves up as trial, judge and jury."

"Well...there were dreadful things going on in the name of religion back then, weren't there? Perhaps they were right to deal harshly with some of those characters?"

"But their victims were human beings Amy. They may have been mistaken in their beliefs but mankind were evolving. It's a part of human existence and we Angels felt it was wrong to intervene in the normal progression of the human race. Our arguments had always been against the evil perpetrated by the Fallen. They were the big danger to the humans. We knew that religious intolerance would sort itself out eventually, so we distanced ourselves from our former allies."

Amy shrugged still not fully accepting his reasoning but what was done was done and couldn't be changed. "And now..." She asked, "Are the Nephilim Fighting Force still a law unto themselves?"

Malchediel grinned, "No, I believe they too have evolved."

"Good...'cos I was thinking of joining them."

"You can't be serious!" An astounded Stephen burst out.

Amy smiled. "Only kidding. After what I witnessed this morning I don't think I have the bottle for it."

Stephen looked from her to Malchediel, "Why? What happened?"

"We bumped into one of my former colleagues." Malchediel announced watching Amy's face for any reaction.

"What? Who?" Stephen had no idea what he was talking about. Amy took up the explanation. "He means we came across a Fallen Angel down at the Lizard."

Stephen's jaw dropped open. "Really? My God! Who was it? Did you know him?" The last was directed at Malchediel.

"Oh yes, I knew him." Malchediel thrust his hands deep into his pockets.

"Well?" Stephen prompted, irritated by Mal's reluctance to share the other Angel's identity.

Amy answered for him, "Asmodeus. His name was Asmodeus."

Stephen drew in a ragged breath, "Bloody Hell! Asmodeus...so he really does exist then?"

"You've heard of him?" Amy was aghast.

"I'll say...One of Lucifer's closest cronies wasn't he?" he looked to Malchediel for confirmation. "And you saw him in the flesh?"

"Look," said Malchediel, "there's no easy way to say this." He paused before continuing, "It's Asmodeus that's been targeting Amy."

Stephen's eyes went straight to Amy then back to Malchediel. "So what happened? Did he try anything?" He looked Amy up and down checking that she wasn't missing any of her limbs.

"No, no, he didn't try anything. He just made it quite clear that he wants me dead." Amy's voice caught on the last word.

"So what did you do?" he demanded of Malchediel. "What did you do to him?"

"Today? Nothing. He knows that I will defend Amy. All we can do now is wait."

"So you let him go? You were face to face with him and you just let him go." Stephen was clearly horrified. Amy saw Malchediel's face harden, a muscle in his jaw beginning to twitch. She stepped forwards placing herself between them. "There was nothing either of us could do Steve." She said quickly. "Asmodeus had the two Guardian Angels with him…the ones that were sent to protect me. He had them chained together and they were injured. One of them was in a bad way. Mal had them to consider. Under the circumstances he handled the situation pretty well."

Stephen continued to glare at Malchediel. After a few moments he turned back to Amy. "So why is he threatening you anyway? What are you supposed to have done to warrant these threats?"

Malchediel turned away from them and carried his mug of tea into the living room leaving Amy and Stephen standing in the kitchen. She pulled one of the chairs out and sat down, then told him what Asmodeus had said about her mother. She described the sorry state of the two Guardians and how Malchediel had sent them back to Raphael. As she finished, Stephen reached across the table to take one of her hands in his. "Do you want to come and stay with us? My Dad has already suggested that he would be glad to have you stay if you want to."

"Thanks Stephen." She said, "But I'll be fine here with Malchediel. He's definitely my safest option. If anything should visualised this moment wondering what it would be like. He was the most beautiful being she had ever encountered and once she had come to terms with his initial arrogance she had come to see a very different caring person behind the bravado. It was a few seconds before she realised that she was holding her breath. She relaxed against him inhaling the very scent of him. She was still amazed at his declaration of his love for her. At last she started to respond to him, her arms going around him, her hands moving slowly up his back. Her fingers absently tracing circular patterns against his sweater. His kiss faltered and a low moan escaped his lips. She found it extremely sensual and as her lips sought his again her hands ceased their caressing motions on his back.

"Don't stop." He murmured as he teasingly tugged her bottom lip between his teeth. "You have no idea how exciting that feels."

All at once it dawned on her why that was so. A low laugh bubbled up inside her chest and he released his hold on her lip.

"As I recall 'sensitive' is how you described it." She said remembering the last time she had gently stroked his back the night of Asmodeus's attack.

He picked up on her train of thought and smiled in response. "And so it is."

She began to move her fingers against his back once more moving slowly upwards to where his wings lay concealed.

Within seconds he began to whisper in a language that she had never heard before. She had no idea what he was saying but the meaning of his words were fairly clear. Words of love are discernible in most languages. He bent to kiss her once more and any reservations that she may have felt, slipped away as she melted into his embrace. His kisses became more urgent as his hands moved under her pyjama top to rest above her hips, his thumbs caressing her abdomen. She could feel the calluses on the tips of his slender fingers against her skin and a part of her mind registered that these must be the result of his angelic cause of his making such a monumental decision.

"You can't know how much I've wanted to hear you say that my love. It's all I've been thinking about for some time." She tilted her head back so that she could see his face. "But knowing what you are giving up fills me with guilt Mal. What if you regret your decision? You said yourself that there would be no going back. If you break contact with your past you would be cast out for ever. We are not talking about a normal human lifetime here. This is for eternity. Would you ever…" Her sentence was cut off by Malchediel placing his forefinger against her lips. She looked into his eyes as a smile curved the corners of his mouth. "Are you trying to make me change my mind?"

She lifted her hand and moved his finger. "I'm scared in case you later wish you hadn't made the wrong decision. Would you hate me for being the reason behind it?"

He regarded her before answering. "The night that I went back I saw my home in a completely different way. I saw it for what it really is. A base. A base from where to embark on the missions that are put before me. I have endured that for thousands of years Amy and have never questioned it before. This mission has been different from any other that I have undertaken." He smiled recalling the interview with Raguel when he was told that he was to protect a Nephilim. "Do you know," He added, "I didn't want to come here. I thought it was demeaning to my station." He still had his arms around her and he gave her waist a gentle squeeze. "Raguel practically had to order me to come. So if anyone is responsible for the present situation it is him."

Somewhat mollified by his reasoning she rested her head against his chest. They stood in silence for a little while drawing comfort from each other's close proximity until Amy lifted her head rising up onto her toes seeking his lips. His hands moved up cupping her face. His mouth momentarily hovered close enough for her to feel the warmth of his breath then with incredible tenderness he kissed her. How often she had always seemed melodious in the past. "For the first time in my life I don't want to return, and that scares me." He gave a despondent laugh. "How ironic; me a Warrior, scared of my own emotions."

She stepped in front of him so that she could see his face clearly. His eyes usually bright with mischief for he frequently teased her with light hearted banter now returned her gaze full of serious intent. "I thought you said that you had no choice in this matter." She said. His comment had sent a surge of hope through her and she wanted clarification about what his options were regarding his impending return. "If you don't return," she went on, "you would face eternal damnation?"

"That about sums it up." He answered.

"Then the decision is made, isn't it?" she asked tentatively.

He looked down into her face and her stomach seemed to turn over under the intensity of his expression. His hand came up and he gently cupped her cheek. She held her breath.

"Is it?" he said quietly. "You think I will go back?"

"You have to don't you? I couldn't contemplate an eternity of damnation for you. All you have ever known is your Heavenly existence. How could you possibly exchange that for an eternity on Earth...Alone?"

"But I wouldn't be alone would I? I would have you."

"Ohh Mal." She murmured, her voice breaking with emotion. "Would that be enough to give up all you know?"

He slipped his hands around her waist and pulled her gently towards him. "Do you love me?" he asked.

"Yes...yes I love you but I think you already know that."

He smiled and bent his face to kiss her lightly on her forehead and letting his lips rest against her skin he whispered, "I love you too Amy. I can't leave you. I can't go back. My life would mean nothing if I couldn't be with you."

A feeling of immense joy flowed through her at his words quickly followed by a terrible guilt for having been the want to face and she had asked pointedly when he thought the summons would come. When he didn't answer immediately, she turned towards him. A fixed steady look on her face.

"Is there something you haven't told me?" she asked.

She was sitting cross-legged on the bed brushing out her hair. They had been sharing the bed since the night of Asmodeus's attack. Mal had been the model of propriety and had not made any attempt to touch her, even when one night, she had, in her sleep turned over and resettled herself next to him, her forehead against his shoulder. He had waited until her breathing was deep and even before easing himself away from her.

He now glanced quickly towards her, taking in her teddy bear motif pyjamas. Sighing he answered, "I have been contacted."

"When?" she asked in surprise.

"The first time, a week ago."

"The first time? How many times have you been recalled?"

"I received the second summons this morning." His voice held no emotion.

"So what have you told them?"

"Nothing. I haven't answered."

"But they won't accept your silence indefinitely, will they?"

He sighed again, "No. You're right I have to answer or I'll just be recalled back without warning."

She placed the hairbrush on the bed and got up walking towards where he stood near the window. She placed her hand on his upper arm stroking his bicep in a comforting manner. "What are you going to do?" she asked quietly.

He looked down at her hand wondering why this benign gesture should send such emotions coursing through his body. As their eyes met she detected the confusion within him and let her hand fall away. He drew a deep breath, "I can't deny it any longer Amy." His voice sounded harsh to her ears and it had

There was no holding back time and in less than ten days Malchediel felt the first tug on his psyche. He was being summoned and he chose to ignore it. At first a wave of panic flowed through him. He wasn't ready for this yet. He told himself that Amy wasn't yet ready to take on the responsibility of her new found telepathic powers without his help. Then why didn't he contact Raguel and explain his concerns? Was it because Raguel would see through his excuses and conclude that this wasn't about Amy's inexperience at all? It was about his own reluctance to consider this mission complete. He didn't want to leave. For the first time in his life he had found somewhere where he would rather be...Someone he would rather be with. And so that first summons went unanswered as he put it out of his mind. He said nothing to Amy either. She was completely immersed in her duo of watercolours of the Helford River scene. She had sketched out the same scene on to two different canvases and was half way through painting the daytime setting. He had accompanied her back to the chosen location one night when there was a full moon and she had taken several photographs of the area so that she would be able to capture the essence of moonlight and water reflections when she was ready to paint the second canvas. He had never seen her so focussed on anything before and he envied her the ignorance of the anxiety that he was feeling knowing that he couldn't hold back the inevitable forever.

It was by now clear that Asmodeus had been acting alone in his vendetta against Amy. There had been no more skirmishes with the Fallen or their accomplices and life for her had settled back into mundane normality. She surprised him one evening by bringing up the subject of his impending return to his life as a Warrior Angel. The one subject that he didn't wrap it around herself in the armchair and he instantly felt guilty taking the bed from her. They were both dressed, what harm could come from sharing the bed. "Amy…I can't let you sleep in the chair. Surely we can share the bed?"

"As you are an Angel pure of thought I'll take you up on that offer." She answered with a smile. She eased herself next to him arranging the throw over both of them before lying back against the pillows. "You know," she said her eyes already closed, "this is the first night for weeks that I can sleep easily." She turned towards him her eyelids flickering open. He was still sitting upright. "Relax Mal," she said soothingly. "It's over. He's gone." He looked down at her, watching as her eyes closed again. She yawned and settled close enough for him to feel the heat of her body. *Relax!* He thought…*some hope.*

Unlike humans, Angels didn't need sleep. They did however achieve a state of dormancy whereby they could recharge their 'batteries' much the same as humans did through their nightly slumber. During this inactive period there was a part of their brain that remained alert. They were never completely comatose, always ready for action should the need arise. Tonight however even this respite was denied him. He spent the first hour of the night watching Amy sleep. She had said that for her this was the first night since he had come into her life when she could relax. Why was it that he couldn't find peace in the steady rise and fall of her chest? He was waiting for something…and he knew instantly when it happened. He felt it in the early hours of the morning. He tried to ignore it and succeeded for a time until the feeling became too insistent. He was being called. They knew that something had happened a few hours ago and the Senate were contacting him for information. Of course they would be aware of the demise of Asmodeus. The death of an Angel could not be hidden even the death of a Fallen Angel. He would have to answer the summons, failure to do so would mean another Angel being sent to check up on him or worse still he would be instantaneously

Chapter Seven

If Amy thought she was the only one desolate at the thought of their impending parting she was mistaken. Malchediel also wondered how he would feel when the time came to say goodbye to his Nephilim charge. He had been aware for some time that his feelings for this earthbound half-Angel were not what they should be. . Initially her vulnerability had engendered a desire to protect-nothing unusual there- he was after all a Warrior. He had not noticed when these feelings towards her had changed and it was with shock that he realised that she had sparked strong sensations of a physical nature within him as she had tended his wound. She was quite oblivious that in Angels the point where their wings sprouted from their shoulders was heavily criss-crossed with nerve endings. He had told her that the area was tender. He didn't explain that they were also areas of strong arousal. He had pulled away from her sharply; knowing that not to have done so would have led who knows where. He had remained outwardly impassive and it was impossible for Amy to know the inner turmoil that her ministrations were causing him.

Good sense dictated that the sooner he returned home the better. Liaisons between Angels and mortals even Nephilim was completely forbidden and had only occurred between the Fallen and mortal women which was how the Nephilim race had first emerged. Any affair between him and Amy would mean immediate banishment from the only home he had ever known. He would join the ranks of the Fallen. Cast out for eternity. As he lay back against the pillows on Amy's bed his outward calm belied the turbulent confusion within.

He was bought out of his thoughts by her voice. "Is there anything you want?" she asked. He looked up noticing the woollen throw draped over her arm. She clearly intended to

does that feel now?" she asked moving back as he turned to face her.

"Much better." He reached for her hand and gave it a gentle squeeze. "Thank you Amy."

He lay back against her pillows as she replaced the unused dressings back into the first aid box. She too was feeling better. Having to call upon her previously unknown Nephilim powers had exhausted her. She was now beginning to feel a sense of exhilaration and it was intoxicating. She set the box on her lap and looked into his eyes. "Is that it now? Is it all over do you think?"

"If it was Asmodeus working alone, and I have no reason to think anyone else was involved then yes it's all over."

"What does that mean for you?" She asked and she wondered if he was able to detect the concern in her voice.

He hesitated in answering her straight away. His eyes remained on hers making her feel uncomfortable. She lowered hers and absently pressed the lid of the first aid box closed although it was already firmly shut. At the sound of his voice she looked back up at him. "Once my work is done I have to return Amy." He said simply.

She nodded and easing herself from the bed she lifted the box and turned away from him lest he see the tears already springing to her eyes. She knew he was waiting for her to say something but she couldn't trust herself not to cry in front of him so she walked from the room under the pretext of putting the first aid box back in the bathroom.

She returned after a few minutes more composed. He hadn't moved from her bed. The room was lit only by the light from the landing and she was glad of the dimness. He started to ease himself up from the bed. "Where are you going?" she asked.

"It's late Amy. I thought you might want to go to bed."

"I do, but I think for once you have earned the right to a proper nights rest. You stay there. I'll take the armchair tonight."

that Angels healed quickly and indeed the hole made by the javelin was clean and did seem to be closing already.

"Come onto the bed. I'll get some surgical dressings to cover the wound." She helped him to his feet and guided him to the bed easing him into a sitting position.

"It's not too bad now. Not as bad as when he sent the heat through it but he probably did me a favour. It did stop the bleeding." He said with an ironic lift of one brow.

For the next half hour Amy cleaned and dressed the wound and Malchediel confessed that he felt much more comfortable. As she had gently cleaned away the blood from his chest they spoke about how she had inexplicably tapped into her previously unknown power of delving into Asmodeus's mind. Malchediel declared that he had never before witnessed such a 'talent' in a Nephilim. He asked her to describe how she had conjured up the water to which she had honestly answered that she had no idea. "I was feeling an enormous rage at what he was doing. I had to stop him. Once his fear of drowning had become apparent everything else just happened. I was as shocked as you." She admitted as she cut a strip of sticking plaster to place over the gauze now covering the wound. As she moved around the bed to check the exit wound on his back she asked, "The flash of bright light...Was that the moment when he died?"

Malchediel didn't turn around as he answered. "That's what happens when an Angel ceases to exist. We just vaporize." She was carefully bathing the exit wound on his back with a wad of cotton wool when he suddenly pulled away from her. "Sorry." She whispered, "I'm trying to be as gentle as I can."

"It's okay. You didn't hurt me. You just touched me where my wings unfurl and it's a sensitive area that's all."

"Oh... right...what...sort of tender you mean?" She didn't notice the tremulous smile that lifted his lips as he answered, "Yes...sort of tender."

She finished applying the dressing to his shoulder. "How

him unsure of whether to touch him or not. "I suppose calling the emergency services is out of the question."

He smiled weakly at her. "Well at least the bleeding has stopped." There was a touch of irony in his voice. "The heat must have cauterised the wound."

As she watched he took three or four deep breaths then steeling himself against the coming pain he pushed forward, caught his breath against the agony of the movement, and pushed forwards again. Amy bit her lip to stop herself crying out as she heard the dragging, sucking sound of his flesh as he pulled free of the javelin which came out of his back still embedded in the doorframe. He staggered forwards and fell to his knees bracing himself on one outstretched arm. She covered the couple of strides to him and dropped down beside him, her hands cupping his face. He closed his eyes and allowed her to hold him close. His breathing was ragged and laboured. She knew that the effort to pull himself free must have been agonising. She gently stroked his hair making soothing sounds each time a groan of pain escaped his lips. They stayed pressed against one another, both on their knees. Eventually Amy pulled back and began unbuttoning his shirt to check the wound beneath. He remained impassive as she eased the blood soaked shirt away from his body. He looked down at her bent head as she examined the wound. "You called me darling." He said quietly.

She stiffened not looking up at him. "No I didn't." she answered after a pause.

"Ohh…" he answered, "My mistake."

"I didn't!" she insisted as she ventured a quick glance at his face knowing full well that her denial was in vain. To save her further embarrassment he changed the subject. "I think we have at last discovered your Nephilim powers Amy, and not a moment too soon." He eased his position resting backwards on his haunches wincing at the pain caused by the movement. Amy was relieved to see that the wound had indeed stopped bleeding. She remembered that he had told her some time ago outside was a girl she had never seen before. Her first glance took in someone of a similar age to herself, fairly tall with short cropped dark hair, her ears sporting several gold earrings.

"Whatever you're selling I'm not interested." Amy said morosely. Not put off in the slightest the girl grinned cheerily. "That's okay...I'm not selling anything." She pulled her shoulder bag around in front of her and delving inside pulled out a small business card. "My name is Ruby Shoreditch. You must be Amy. My goodness you have been difficult to track down I have to say. She held out the card to Amy who took it with little interest. "Look...I'm not even dressed yet. I'm not feeling too good. What do you want?" She knew she was being incredibly rude but she really didn't care. Not to be put off the girl's grin broadened. "My card confirms my identity."

Amy sighed pointedly and looked down at the card in her hand. It did indeed show the name *Ruby Shoreditch* across the middle with a six digit number in the bottom right hand corner but what had instantly caught Amy's eye were the four bold letters at the top **N.F.F.O.** Her jaw dropped open and as she looked up at her visitor's grinning face Ruby held out her hand, "Nephilim Fighting Force Officer Shoreditch...Pleased to meet you. May I come in?"

AMY
NEPHILIM FREEDOM FIGHTER

BOOK TWO

WINGS UNFURLED SERIES

She called out to him using her mind...

'MALCHEDIEL!'

Contents

Prologue

It took a little while for Ralph to notice the flashing red light on the black phone indicating an incoming call. It was his turn to man the Control Room that evening and the last thing he was expecting was a call on the phone that had been pushed to the back of the desk. No one had rung that number for over five years, ever since the new phone system had been installed. Someone was using it now though; the steady blinking light was testament to that. He frowned staring at it until it stopped flashing displaying instead, a steady red glow.

"Ilya!" he called, "Ilya I think you need to come and see this."

A blonde head appeared at the doorway to the kitchen area, "What's up?" the two heavily accented words clearly denoting his Russian heritage.

"Someone has just rung on the black phone."

"No way…No-one has used that phone for years."

Ralph turned to face his colleague, "Well someone has used it now." he said as he pulled the phone towards him. He waited to see if it would ring again but when the red light remained constant for a further couple of minutes he lifted the receiver and dialled one four seven one and listened. "Number withheld." he said replacing the receiver. Fishing his cell-phone out of his pocket he dialled his Supervisor's number.

Within ten minutes Doctor Steenbergen had arrived in the control room.

"I suppose it could have been a wrong number." He suggested.

"That is possible." Ralph answered, "But it would be interesting to trace it somehow. It's strange that it hasn't been used for what…five or six years."

At that moment the door opened and Ruby casually walked in. The Doctor, Ralph and Ilya all turned to see who had entered the Control Room.

Perhaps it was time to come clean with Ruby. She worked for the same organisation that her mother had belonged to. She surely could be trusted and when all was said and done it would be such a relief to share the happenings of the past few weeks with someone. Amy took a deep breath. Standing up she reached for the teapot. "I think we need some fresh tea. I haven't been completely honest with you up until now. There is so much I have to tell you."

Ruby's eyes widened. "I knew you were holding something back." She said with a grin.

Chapter Two

Several cups of tea later Ruby was fully conversant with all that had happened to Amy since Malchediel first walked into her shop some weeks before. When Amy first spoke his name Ruby's mouth dropped open. "Malchediel...as in the warrior Malchediel!" she exclaimed.

Amy nodded. "Clearly you know his name, which was more than I did when we first met." She went on to explain how a few days after their first meeting he suddenly appeared to rescue her from a rock fall at the beach where she had set up her painting easel. It was then that she found out he was an Angel. "That was the first time I saw his wings. I couldn't believe my eyes. I had never believed in Angels before then."

Ruby's eyes were as large as saucers. "You must be the only Nephilim alive that can admit to that. Let's face it we wouldn't exist if it weren't for Angels."

"Well...my upbringing was sadly lacking in Angelic education so you can imagine how shocked I was when I first saw those wings and then when he retracted them I thought I was losing the plot."

Ruby laughed. "Yeah, I can imagine the impact that must have had on you." Her face became serious and she leaned forward conspiratorially, "What did he look like...I bet he was fantastic."

Amy was bought up short by the question. An image of Malchediel flashed into her mind unbidden. She had been trying not to conjure up images of him for the last three days; it only resulted in a fresh bout of tears when she did. She lifted her mug to her lips only to discover that she had already drained it. She placed it back on the table acutely aware that Ruby was waiting for an answer. Unsuccessfully she willed the tears not to well up in her eyes. Ruby was watching her waiting for an answer to her question. All at once realisation dawned on her. "Oh my God!" she cried, "It was him wasn't it? You said there were several differences between the two of you...the guy you broke up with...It was him...you fell for an Angel. Oh Hellfire Amy..." She ran out of words. She just looked at her friend in astonishment. Amy put her head in her hands determined to fight back the tears that were threatening to fall.

Ruby, aware of the other girl's misery acted quickly to mask her shock at the revelation of Amy's mysterious lover. "Okay..." she said, her voice returning to a normal pitch, "What was the reason for his being sent here?"

Amy took a couple of deep breaths and lowering her hands went on to explain that he had been told that she was under some sort of threat and he was to unravel the mystery and deal with it.

It was mid-afternoon by the time Ruby knew the full story. When Asmodeus was revealed as the one behind the threat to Amy's life Ruby scowled. *'So...'* Amy thought, *'She's heard of Asmodeus as well as Malchediel.''*

Ruby listened in silence until Amy described how she had killed Asmodeus herself when he launched his attack on her and Malchediel. "So that's how you discovered your latent Nephilim power, sensing his fear of water and conjuring up enough to drown him. Wow ...Amy that's amazing."

"If Malchediel hadn't been injured by Asmodeus in the attack I probably would never have had to use the telepathic skills that had lain dormant. I was so enraged to see Mal pinned up against the wall by Asmodeus's spear that when visions of him floundering in water raced through my mind I just knew what to do. It seemed easy at the time to create the means of destroying him once and for all. It was only later that the enormity of what I had done sank in."

"Ohh...wow! I can't wait for the Doctor and the others to meet you. I can't imagine what they'll make of that story."

"What do you mean? Are they coming here as well?" Amy asked in surprise.

"No…I'm going to take you to our headquarters." She grinned at Amy, "It's about time you found out about your Nephilim background. You'll need to pack a few things…just enough for a few days."

Amy looked at her in astonishment. Ruby laughed at her expression. "Look at it as a way of finding out what sort of life your mother led before you were born." she said.

That comment was enough reason for Amy to decide that she would indeed accompany Ruby back to the Nephilim Fighting Force Command Centre as soon as possible. "I don't even know where your headquarters are." she said.

"I'm based in the south west." Ruby answered as she stood to carry the breakfast dishes over to the kitchen sink, "Head Office is obviously in London. There are various other bases around the U.K."

"So where is the south west office located?"

Ruby laughed, "You make it sound like a local authority department. All our bases are private country houses in parkland away from prying eyes. Ours is on the outskirts of Bath."

"Sounds like a pretty decent place to work." Amy said with a smile.

"You wouldn't believe it." Ruby smirked.

For the first time in days Amy had something to look forward to. She packed a weekend case with enough clothes to last three or four days and a toilet bag with the essentials that she would need. She telephoned Stephen's home knowing that he would be working at the shop in Falmouth, She felt a little guilty about not speaking to him but she knew that he would most likely try to dissuade her from leaving before he was able to vet the Nephilim she was travelling with. Since the arrival of Malchediel he had set himself up as her chief protector and advisor. She was aware that he had always had 'a bit of a thing' for her but Malchediel's presence had tipped that over into almost an obsession. She spoke to Stephen's father explaining that an Officer from the Nephilim Fighting Force had contacted her and invited her to visit the South Western headquarters in Bath. In contrast with his son, Alex Goodrich was all in favour of Amy visiting the Organisation where her mother once worked. "I'm sure you will find it very informative. There are bound to be people there who will remember your mother. It will be good to find out about her life...goodness knows you know so little about her. Keep in touch by phone and let us know how you get on. We'll see you when you get back my dear."

With that done, she locked up the cottage and turned to the car parked out at the front, a sleek black Mercedes SLK. Her jaw dropped as Ruby pressed the key fob. The car bleeped as the central locking engaged. Ruby glanced across taking in her surprised look of admiration. She grinned. "Not bad is it?" she smirked.

"How much do they pay you?" Amy gasped. "I could never afford a car like this in a thousand years."

"I don't own it." Ruby laughed. "It's one of the fleet cars. Any one of us can drive it." She gave Amy a devilish look, "nice though isn't it?"

During the drive up through Cornwall, Devon and Somerset Ruby kept up a steady stream of conversation about herself, the Organisation she belonged to and the people she worked with. By the time they reached the outskirts of Bath Amy knew that she and Ruby were going to be firm friends. Their personalities were very different. Ruby was an outgoing, confident individual, an extrovert of the highest order. She openly admitted to having an extremely active sex life. "What about you?" she asked glancing across at Amy who was quite taken aback at the suddenness of the question. "Me? Oh...um...well...there'd been no one special before Malchediel." She spluttered. "Since Dad died I really haven't had much time for romance...um...I had been trying to build up my the fact that Mal's had been more golden and a good deal longer than Ilyas'.

"Amy's going to be staying for a few days. I'm just showing her around." With that she linked her arm with Amy's, and turned to head back the way they had entered.

"It was nice meeting you. Perhaps I'll see you again." Amy called over her shoulder. Ilya acknowledged her comment with a wave of his hand before he turned too to make his way back to the basket-ball hoop.

Once back in the corridor Amy asked, "Ilya? I gather he is a Russian?"

"Yeah. He came over from Moscow on a month's secondment. That was three years ago." She giggled, "He obviously likes it here."

"He seems nice." Amy ventured.

"Yeah, he is quite nice." Ruby answered, "Unless you're a demon or goblin. He's lethal in hand to hand combat."

Amy lifted an eyebrow but said nothing. *Those muscles are not just for show then.* She thought.

Also housed in the gymnasium wing was a swimming pool. It was in darkness but Ruby flicked on one row of lights illuminating the end where they stood looking over the still water. "The facilities here are amazing Ruby. Can anyone use them?"

"Sure. The Doctor likes all of us to keep fit and healthy. You never know when we will be called out in an emergency."

"I assume you mean if and when the 'bad guys' decide to launch an attack."

Ruby glanced at Amy nodding. "Of course..." She said thoughtfully, "You've been at the receiving end of one of those, haven't you?"

Amy didn't care to reminisce. "Where next?" She asked with a smile.

The tour continued taking in all the ground floor rooms including the dining room, the board room which Ruby explained was used whenever the Doctor called a meeting of all the staff and officers on duty. This room was dominated by a huge mahogany table flanked each side by at least twelve chairs. The last room they viewed on the ground floor was the 'armoury.' Amy was taken aback by the array of weaponry stored here. All four walls were lined with racks holding various firearms and other almost medieval-looking weapons including several mace, spears and axes. There was also a dozen or so metal lockers each bearing someone's name. Amy stood just inside the door open-mouthed taking in all the paraphernalia. "My God!" she breathed.

Ruby chuckled leading the way to one of the lockers. It had her name on it. She placed an index finger on an electronic pad on the door which immediately sprang open. The two girls' eyes met, Ruby's sparkling with amusement. Amy grinned back, "More electronic security gadgets?" she speculated. She peered around the locker door taking in the contents. Hanging inside was combat gear all camouflaged in shades of green and grey. Ruby lifted out what Amy recognised as a body-

armoured vest. "Have you ever felt the weight of one of these?" she asked.

Amy took the hanger from her acknowledging how heavy it was with a slight grimace.

Ruby laughed taking it back to hang away again. On the floor of the locker stood a pair of heavy combat boots alongside what appeared to be stout leather shin pads and a pair of similar re-enforced sleeves. "What on earth are those? Amy asked.

Ruby chuckled. "Those," she pointed to the sleeves, "are called vambrace. They protect my forearms. And those," her finger moved across to the shin-pads, "are Greaves."

Suddenly Amy became aware that there was more to her new friend than the multi-ear ringed chatty teenager that she had come to know over the past few hours. She turned a solemn face towards the other girl. "My God Ruby! You actually need all this body armour to be a member of the N.F.F?"

Ruby looked at her in astonishment. "We don't 'play-act' at this Amy. It's for real. We're like the regular army...we just do it in secret. We volunteer for this and we train hard. These..." she said indicating the contents of the locker with a flourish of her hand "are the tools we use." She gave Amy a hard look. "Have you been put off by all this?" she asked.

Amy returned the look with a questioning lift to her brow. "You really thought I was considering joining the Organisation?"

With a grin Ruby answered, "You're your mother's daughter...of course I did."

She closed the locker door and with a quick change of subject said, "I'll show you upstairs now."

As Amy followed her out of the Armoury the seed of Ruby's suggestion began to germinate...just as Ruby had intended.

The first floor contained all the bedrooms of which there were twenty two; all, Ruby stated smugly had en-suite facilities.

"So how many people live here?" Amy asked in surprise.

"In the main house just the Doc, Ilya and me. There are two resident staff members, Marcia, the Housekeeper and her husband Jack who deals with all the Maintenance around the house and gardens but they have their own house in the grounds."

"I think I probably saw Jack earlier. Was that him cutting the grass?" Amy asked.

Ruby chuckled, "That would be him. We can't get him off that tractor mower since the Doctor bought it. It's his new toy."

Amy smiled at Ruby's comment. "Are they Nephilim like us...Marcia and Jack?"

"They are but they don't take part in active service. If the subject is bought up Jack will say that they're too old for it now but between you and me I think it has more to do with the fact that their only son was killed two years ago during an attack on a group of off-duty officers in London. Jack was devastated. Poor Marcia didn't even have time to grieve properly 'cos Jack had a breakdown over it. She had to care for him for over six months until he was able to cope with life again." She was silent for a moment or two clearly remembering the difficult time. "We were all walking on egg shells for a while trying not to bring up any subject that would remind them of their loss."

Amy listened in silence, and then Ruby went on, "As he was recovering Marcia made it clear that for the two of them there would be no more active service. They only had each other and she didn't think Jack could cope with any more stress. At that time the Doctor was employing staff through an agency. Because of the secret nature of our work here, we couldn't trust outsiders on a permanent basis so the staff was changed regularly before they became aware of what was going on in the Organisation. It seemed that the answer to Marcia and Jacks' predicament was staring the Doctor in the face. He offered the positions to them on a permanent basis. It's worked perfectly for everyone concerned."

As they were chatting together Ruby was showing Amy the rest of the empty bedrooms opening each door as they went along the upstairs corridor. All the rooms were furnished much the same as the one allocated to her. "Are any of these rooms ever occupied?" Amy asked.

"Oh yes...we often have visiting members ...you know like from other bases. I told you that we have bases around the U.K. as well as in other countries. We often visit one another and there is a yearly AGM that is hosted by a different region each year. It's great when the house is fully occupied. It can be boring when it's just me, the Doc and Ilya." She gave Amy a furtive glance, "That's why I'm hoping you will consider staying here."

Amy made no comment and Ruby turned away walking towards the next bedroom door. It wasn't that Amy dismissed the idea of living at the Manor out-of-hand, but there was a lot to consider. She already had a home in Cornwall, a small business that gave her a modest income and a quiet way of life that suited her. To move into the Manor was not only a change of address, it was also a complete change of lifestyle. Certainly she would be following in her mother's footsteps but she hadn't been bought up to be a guerrilla fighter. True she had risen to the challenge when threatened by Asmodeus but that had been initiated by her rage at Malchediel's injury. When faced with violence again would she just freeze or perhaps turn tail and flee?

Dinner that evening was served in the dining room. The long table was set only at one end for the Doctor, Ilya, Ruby and Amy. Marcia served them a three course dinner commencing with Minestrone Soup. As she set his bowl in front of him, the Doctor asked the Housekeeper who was manning the control room that evening.

"Charlotte is on tonight." she said, "I've already served her soup."

"I'm taking over from her at midnight." offered Ilya. "I doubt there will be anything going on. I have a good book that I'm hoping to finish."

The Doctor broke into his bread roll nodding at Ilyas' comment. "It's been very quiet over the past few months. I don't know whether to be relieved or worry that it's the lull before the storm."

Ilya chuckled as he glanced at Amy's look of concern. "The Doctor jests Amy..." he said smiling, "He revels in being a pessimist. We haven't had a storm, as he puts it, for years now."

Amy returned his smile. She liked Ilya. He had a very laid back personality and his Russian accent was attractive to listen

She could feel her cheeks colouring under his gaze, "You're not the first person to tell me that." She said.

His gaze lingered on her face before he asked, "Are you going to join us Amy?" then a smile lifted the corners of his mouth, "We could always do with another Monkshood on the team."

She returned his smile saying, "Ahh but I'm a Bernstein not a Monkshood."

His smile faltered slightly then with a lift of his eyebrow he countered, "From where I'm standing you are definitely a Monkshood." He said no more but his comment had left an impression never the less.

She went to bed that night with nothing resolved about her future. She knew that she would have a home at the Manor should she choose to join the organisation and it was tempting, she had to admit. She acknowledged that if Ruby hadn't turned up on her doorstep she would most likely still be sunk in depression all alone in her cottage in Cornwall living through each day in a haze of misery? Since arriving there had been long periods when she had almost forgotten the trauma of Malchediel's abduction. She also had to come to terms with the fact that he hadn't tried to return to her. Perhaps she needed to move on and it would be easier if she had a goal to aim for. Was the Organisation going to provide that goal for her?

Chapter Three

Malchediel handled his abduction in a completely different way to Amy. He had raged against his former comrades for their part in separating him from her. They had clearly planned his kidnap and had caught him unprepared. What **they** were unprepared for was his fury at being unceremoniously dragged away from her. When he found himself locked in his own quarters unable to overcome their combined Celestial powers to escape, he unleashed his anger on the contents of his room, smashing everything in an unbridled assault until he was exhausted, finally sinking to the floor in despair to await Nemamiah's appearance for surely he would come and explain his actions. When at last they did come face to face, Malchediel launched another attack on what he now considered a former friend. When Nemamiah refused to fight back, the anger and resentment seemed pointless and Malchediel's temper drained away as he waited for Nememiah to explain why they had removed him from the girl he loved.

He was in no mood for Nememiah's excuses and claimed that he would return to Amy as soon as he was able. It was then that Nemamiah hit him with the news that Amy had returned his feather. The feather that he had given her with the instruction that if ever she should need him, for whatever reason, she only had to snap the calamus and he would be aware of it. He had told her that as soon as he sensed the break in the quill he would come to her. To have Nemamiah return the unbroken feather to him could only mean that she had no further need of it. She would never call upon him. She had no further need of him. In all the millennia that he had been alive he had never had his heart broken but he felt it slowly shatter at that moment as he held the last link that he had to the girl who had stolen his heart. He couldn't understand why she had returned it. Nemamiah said that it was because she realised that their romance was nothing more than wishful thinking.

Only Fallen Angels mated with mortals. She knew no good would come of their relationship. After all he was immortal and any life they may have together would be a fleeting moment in time for him, leaving him alone and an outcast when she died which of course she would in time.

Oh, how he was hurting. He told Nemamiah to leave him. He had nothing more to say to his former friend. He sat amongst the debris of his room holding the feather as his heartbreak washed over him. Hour after hour he remained immobile slowly rotating the single piece of plumage between his fingers. Eventually he concluded that there was only one course open to him now. He was a Warrior Angel. That was what he was created for...to fight evil. Who needed love? He would henceforth devote himself to what he was best at. From that moment he hardened his heart. He now realised why it was forbidden for Angels and Mortals to form any sort of romantic relationship. It could only end in disaster.

Nemamiah, Paschar and Qaphsiel realising that he now accepted the inevitable released him from his one-room prison and they attempted to draw him back into the arms of their brotherhood. For some time he held himself apart from them unable to regain the easy camaraderie that had existed before. All three observed the detached way he handled his first mission following his abduction. He seemed not to care if he put himself in danger. Injury or even death no longer bothered him; indeed it was as though fear no longer governed his actions. Was he courting danger as a means to end his misery? His friends now watched his back as he had once watched theirs, hoping that the old Malchediel would eventually resurface.

Only once did Nemamiah mention Amy to him, some three or four weeks following his return. Mal's face hardened and he glared at his friend. "I have no wish to discuss her with you Nem." He said coldly, "It's over. Don't bring it up again." And with that he abruptly rose from the bench where they had been sitting and strode back into the building. Nemamiah had only enquired if Malchediel wanted him to surreptitiously check up on Amy to make sure she was alright. He knew that Malchediel contrary to his outward impression of hardening his heart to what had happened was nursing his hurt in solitude. He had thought that if he could bring news that Amy was getting on with her life it would ease his friends torment. It had been a mistake, one he wouldn't repeat.

As time went by the tension between the four of them eased but they couldn't seem to regain their former easy-going relationship. After every mission there would always have been a period of light-hearted banter, a time to 'wind down' after the exertion of battle. Malchediel would always have been the first to instigate the verbal banter that sometimes developed into a bout of horseplay. Now, once their injuries (if there were any) had been treated Malchediel would return to his quarters alone.

Whereas the three friends missed the old Malchediel, Raguel, who had also noticed a change in his behaviour, was gratified by it. A few weeks following his return, Malchediel was summoned before his overseer once more. This time when he entered Raguel's office he was greeted with a smile. The expression didn't sit easily on the overseer's face. Mal had only ever seen Raguel smile at him when he had been able to get the better of him over some disciplinary matter. This time however the smile almost bordered on friendliness. Raguel leaned back in his chair eyeing Malchediel making the Warrior Angel feel uncomfortable.

"I have noticed a change in your attitude since you returned to us after your little stint of guardianship Malchediel."

Mal's eyes which had been focussed on the papers on Raguel's desk lifted to meet those of the Overseer. After a moment he dropped them back to the desk, waiting.

"I like the change. Your attitude to your work is greatly improved. It seems that my decision to send you on that mission was the right one."

Malchediel's eyes snapped back to Raguel's face. Surely he wasn't intending to repeat the assignment. Was he thinking of sending Mal on another Guardianship mission? He had never heard of an Angel's vocation being changed before. Each was created for a specific purpose. He was a Warrior built for fighting. Surely Raguel couldn't change his status? Mal's eyes must surely have displayed some of the anxiety that he was feeling. Raguel's smile almost held a touch of warmth, "You once told me that you were the best Warrior we have. I have never verbally agreed with you in the past because quite frankly your attitude had always let you down." He tilted his head to one side meeting Malchediel's gaze. He paused for a moment then went on, "With your change of attitude I am thinking that you now have the maturity to eventually command a cohort of your own."

Malchediel's brows dipped into a frown. This was the last thing he was expecting.

"I...I don't know what to say."

Raguel leaned forward, resting his forearms on the desk and linking his fingers casually together. "I was always aware that you were the best we had." He said keeping his eyes on Malchediel's face, "I just wasn't going to admit it to you before now." He unclasped his fingers and pushed himself backwards in his chair once more as he drummed his palms against the edge of his desk. Mal sensed that the interview was over and his shoulders at last relaxed. Raguel assumed a business-like mood once more. "Keep up the good work Malchediel." He said, "We will talk about this again sometime. I just wanted you to know that your conduct has not gone unnoticed. You may go."

As Malchediel descended the stairs returning to his quarters he smiled inwardly to himself. At a time when he felt he had little to smile about, the irony of the situation was not lost on him. To have been offered his own cohort in the past, before his disastrous liaison with Amy, would have filled him with pride. Now...it meant nothing. There was only one thing he desired now and it was the one thing he could not have.

the cushioned chair wing she began to feel that this could indeed be her new home.

She didn't sleep well that night. There was too much to think about. Most of the guests would be leaving tomorrow following the Christmas festivities. She too needed to return to Falmouth. She owed it to her new friends to confirm whether the return would be permanent or just to tie up loose ends enabling her to start a new life with them. The decision would have to be made before she left again.

By Boxing Day morning she had come to a decision and after breakfast she made for the Doctor's office and knocked on his door.

Chapter Five

After her interview with the Doctor, Amy went straight up to Ruby's room to let her know that she had decided that once everything back in Cornwall had been sorted out she would be returning as a resident member of the N.F.F. Needless to say Ruby was beside herself with delight and Amy declared that her smile was in danger of splitting her face in two. Together they made plans to return to Falmouth within the next two days. Amy was getting an inkling that Ruby's enthusiasm had quite a lot to do with seeing Stephen again.

By the twenty seventh of December the Manor had shed its extra guests and returned to normal. All through the Christmas period there had been no let-up in their vigilance in monitoring Demon activity. There were sporadic attacks, always around areas of water. The Doctor was concerned about this new aspect of activity and he was in regular contact with other N.F.F. headquarters especially the London base that was experiencing heavier than usual nightly attacks. There had been several murders especially around the River Thames and these had been reported in the press as linked to drug trafficking although senior N.F.F. officers were sceptical about this.

Amy and Ruby decided to drive back to Cornwall on the twenty ninth of December. Stephen had been in touch and suggested the girls join him and several friends to celebrate the New Year with a 'pub crawl.' It didn't particularly appeal to Amy but Ruby was all for it.

Once back, the first thing Amy did was to contact the letting agency for the little shop she occupied in Falmouth to give notice that when the lease came up for renewal at the end of February she would vacate the premises. That gave her plenty of time to remove all of her stock back to the cottage and clean up allowing the agents to re-let the shop.

She decided to start emptying the shop straight away, dropping down the rear seats of her little car so that she and Ruby could stack as many canvases into the back as possible. She estimated that it would take at least three runs backwards and forwards from shop to cottage before all the paintings were safely stowed at her home.

"Do you want me to stop here at the shop while you run them back?" Ruby offered when they had loaded the first batch into her car.

"Okay, if you don't mind? It should only take me about three quarters of an hour and I'll be back for the second load. It'll save me locking up each time if you wait here." It had not occurred to Amy that there may have been an ulterior motive to Ruby's suggestion and it was only when she returned from the first run that she found Stephen inside the shop chatting away to Ruby who was sitting cross legged on the bench twirling a lock of her short dark hair suggestively around her finger as she listened to his describing the night-life of Truro. Amy smiled to herself as she entered the shop. Stephen had been standing sideways on to Ruby, his upper body leaning in towards her indicating a more than casual exchange going on. As the little door-bell tinkled he pulled back rapidly making the whole situation look even more furtive. Ruby showed no such embarrassment smiling broadly at Amy. "Wotcha, we've sorted out another pile of canvases ready for you." She nodded towards a stack of Amy's paintings resting against the bench.

"Um...yes...yes I'll carry them out for you Amy." Stephen stammered quickly moving away from Ruby to lift up the first three canvases as Amy reached for the door to open it for him.

"I'm parked on double yellow lines but I've left the hazard lights on." She said holding the door open.

Stephen scooted through but not before Amy noticed his reddened cheeks. As she let the door swing to she grinned at Ruby, "Not interrupting anything was I?"

"Not yet." Ruby smiled back, "He'd only been here about ten minutes. Don't rush back on the next run."

"You're awful Ruby. Did you see how embarrassed he looked when I walked in?

Ruby laughed heartily as she too picked up two more canvases to carry outside to Amy's car.

By the thirty first of December the shop premises were empty and as Amy stood in the middle of the room she felt a pang of sadness as she surveyed the bare walls and work surfaces. This little business had been the mainstay of her life since the death of her father and although she was looking forward to the next phase of her life within the N.F.F. she had fond memories of Falmouth and Cornwall. Not only that but with the move from Cornwall she was cutting the last link with Malchediel. She sighed as she returned the sweeping brush to the cupboard. She needed a fresh start, a challenge, something that would occupy her fully so that she didn't dwell on the past.

She looked around her, satisfied that everything was tidy and that the premises could be re-let without any delays. At that moment Ruby bustled into the shop laden down with shopping bags. "Wait till you see the dress I've got for tonight." She said excitedly. "I didn't think there'd be anything suitable in a small town like this but that little boutique had this... and it's in my size." She pulled a black dress from one of the bags with a flourish shaking it out for Amy to see. "If he doesn't fancy me in this tonight then he has to be gay." She exclaimed.

Amy laughed as she reached out to touch the silky dress that was being thrust at her. "It's lovely Ruby. I hope you're not planning to seduce poor Steve tonight. I think he probably needs a little fore warning."

Ruby grinned, "Well if we're going back shortly, time is of the essence." She said and Amy wasn't altogether sure if she was joking.

All in all it was a good way to welcome in the New Year. Stephen had rounded up about a dozen friends and they all met at 'The Rose' public house at a little after eight o'clock. Most people had left their cars at home with a view to walking to their various places of abode at the end of the evening. Only Stephen and Amy lived too far away to attempt getting home on foot so he had arranged with his father to pick them up. He had his mobile phone and providing it wasn't any later that 2 a.m. Alex said he would wait up until he heard from them. They managed to cram in five different pubs before ending up at The Swan where the guys had to fight their way to the bar and it was impossible to hold any sort of conversation above the raucous singing and laughing. Amy amused herself watching Ruby's unbounded flirting with Steve. At first he seemed embarrassed. He kept glancing across at Amy to gauge her reaction to which she smiled warmly back at him in an attempt to convey that she was by no means upset by what was going on. After all she had never harboured any romantic feelings towards him and if he should develop a relationship with Ruby it was certainly with her blessing. As the alcohol flowed and the merrymaking became less inhibited she noticed that Ruby was winning the battle. By midnight the two had become inseparable and the 'Happy New Year' kiss became quite a clinch. She was happy for them but it bought home to her that there was no-one special in her own life and she, for a brief moment, imagined what it would be like to have Malchediel here with her now. As soon as the thought had occurred to her she dismissed it. How foolish to fantasize celebrating the New Year with an Angel. Would she ever stop thinking about what might have been? She turned as she felt someone tap her shoulder just in time to be assaulted by a pair of wet eager lips bearing down to her for a celebratory kiss. She just had time to turn her cheek towards the 'sink plunger' onslaught, before dodging under the stranger's arm and squeezing towards the door leading to the Ladies loo. Ten minutes away from the bar should be enough for the wild round of kissing and groping to die down and then she could slip back in. The toilets were across an outdoor courtyard. There was one light illuminating the area and before she slipped inside the toilet, she caught started back the way he came breaking into a run after a few strides. He extended his wings as he built up speed passing the elderly lady who had been down by the Harbour earlier. Once again as his feet left the ground she was blasted with another wave of cold air that blew her coat around her legs. He was already out of earshot as she muttered under her breath, "Bloody weather!"

Within ten minutes he was landing once more, this time, in the lane some fifty metres away from Amy's cottage. He approached carefully just in case she was outside or maybe at a window. Her car was missing. His heart sank yet again. Where was she? He walked up the drive and went around to the back of the cottage listening all the time for any sounds from within…nothing. He wasn't just going to leave. He walked up to the door, sensing that there was no-one inside. Without hesitation he passed through the door and stood just inside, listening. It was cold. There was no heating on. He carried on through the kitchen and into the living room savouring all the ambience of her home. It was just as he remembered. His heart felt heavy in his chest and his breath caught in his throat as disappointment and despair swept through him. All he wanted was to see her. All this way for nothing. He went upstairs just to be in her bedroom. He stood in the doorway looking around the room. His eyes strayed to the wardrobe where she had crouched down in fear on the night of Asmodeus's attack, then moved to the bed across from the doorway. His mind went back to the night of his abduction, the night he was going to make love to her for the first time. He closed his eyes and let his mind drift back to that night. Amy, on the bed watching him as he undressed, her face flushed, her hair tumbled over her shoulders. He could feel the longing that he had felt that night. She was willing, lifting her arms so that he could pull her pyjama top over her head. She was beautiful and he was going to make love to her.

He opened his eyes before the memory of his three companions bursting into the room could spoil the image of Amy, semi naked wanting him as much as he wanted her.

The bed that night was rumpled from their exertions. Tonight it was neatly made up and empty. A solitary tear tracked slowly down his cheek... he so desperately wanted to see her again.

He turned to the wardrobe and opened it, finding it half empty. The coat-hangers swinging idly with the motion of his opening the door. He raised his eyes to the top of the wardrobe where her red suitcase normally sat. That too was missing. She wasn't just out...she had left, taking some of her clothes with her.

He let out a moan of frustration before walking back to the bed and sitting down upon the quilt. He sat motionless for hours as the sun slowly sank over the horizon eventually to be replaced by the moon. It was a little before midnight when he finally stood. He straightened the duvet before unfurling his wings and passing through the bedroom wall he flew out into the cold night air.

He had a mission to complete. This had always been a 'fool's errand'. Why couldn't he accept that it was over? His life was not with her. He was a Warrior Angel.

He circled the town of Falmouth a couple of times in the crazy hope of detecting her presence below before reason asserted itself that she wouldn't have needed a suitcase if she was in town. He had to face the possibility that she was somewhere miles away unaware of his desperation just to catch a glimpse of her. He let out a howl of frustration before deciding that he had wasted enough time. She was clearly getting on with her life...he needed to do the same. He became aware of the damp night air coming up from the English Channel below and turning eastward resumed his coastal patrol of the island of Britannia. As dawn broke he hovered above Portsmouth watching for any strange activity amongst the naval ships below. When satisfied that all seemed normal he moved on flying northwards around the Straits of Dover. He turned westward again following the Thames estuary towards London. He reasoned that if he were one of the Fallen bent on creating havoc on Earth it would be sensible to target heavily populated areas. He was within sight of the Thames barrage and beginning to think of turning around and continuing back up the east coast when without warning a blast of Demon activity burst up from the river below. The commotion of evil hit him carrying him upwards for several hundred feet buffeting him from left to right. He was totally unprepared for the gust of hot air and turbulence that tumbled him over and over as he fought to right himself, his wings straining against the tempest. As he struggled to regain control he scanned the area below but could see nothing. There was no sign of either Fallen Angels or demons of any kind but he knew the signs. There had been a presence of considerable force around the mighty Thames within the past few hours. He was now flying higher than he had before and the buffeting against his body eased. He needed to complete his reconnaissance and return with his report. Something was definitely going on. The power of the manifestation around London could only mean that some sort of attack was possible if not imminent.

Evidence of demonic presence around the capital city of Britannia had shocked Malchediel not only by its existence but more worryingly by its strength of number. The buffeting that his body had experienced from the waves of ethereal heat emanating from below could only have been produced from huge numbers of malign beings. He continued his patrol along the north east and back into the realm of Caledonia skirting the Northern Isles but detected no further Demonic power. If an attack were to come would it therefore be centred on the most heavily populated area of the country? And if such an attack were to be mounted against the unsuspecting humans, Malchediel reasoned that other countries would surely be targeted also. It would be prudent for other heavily populated areas to be assessed for possible attacks. He needed to return as quickly as possible with his report.

It had been thousands of years since Lucifer and his generals had mounted a revolt of any significance. There had always been skirmishes which proved the need for the likes of Malchediel and his fellow Warriors but with hindsight was that just the Fallen flexing their muscles for 'the big one.' – The next mighty battle between good and evil, with Earth as the battleground? Mal remembered the first Angelic revolt which had taken place in Heaven. He had lost many friends to Lucifer's insane attack upon the Creator. Up until that time he had many sympathies with those that would become known as the Fallen. He had quickly decided to remain faithful to Michael, God's new 'right hand' a position vacated by Lucifer himself. He had never regretted that decision hating the carnage that Lucifer's fall had left in its wake.

His aerial assessment of Britannia now complete he turned for home eager to pass on his findings to Raguel. He was thankful that the only areas that caused him concern were around Liverpool and more worryingly London. Thank the saints that Cornwall, where Amy lived had shown no presence to concern him. She at least would be safe if any attack should come.

Chapter Seven

The N.F.F, lacking Malchediel's Angelic abilities were unable to ascertain the level of risk posed by the Fallen Angels and the Demonic creatures working for them but they were aware that something was brewing. As Nephilim they had descended from Angels and possessed - albeit at a reduced level – a certain amount of power denied to normal humans. By sharing information with other forces, both national and global, they had come to the conclusion that the sporadic attacks had all been around water, either rivers or coastal areas. As yet they had no idea why this should be or what to expect next. They could only wait keeping themselves alert for whatever was coming.

Training was stepped up, not just the physical exercise side but also each officer was encouraged to hone his or her special skill. This gave Amy and Ruby a chance to work together combining Amy's talent for telepathy and Ruby's skill at changing her appearance at will.

Following her little demonstration in the classroom a few weeks previously there was no shortage of volunteers to act as guinea pigs for Amy and Ruby. Some of them were sure that Amy would be unable to detect their individual private fear therefor putting themselves forward to prove a point. Without exception she foiled them every time picking up on even the most obscure anxiety like Cassie's fear of birds, when she was able to conjure a small snowstorm of feathers to float down around the girl's shoulders. Her shrieks only subsided when Amy waved her arm above Cassie's head dispelling the vision of falling feathers. When any of the volunteers displayed a fear of either a person or an animal of some kind, a whispered

Malchediel's expression hardened once more. He moved closer to Stephen so that they were eye to eye. "I don't have to explain myself to you but it was she who called time on..." he hesitated searching for the right words, "...on us." He finished.

Stephen said nothing. What could be gained by continuing this exchange? Malchediel nervously tapped his helmet against his thigh. "Do you know where she is now?" he asked keeping his gaze locked on that of the younger man.

Stephen sighed, "She is based in Bath...a place called St Alexandra Hall."

Malchediel nodded before turning away.

"Are you going there?" Stephen asked quickly.

Without turning back Malchediel answered, "I don't know...maybe." He stopped to replace his helmet before turning back to Stephen, "I honestly don't know." And with that he walked back down the alley to the High Street before taking to the air. By the time Stephen reached the pavement there was no sign of him.

Malchediel circled the town ignoring the incessant rain. What should he do? He could be in Bath in minutes but what would that achieve? Nothing had altered apart from the fact that he now knew that Amy had followed her mother's lead and joined the N.F.F. She had still spurned him, leaving him to nurse a broken heart. It hadn't taken her long to find a new life style. She hadn't even waited a reasonable length of time to see if he would return to her. His short confrontation with Stephen had altered nothing, in fact it emphasised how quickly Amy had forgotten him, to move on with her life. Finally he decided to head back to the south east. As he flew over the Cornish/Devon border he considered the devastation below. Most of the low lying land was under water. Rather than cut across country he decided to follow the coastline. Again he detected areas where the sea had reclaimed land where soft sandstone had crumbled causing countless landslips along the seaboard. He coasted around Bigbury Bay and it was here that he picked up a tingling sensation telling him that something was amiss ahead of him. He hesitated...what to do? After a moments' indecision he decided to check it out. A slight delay would not inconvenience him too greatly. Within minutes he was above the rugged coastline known as Bolt Head. He didn't know what made him fly lower to check out the ground below but as he skirted the treeline he became acutely aware of Demon presence. He could feel the heat rising up to meet him. A smile slowly spread over his face...he was after all a Warrior and he could feel the pull of the hunt.

Just above the canopy of the trees, he hovered sensing out what was below. It was still daylight, at least another hour before the light would start to fade. The supernatural beings sent out by the Fallen were becoming brazen. They usually only manifested after dark. Could it be they were beginning to detect that they were winning the battle. Malchediel felt the anticipation of a coming conflict with the Demons below. He was alone with no backup but with the blood zinging through his veins he followed his instinct and headed downwards seeking his prey.

He stood in the shade of the trees listening. He held off retracting his wings whilst trying to detect any sounds to confirm where the Demons were. After a moment or two he heard a commotion off to his right, about a hundred metres away. His wings instantly began to fold flat against his back. He may yet need them but he was not going to risk any injury to them in his pursuit of the enemy. With head down he charged through the trees carefully dodging the exposed tree roots.

Chapter Nine

By Saturday Amy's team had cleared the area that they had been patrolling and for the next two days, no Demon activity had been detected. Ralph decided to send them north across the border into Devon where a new anomaly had manifested itself pouring forth more Demons. Strangely it was in a fairly unpopulated area. It would seem that the Fallen were tiring of seeing their minions slaughtered before they were able to cause too much devastation. Their new ploy was to amass a huge force of Demons away from populated areas where they would be held before being unleashed upon the unsuspecting population.

Ilya parked the Land Rover at the end of a coastal track known as Prawle Point. It was from this isolated area that Ralph had been detecting strange readings on his equipment. Before they left the vehicle, Ilya checked in with Ralph.

Cell phone reception wasn't marvellous but they gathered that they were not far from the Last recorded sighting of Demons. As the three of them donned the heavy body armour that afforded them some protection from the vicious claws and teeth of the Demons and Goblins, Amy acknowledged that for the first time this wasn't a training session. This was for real.

"Okay...are you two happy to split up and monitor the surrounding area?" Ilya suggested as he delved into the rear of the vehicle. He looked up acknowledging nods from Mark and Amy. "Right, stay within shouting distance." He added handing out pistols and ammunition. Don't forget always aim for the middle of the body. That's the only way to stop them dead."

Amy knew this instruction was meant for her. She was the newest recruit to the team and had only limited experience in the hunt. She nodded again to Ilya who added, "Any problems...drop to the ground and shout for help." Turning to include Mark he added, "If either of you hears a call for help, respond immediately. Don't forget they're fairly stupid creatures but they're deadly." He eyeballed both his comrades to give his words emphasis. Mark gave a curt, "Yep." whilst Amy acknowledged with a muttered, "Sure."

The light was beginning to fade as Amy worked her way eastward. All her senses were heightened and it crossed her mind that her mother must have experienced these feeling many times when she was about Amy's age. She walked on, frequently stopping to listen for any sounds but detected nothing that gave her any idea if there were Demons close by. From time to time she picked up a sound that to anyone else would pass as a bird call but she knew that it was Ilya who had perfected this art of mimicry. She smiled comforted by the knowledge that he was within calling distance. Stealthily she moved on through the bracken trying to keep her movements as quiet as she could. Suddenly to her left there was the crack of gunfire, a shout of warning from Mark followed by the explosive sounds of something crashing through the undergrowth. The adrenaline spiked through Amy's body as she turned to face the oncoming noise. It seemed like several minutes as she tensed waiting for whatever was coming towards her. In reality it was more like seconds. With her handgun raised and cocked she dropped to her knees eyes focussed dead ahead. Holding her weapon in both hands she waited. Suddenly a Demon crashed through the undergrowth not twenty metres in front of her. It was huge at such close quarters. The smell of the creature hit her as soon as it appeared and she had to swallow rapidly to quell the nausea caused by the decaying stench. Remembering her training she aimed dead at its middle and as it lumbered towards her howling, she squeezed the trigger. She fought the desire to close her eyes as it toppled towards her, a startled look in its eyes. She could see a wound high on its shoulder. Clearly Mark had wounded it which was why it was hurtling through the chest high bracken towards her. Falling backwards Amy scrambled away putting as much distance between her and the crazed Demon as it continued to fall towards her. Then as its life-force left its body it disintegrated into thousands of slimy pieces before disappearing completely. Amy had come up against the rough bark of a tree where she sat propped, breathing heavily. Within seconds Mark closely followed by Ilya came running from the same direction of the Demon. Of course there was nothing to see but both men wrinkled their noses at the pervading Demon odour.

Ilya went down on one knee in front of Amy. Reaching out he rested his hand on her shoulder. "You okay?" he asked his eyes going over her to check for any sign of injury. Amy gave a nervous laugh and her senior officer knew how close to tears she was. He squeezed her shoulder smiling warmly at her. "Your first kill is always mind-blowing...you did well."

She nodded not trusting herself to speak in case she cried. He was right. She was terrified. She was also exhilarated. She could feel the blood pumping through her veins...Oh Wow she was a Nephilim Officer. The thought hit her like a sledgehammer. Ilya was watching her, his hand still resting on her shoulder, "Think you can stand Officer Bernstein?" he asked getting up to help her to her feet.

Her breathing now under control she stood. "Oh my God I was so scared Ilya."

"That's nothing to be ashamed of Amy. Only a fool wouldn't be afraid when confronted by one of those things." Then turning to Mark who was still standing off to one side added, "I saw it come at you. It didn't give you any time to get a good aim. Luckily, wounding it caused it to swing away from you..." He sniffed the air, "My God they stink." He looked back to Amy, "Are you feeling up to carrying on with the hunt. There are bound to be more of them around. They'll have heard the gunfire so they know we're here."

He buckled his armour back on but left his helmet on the floor then without a word to her he walked to the mouth of the cave. He stood for several moments looking out over the sea. Then still not looking at her he called over his shoulder, "Are you hungry?"

The question surprised her. It wasn't what she expected. "Um...yes...I am."

He nodded. She waited but he said no more. She tested her injured ankle, found she could put a little weight on it now and slowly hobbled up to stand behind him. She hesitated for a few seconds, her eyes taking in the woven texture of the breastplate straps criss-crossing his back. He must have known she was behind him but he didn't turn around. She reached out a hand and touched his shoulder. Immediately he stiffened. "Don't!" he said abruptly, and her hand dropped back to her side as tears sprang up in her eyes.

"I'll go and find something for you to eat." he added. Not waiting for her reply his wings sprang forth and he took to the air swooping down just above the water and then swung right disappearing from view.

Amy continued to stand at the mouth of the cave looking out over the water, the tears falling freely now that he wasn't there to witness them. The last time he had seen her he had called out that he loved her. That was moments before he had been dragged away from her by his friends. Now he seemed to hate her. How could that be? She feared it was all due to her returning his feather via Nemamiah. Why the hell had she done that? From the moment that Nemamiah had left her alone weeping at the cottage, she questioned why she had decided to hand over the plucked feather. How devastated Malchediel must have felt to have that one last link returned to him. Sighing, she wandered back to where her body vest lay next to his helmet. She needed to get in touch with Ilya to let him know that she was safe. Her cell phone had been submerged in water...would it still work? She searched the pocket in which it was normally kept and on finding it empty she checked the other three pockets but the phone was missing. So…it was irrelevant whether it was water damaged or not, she had lost it. Could things get any worse? She doubted it.

By the time he returned she was sitting on the floor of the cave, her back against the rough stone wall. She was holding his helmet between her raised knees, slowly turning it around, deep in thought. As he landed just inside the entrance, his wings beating rapidly braking his fast decent she looked up startled by the sudden intrusion into her thoughts. He stood motionless watching her toying with his helmet and as their eyes met she gave a hesitant smile. She was again dismayed when he didn't return her friendly greeting. Without a word he walked towards her and she saw that he had a crusty baguette in one hand and a bottle of spring water in the other. Despite the tension that was clearly radiating between them, a bubble of uncontrollable laughter rose up within her at the sight of an Angel in full body armour holding what was to be her breakfast in his hands. He stopped as she giggled at him. Following her eyes, he looked down at the items in his hands which had been the cause of her mirth. She was gladdened to see his lips quirk at the realisation of why she was amused.

"Ohhh…Malchediel." She murmured; a catch in her voice. "That's the first time you've smiled at me since you saw me yesterday."

He walked the few steps towards her and dropped to his knees holding out the food to her, his face once more serious. "I haven't had much to smile about for a while now." He said.

She placed his helmet on the floor next to her and he laid the bread in her lap. Looking up into her face he saw that she was watching him. "Is this all about me returning the feather Mal? Are you angry with me?"

His heart turned over on hearing her call him Mal. No one else made his name sound the way she did. He sat back on his heels looking into the face that he thought he would never see again and his resolve not to let her back into his heart wavered. Not taking his eyes from hers, he exhaled sharply. Ignoring the bread in her lap she reached out and caught his hand resting on his thigh. "It was the feather wasn't it?" she questioned, "I don't know why I did that. As soon as Nemamiah left me I regretted it but it was too late then." A tear slipped down her cheek and she hiccupped, "It seemed the right thing to do at the time...you know... when he said that you wouldn't be allowed to return if you came back to me a second time. You would be deemed a Fallen Angel and...and my lifespan was nothing compared to your immortality. You would be an outcast forever." Her word tumbled over one another in her haste to make him understand the pressure she had been under. "He wanted me to write to you telling you not to try to come back to me...that it was over between us." Another tear rolled down her cheek and she dashed it away with her fingers. "I told him I could never do that. I couldn't write those words...it seemed easier just to return your feather. I knew you would understand the message behind it. He made it sound like I was doing the kindest thing. Keeping you with me would have been selfish." She was crying freely now. "It broke my heart but that didn't matter because I was freeing you to go back to the only life you had ever known." She caught her breath trying to stifle the tears but she kept her eyes on his. His lips parted but it was several seconds before he spoke. "We had discussed the consequences of my decision Amy. We both knew what it would mean if I stayed with you. Why did you change your mind once Paschar and Qaphsiel had hauled me away?" He frowned as a thought occurred to him, "Did Nemamiah threaten you in some way?"

She squeezed his hand, "No...no. He was very kind to me. It was just that he made me feel so selfish for expecting you to give everything up for me."

Malchediel caught his bottom lip between his teeth looking at her thoughtfully.

She sniffed looking at him quizzically, "What?" she asked, "What are you thinking?"

His frown deepened, "Did he touch you?" he asked.

What? What do you mean?"

"A simple question Amy. Did he touch you in any way?"

She felt her face start to colour up. What was he suggesting? She made to pull her hand away from his, and in an instant he realised what she was thinking. He caught her hand before she had time to pull away completely and she was startled to feel a weird pulse of electricity pass through their fingers.

"Oh!" she cried.

"Yes!" he exclaimed, "You felt that didn't you? Did Nemamiah touch you when you were alone with him? Did you feel anything like that with him?" His eyes were bright with a burning intensity waiting for her answer.

"Yes...yes. I had forgotten all about it. He held my hand as he was telling me about what life as a Fallen Angel would be like if you came back to me."

Malchediel slowly shook his head as comprehension of what she had revealed sank in. "I didn't realise he could be so devious." He said quietly. He could see that Amy was confused. "It's a little Angelic gift we have." He smiled thinking about his friend's act of deception. "We are able to temporarily override a subject's willpower just by touch, implanting our resolve in its place. In short he made you believe that it was wrong to keep me with you... he overrode your decision implanting doubt in its place." He shook his head once more in disbelief at what his friend had done. "I should have hit him when I had the chance...when he gave me the feather. It never occurred to me that he could be so underhand...the..." he left his opinion of his friend unsaid.

Now it was Amy's' turn to shake her head. "I didn't know. That was why once he had gone; I started to regret what I had done. His temporary power over me must have waned." She looked down at their interlinked fingers. "I suppose I should hate him for what he did, but it just emphasises how much he thinks of you Mal. He must have been willing to do anything to stop you from leaving your former life."

They sat for a few moments, both thinking about this startling revelation before Malchediel added, "I think I'll still hit him the next time I see him." But he smiled as he spoke. He looked down at the bread in Amy's lap. Cupping her face in his hand he said, "Eat your breakfast. It took quite a bit of subterfuge to get it for you."

Her eyes widened, "My goodness…you didn't have to steal it did you?" she asked with a wicked smile on her face.

He grinned back at her. "Even Angels sometimes have to resort to small acts of criminality. With what's going on out there…" he continued, the smile fading, "I think this is a minor offence."

Amy was ravenous and she broke off a piece of the baguette and started eating. The bread was delicious washed down with the bottled water. They sat side by side as she ate still holding hands. Amy was wallowing in a glow of euphoria. Malchediel was back with her. His earlier hostility now explained away transposing him into the Malchediel she remembered. With her mouth still full she asked, "Did you see anyone while you were out there?"

"A few people." He answered, "Luckily there was a delivery van outside a grocery store. I waited until the driver went inside laden with boxes. He left the rear doors of the vehicle open. Your breakfast was there for the taking. I was invisible to anyone around but I had long gone before he came out of the shop anyway."

"You didn't see anyone else then?" she asked before taking a long drink from the bottle. "I was with two other members of the N.F.F. before you found me."

He shifted his position, crossing his long legs before answering. "Amy, there was no sign of anyone anywhere near you when I found you. You were quite alone…well apart from the Demon that is." He made an impatient sound. "I can't

Just as Ralph approached from behind, Malchediel whispered, "I have never been more sure of anything." Then standing he turned to face the team leader, "I have to return to my comrades but if you feel that I can be of benefit to you I should like to return to...I think Amy said it was Saint Alexandra Hall?" he looked expectantly at Ralph.

"Yes! Yes...of course we would be esteemed to have you with us. We are under no illusion as to how serious this conflict could be. Your presence would be most welcome...most welcome." Then he added, "Would any others be accompanying you?"

Malchediel smiled, "I think that would be most unlikely. Angels and Nephilim parted company some time ago. It had become an uneasy alliance. I have a vested interest in Amy's safety so I will be returning to you alone."

At his words Amy felt her face begin to burn and she was relieved to be inside the vehicle where Ralph couldn't see her. She heard Ralph's response, "I see." And then heard him call to the others in the yard, "Are we all ready?" There were several muffled responses as Ralph walked to the driver's door. Malchediel bent back down looking into the car's interior and before Ralph had time to open his door, whispered, "I will see you soon Amy...you take my heart with you."

Amy reached out to him and he briefly held her hand before stepping back away from the vehicle.

Within minutes everyone was on board and six engines simultaneously burst into life. Several pairs of eyes went to the Angel standing alone as slowly he unfurled his wings. Ruby who was now sitting next to Amy responded with, "Bloody Hell...that is amazing!"

Amy said nothing as the cars started forward towards the gateway but she kept her eyes on Malchediel as he retrieved his armour and started to put it on.

Once they were back at St Alexandra Hall Doctor Steenbergen checked Amy's ankle confirming Ralph's earlier diagnosis that she had sprained it and a few days rest should see it healed. That done he and Ralph made their way to the Doctor's office where they remained for over an hour whilst Ralph conveyed all that had happened down in Devon to his commanding officer.

Amy and Ruby were sitting in the drawing room when the Doctor sought them out some time later. "Ruby, my dear," he addressed them, "would you mind if I had a word with Amy?"

Ruby got up from the sofa next to Amy and taking her teacup with her moved to the window seat out of earshot. The Doctor smiled warmly at Amy before taking the chair opposite her. "Ralph has been filling me in with all that has happened over the last few days Amy. It seems that we owe a certain Angel a great deal of gratitude for saving your life." His eyes never left Amy's face as he spoke and he was very aware of the flush that crept over her cheeks. She cleared her throat nervously and flicking at some imagined fluff on her trousers answered with downcast eyes. "Yes...yes it was lucky he was in the area." When the Doctor remained silent she hesitantly looked up into his face.

"Yes wasn't it?" he smiled. "And a coincidence that it happened to be Malchediel...an Angel you are already acquainted with?"

She remained silent. What could she say to his observation? He waited for a moment or two giving her time to add a comment then he went on briskly "Ralph tells me he may be joining us at the Hall once he has made his report to the rest of his team. His assistance will be most appreciated Amy. When word gets out that we have an Angel working with us we will be the envy of all the other bases." He leaned forward in his chair before asking, "Your first experience of active service must have been very frightening for you Amy." He said and she was surprised and not a little relieved at the change of subject.

"Yes, yes it was. I'm afraid I made the mistake of letting myself become separated from the rest of the team." She smiled tremulously. "I won't let that happen again."

The Doctor returned her smile warmly, "We all make mistakes Amy. As long as we learn from them, that's the important thing." He surveyed her across the small space dividing them. "I must thank Malchediel when we meet. I don't take kindly to the idea of losing valued officers." Rising from his chair he patted her shoulder before making his way back to his office.

Over the next ten days the swelling around Amy's ankle subsided and things were very quiet in the south west of the country. No so around the London area where there had been severe flooding when inexplicably flood defences had failed. There had fortunately only been four reported fatalities but damage was extensive and the regular army had been drafted in to help with the clear-up.

It was in the early hours one morning when Malchediel arrived unannounced at St Alexandra Hall. Effortlessly he entered Amy's room whilst it was still dark. The house and its occupants were silent and sleeping. Retracting his wings he stood contemplating the sleeping girl. Eventually he turned to the winged easy chair opposite the door and sat quietly waiting for her to wake. With little else to do, he mulled over his last conversation with his friend Nemamiah. They had, he realised, reached an unspoken acceptance that his affection for Amy was not a thing of the past. When Malchediel had casually mentioned that he was returning to the south west of Britain, Nemamiah's jaw had tightened flashing a scowl in the other's direction. Malchediel returned a stony glare stilling any comment on the matter. After a moment Nemamiah had ventured one questioning word, "Cornwall?"

"No. As it happens, I am visiting a Nephilim stronghold near to a City called Bath."

Nemamiah hadn't been easily fooled. "So, she is following in her mother's footsteps?"

At that, Malchediel had made an impatient sound causing his friend to raise both hands in a placating gesture. "Your reaction confirms my suspicions Mal." Sitting relaxed in the armchair, Malchediel recalled how his friend's hands had dropped to his sides sighing, "I know the past few months haven't been easy for you, and I am aware that you have tried to forget this girl." He had held the other's gaze. "You can't...can you?" he had asked quietly.

Malchediel had looked away, taking a deep breath before asking, "Are you going to inform Raguel?"

"What would be the point Mal?" was the others answer, the sadness evident in his voice. "You can't help how you feel. We intervened once hoping that it was just a passing infatuation, but it has gone beyond that." He had waited for Mal to look back at him before adding, "Hasn't it?"

Malchediel now glanced towards Amy's bed remembering how he and Nemamiah had stood looking at one another before he had dropped his eyes once more.

"We won't interfere a second time and I believe you have made a decision already." Nem had then paused before adding, "Is she worth it?"

Malchediel's eyes snapped back up, "Yes...yes she is."

Nemamiah had smiled but it was a smile tinged with sadness. "Then I wish you luck my friend." He grasped the other's arm briefly before turning away.

Now sitting in the darkened room Malchediel wondered if he would ever see his friend again. In truth he felt only relief at Nemamiah's confirmation that he would not be prevented from leaving the only life he had ever known to be with the girl he had fallen in love with. The decision had been made and the die was cast. He had no idea what would happen next but his uncertainties were soothed by the sounds of Amy's steady breathing.

As dawn began to lighten the room, Amy stirred turning so that she was facing Malchediel's chair. He held his breath as she repositioned herself, one arm coming up to rest on the pillow in front of her face. He waited and then thinking that she had settled back into sleep, he let out the breath he had been holding. As he watched her face, she slowly opened one eye, looked at him and then closed it again. Within seconds both eyed snapped open as she moved her arm so that she could focus on him unobscured. He smiled at her. She pushed herself up on her elbows blinking sleepily at him. "Mal?"

His smile broadened, "I have come to reclaim my heart." He grinned, "I hope you have taken good care of it." He pushed himself up from the chair and stood looking down into her bemused face.

She frowned pushing her hair away from her face. "What..."

Within two strides he was at her bedside and dropping down to his knees his arms went around her, holding her, his face against her throat. Tentatively she raised her arms so that she could hold his face easing him away so that she could see him clearly. "Ohh Mal...Oh my love...you're back." She licked her lips before seeking his, melting into the depth of his kiss. A fleeting thought occurred...was she dreaming? She had gone to sleep thinking about their last encounter in the bedroom of her cottage when he had declared his love for her. Was this a cruel dream...a continuation of their passionate prelude to lovemaking...but that had not happened...he had been taken from her. She pulled back from him searching his face. As if sensing her thoughts he smiled at her confusion. "No interruptions this time Amy."

With those words she shook away the final remnants of sleep. She wasn't dreaming. He was here and he had said that this time there would be no intrusions from other Angels. She trailed her fingers through his tousled hair relishing in the silky softness. "I have taken very good care of your heart." She replaced the glass. "I should imagine you feel as though you have been kicked by a horse...am I right?"

She nodded, feeling too drained to speak. Taking a deep breath she croaked one word, "When?"

He sat back down next to her bed. "When? When did it happen?" He smoothed her hair away from her face. "Two days ago. You have been unconscious for two days."

She blinked in surprise then asked, "How..."

"You could always try telepathy Amy." He suggested with a smile.

She tried to smile back but her cracked lips were sore.

'I hurt everywhere Mal...How did I get here? I remember the Demon and the Angel...his creator. Something hit me in the neck. It hurt like Hell...What was it?'

Malchediel smiled, "Take your time Amy. One question at a time. The Fallen Angel killed his own Demon because it had failed him. They don't get a second chance. When it exploded, one of its spines hit you and embedded itself in your neck. Have you never had instruction about Demons?" He asked.

Her blank stare answered for her.

His lips tightened in anger. "You should never have been put in such a dangerous position. So you didn't know about the poisonous spines on a Demon's tail then?"

There was a barely perceived shake of her head.

He let out a none too Angelic expletive. "If you attempt to pull the spine out the barb will break off and poison floods into your system. If you had left it until I could cut it all out there would have been no problem...You're lucky to be alive Amy." He lifted her hand to his lips and kissed her knuckles tenderly.

'So how did I survive?'

"Raphael intervened for me. He saved your life." He continued to hold her hand against his lips as he added, "I thought you were going to die."

She wanted to touch him...to cup his cheek with her hand but she felt so weak. Her eyes filled with tears. *'I love you.'*

"I love you too." He reached across to wipe a tear that had rolled slowly across her cheek. "Don't ask me why, but Raphael gained permission from the great Michael to heal you."

She frowned at his comment.

"He is only supposed to heal Angels Amy but Michael agreed to Raphael helping you. Thank the Saints that he did." He pressed his lips to the back of her hand again. "Now sleep my love. I'll stay here."

It was another three days before Malchediel allowed Amy to get up. As each day went by her strength returned until by the end of the week she declared that she was so bored cooped up in bed she was in danger of dying of tedium.

During the time of her recovery, teams of Nephilim scoured the south west eliminating pockets of Demons as they appeared. The Doctor asked Malchediel to instruct his teams on fighting strategies when it became apparent that their knowledge of the Fallen and Demon capabilities was flawed. It had been known that the tail spines were dangerous to mortals and many Nephilim had lost their lives by removing embedded spines without realising that it was only by leaving the broken barbs in the skin that the poison was released.

Malchediel accompanied the Nephilim whenever they were called out but immediately went back to Amy's room on his return to the Hall. Ruby too spent as much time with Amy as she could and was delighted when the Doctor pronounced her friend well enough to leave her sick-bed.

Malchediel never regretted his decision to break ranks with his former life. If he had ever questioned his love for Amy, the shock of her almost dying in his arms only strengthened his professed love for her. He did however miss his former companions. He had been cut adrift from not only companionship but also communication. He was now unable to glean information of what was going on. To a Warrior Angel this intelligence was crucial to their success against the Fallen.

Three weeks following her almost fatal accident, Doctor Steenbergen gave in to her persistent nagging and allowed her to return to duty. During her recovery she had moped about the Hall every day as the others went out on manoeuvres. She would walk around the grounds waiting for their return. There was always de-briefing sessions in the Doctor's office following these exercises and Amy would wait impatiently for Malchediel to come back to the room they now openly shared together. Her intention of just probing for information about the days' events was usually side-tracked by his taking her to bed first.

All her pre-conceived impressions of Angelic purity had been blown sky-high since knowing him. As she had said to him the first morning they had woken up together, "You are one sexy Angel."

His reply had been "I aim to please." causing her to roll her eyes at him. Each time they made love he would conclude with the strange act of placing his hand on her abdomen causing the fleeting sensation of heat to flow through her. She remembered him telling her once, that female Angels could not conceive but the mere fact that there were Nephilim across the planet confirmed that male Angels were fertile and could father healthy children. With the uncertainty of the present Global situation Amy was only too happy to let him continue with his bizarre form of birth control.

Once she was back on active service Malchediel watched her like a hawk, never straying too far from her. The sporadic attacks continued neither abating nor intensifying giving rise to Malchediel questioning the Fallens' commitment to all-out annihilation. He confided to the Doctor one evening as they sat together, "They have the power to escalate these attacks. Something is holding them back from the final push. Some would suggest that perhaps they have over-reached themselves, but I am beginning to think that they really don't have the heart to destroy humanity."

"If that is the case, what do you think will happen next?"

Malchediel slowly shook his head, "I wish I could answer that question. I don't know if my former brethren have any better insight into this seemingly impossible situation. It is becoming a no-win conflict. I have no idea where it will all end."

It was some six weeks later that matters came to a head. Early one morning just as the eastern sky was bathed in a red glow heralding a magnificent dawn; Amy woke early and turned towards Malchediel gently stroking her fingertips across his chest. It was all the indication he needed. He gathered her into his arms kissing her tenderly. Her eager response fuelled his passion and as the rest of the Hall's occupants slept on, he made love to her. As she lay afterwards flushed and contented in his arms he reached his hand across but before he could lay it on her abdomen she caught it and lacing her own fingers through his she proceeded to kiss each of his knuckles in turn saying deliberately, "I – Love – You - So - Much." Each word punctuated by a kiss. Her lips were still resting against the knuckle of his little finger when suddenly they both became aware of shouting and running footsteps from the corridor outside their room. They were both out of bed in an instant. Amy grabbed her wrap and quickly tied the belt before opening the door. Ilya appeared to be knocking each bedroom door shouting, "Wake up...wake up! We are under attack!" When he saw Amy in the doorway he yelled. "Get dressed! Quickly...They're in the grounds!" Amy turned just as Malchediel wearing only boxer shorts strode passed her.

"Ilya...Who? Who is attacking?"

By now several doors had opened as bleary eyed Nephilim stood perplexed in their doorways.

"Demons...dozens of them." Ilya shouted. "There are Angels with them this time as well!"

At this, there were several voices shouting at once. Suddenly the Doctor's voice boomed out above the cacophony.

"Everyone! Get dressed. Body Armour too. Bloody Hell they've managed to infiltrate the grounds. Quickly…Now!"

Malchediel caught Amy's hand and pulled her back into the bedroom kicking the door to with his foot. She stared up at him taking in his ashen pallor and wide eyes. "I suppose it's pointless to ask you to stay here." He said shortly.

"Are you going out there?" she asked.

"Of course! That's what I'm here for."

"Then I'm going as well."

He snorted at her answer although it was what he expected. "Then stay close to me…Do you understand?"

She nodded easing her wrist from his grasp.

Within minutes they were dressed and on their way downstairs. The whole house was now awake. Several officers already in the Armoury collecting body armour and weapons.

As Amy passed the Doctor's office she peered in. He was on the phone doubtless calling up reinforcements. Malchediel, without waiting for an invitation strode into the office. The Doctor acknowledged him with a curt nod but carried on speaking into the receiver.

"Get your body armour on quickly." Mal called to Amy over his shoulder, "And get a jacket for me while you're there."

Amy dashed into the Armoury almost colliding with Ruby who was already kitted up and now selecting weapons from one of the wall cupboards.

As she opened her locker she asked, "How can we be under attack Ruby? I thought the grounds were protected."

"Christ knows." Ruby answered without looking up. She was trying to fasten the buckle of the weapons belt across her chest and Amy saw that it was laden with several of Ruby's favourite weapons, the five pointed spinning stars. Amy knew that Ruby was quite an expert with this particular weapon. "This could be serious Amy. Only someone powerful could override all the supernatural protection that the Nephilim bases have in place. This has never been known before." She looked up at Amy satisfied that she now had enough weaponry to defend

Nephilim present, began to change shape before them. He rose up growing to enormous proportions, changing appearance from an Angel of some beauty to a monstrous twenty foot red beast complete with tail and horns before being swallowed up in a swirling mass of sulphurous smoke. As the smoke slowly dispersed there was no sign of him.

Amy started as his voice reached inside her mind. *'Goodbye child of mine.'*

The anomaly shimmered and disappeared. Everyone started talking at once discussing the implications of what had just occurred within the grounds of a county house mansion in Somerset.

"Quiet everyone!" Ralph shouted suddenly, pulling his mobile phone from his pocket. Putting it to his ear he listened nodding from time to time. "Yes...okay we are on our way back now." Pocketing the phone he called out to all, "That was the Doctor. He's taken four calls so far from various bases reporting a sudden cessation of hostilities. The anomalies are all disappearing as we speak. My God I believe it's all over.

Malchediel turned to Amy pulling her close, "By all the Saints Amy what on earth were you two discussing? I can normally pick up on your thoughts but he blocked me out completely."

She leaned into him, resting her head against his chest, "I can't believe I was exchanging thoughts with Lucifer." she said in wonder. Pulling on his hand she turned to follow the Nephilim officers who had already started to plod back to the Hall. You're not going to believe what he told me. I can barely believe it myself."

They hung back from the others letting the gap between them lengthen as she divulged all that Lucifer had told her of her origins. As they walked together hand in hand, talking quietly, neither of them was aware of the small cluster of cells busily dividing within Amy's uterus.

Author's Note:

This has been a work of fiction. However all the Angelic names both Celestial and Fallen are real. I therefore apologise for having cast Malchediel as a Fallen Angel for the purpose of the story. To my knowledge he is as he has always been a 'Warrior Angel.'

If you have enjoyed this book please review and rate it. Authors rely heavily on Readers comments.

You can visit my blog at kindlebooksbymaureen.co.uk

Contact me at maureenjiturner@btinternet.com

Other books by Maureen Turner:

Wings Unfurled series:
Book One – 'Malchediel – Warrior Angel' (e book)
Book Two – 'Amy – Nephilim Freedom Fighter' (e book)

'First Breath'
(Hardback and Paperback available through Authorhouse and Amazon and e book format)

Do Androids Dream? (e book)

Purgatory – 12 short stories (Paperback available through FeedARead and Amazon and e book)

Acknowledgements:

Thanks go to: My husband Gary.
Demelza and Paul.
Sue Bowen.
Kimberley.
For their support

Cover titles by Paul Wilkes

brouillard, il ressent un besoin d'ivresse, ses pas le mènent dans les bouges où il aime fréquenter les acrobates et les tziganes. En ces années-là, fait remarquer Angelo Maria Ripellino, Blok s'abandonne sans retenue à l'univers des gens du voyage. «Non seulement ses lettres, ses vers, ses carnets regorgent de références aux bohémiens, mais la romance tzigane devient sa forme poétique principale.» Cette fascination avait déjà été celle de Pouchkine. Elle devient chez Blok un élément de son destin. En 1914, il s'éprend de Lioubov Alexandra Delmas, au physique de gitane rousse, interprète de Carmen au Théâtre du Drame musical.

La révolte intérieure de Blok, sa nausée devant les mœurs bourgeoises, son attente impatiente d'une vie neuve et d'un monde régénéré, faisaient de lui un homme prêt à accepter la débâcle de sa propre classe. Il accueillit comme une aurore le processus révolutionnaire de l'année 1917. En janvier 1918, il écrivit coup sur coup, et chaque fois d'un seul souffle, deux poèmes qui, par leur ampleur et leur puissance, se hissent au rang de chefs-d'œuvre : Les Douze *et* Les Scythes. *Le cycle des* Douze *s'est imposé à Blok sur un mode visionnaire : il les avait vus en songe, ces gardes rouges qui vont dans les rues glacées de Petrograd et prennent figure d'apôtres derrière un Christ couronné de neige et portant l'étendard cramoisi. Angelo Maria Ripellino a décrit avec une impeccable précision le style génial et déroutant de ce poème : «L'écriture, violemment secouée de syncopes et de ruptures, de sautes métriques, d'âpres dissonances (sifflements, aboiements du vent, piétinement, balles qui crépitent), mêle dans une pâte lexicale insolite des slogans d'affiche politique et des formules de prière, des constructions d'odes* solennelles et des injures des rues, les termes grossiers du slang prolétarien et des accents de romance.» Ce poème suscita chez les uns l'enthousiasme, chez les autres la stupeur et la réprobation. Mandelstam estima qu'il s'agissait de la plus étonnante et de la plus décisive des œuvres de Blok et qualifia les critiques réticents de commentateurs oiseux.

Trois ans plus tard, quelques mois avant sa mort, Blok prononça un discours à la mémoire de Pouchkine. De ce texte admirable, intitulé De la mission du poète, et au regard de ce qu'allait être la suite des événements, nous citerons au moins ces mots qui, comme Janus, lorgnent à la fois en amont et en aval de l'Histoire: «Aucune censure au monde ne peut entraver l'action fondamentale de la poésie.»

*

«Ma bouche ne sait plus sourire / Le vent d'hiver glace mes lèvres. / C'est lorsqu'une espérance expire / Qu'une chanson de plus s'élève.» Anna Akhmatova écrivit ces vers en 1915. Ils s'inscrivent dans le registre de la lyrique amoureuse et des déceptions du cœur, en accord avec la tonalité dominante de ses premiers livres, mais on ne peut s'empêcher d'y entendre d'autres résonances, quand on songe aux tribulations d'Anna Akhmatova, dès 1921 lorsque fut exécuté son ex-mari, le poète acméiste Nikolaï Goumiliov, et plus encore sous la terreur stalinienne. Au lendemain de la mort de Goumiliov, accusé de conspiration monarchiste, le bruit courut qu'Anna Akhmatova s'était suicidée. Marina Tsvétaïéva lui écrivit peu après: «À ma connaissance, votre seul ami (l'ami, c'est celui

qui agit) parmi les poètes s'est révélé être Maïakovski
— il errait dans le Café des poètes avec un air de taureau
mis à mort. Tué par la douleur, *c'est vraiment l'air qu'il*
avait…» En 1939, *dédiant un poème à la mémoire de*
l'auteur du Nuage en pantalon, *elle notera:* «*À Vladi-*
mir Maïakovski, le seul des poètes de Moscou à s'être
inquiété de vérifier la soi-disant mort d'Akhmatova.»

La poésie d'Akhmatova se distingue par sa netteté lim-
pide, sa légèreté, sa retenue, mais aussi par sa manière
d'unir une élégance altière à des éléments de la tradition
populaire, principalement dans le rythme et l'intonation.
Le critique Nikolaï Nedobrovo, qui fut amoureux d'elle,
avait écrit en 1915 un commentaire sur son poème «La
vraie tendresse», et son approche était si juste qu'Anna
Akhmatova conserva cet article toute sa vie. Nedobrovo
relevait en particulier que «chaque nuance de la significa-
tion intérieure du mot, chaque élément de chaque
expression et chaque inflexion de la structure du vers et
de sa sonorité […] tout converge et contribue au même but,
et l'économie de moyens est telle que ce que le rythme
effectue, par exemple, aucun signifiant ne le reprend.»
La poésie était pour Anna Akhmatova une affaire de pré-
cision: «Il faut, disait-elle, que dans le vers chaque mot
soit à sa place, comme s'il y était déjà depuis mille ans,
mais que le lecteur l'entende pour la première fois. C'est
très difficile, mais quand on y parvient, les gens disent:
"C'est de moi qu'il s'agit. C'est comme si c'était moi qui
l'avais écrit."»

D'un poète de l'inquiétude amoureuse, l'Histoire allait
faire un poète d'une impressionnante envergure civique.
La mémoire de quelques amis fut le garant de la sur-
vie de nombre de ses poèmes qui ne pouvaient être

*confiés au papier. Après la deuxième édition d'*Anno
Domini MCMXXI *en 1923, il lui fut impossible de
publier aucun livre pendant dix-sept ans. Même calom-
niée, même réduite au silence, Anna Akhmatova ne se
sépara jamais de son peuple. Sa vie en témoigne autant
que ses poèmes. Dès les premiers jours du siège de Leningrad par les armées hitlériennes, elle prit part à la lutte
patriotique : masque à gaz en bandoulière, elle monta la
garde devant un édifice de la ville comme un simple sol-
dat de la défense antiaérienne. Olga Bergoltz se souvient
de l'avoir vue coudre des sacs de sable et de l'avoir
entendue adresser aux femmes de Leningrad un vibrant
appel radiophonique au courage et à la résistance. Le
siège de la ville débuta le 8 septembre 1941. Il devait
durer 900 jours. En octobre, 10 000 citadins perdirent la
vie. En janvier 1942, ils étaient 10 000 par jour, affamés
et squelettiques, à périr de mort lente.*

*Comme nombre d'artistes et d'écrivains, Anna Akh-
matova n'a pas vécu à Leningrad pendant tout le blocus.
Fin septembre 1941, elle fut évacuée vers Moscou, d'où
elle partit rapidement pour Tchistopol, avant de trouver
refuge à Tachkent, en Ouzbékistan. La période de la
guerre s'accompagna d'un relatif dégel dans le domaine
de la censure. Entre 1940 et 1946, trois volumes antho-
logiques d'Anna Akhmatova voient le jour, à Leningrad
en 1940, à Tachkent en 1943 et à Moscou en 1946, ce
dernier volume imprimé à 100 000 exemplaires. Elle est
admise à l'Union des écrivains. Et dans Leningrad assié-
gée, elle incarne en quelque manière la réconciliation
nationale : ses poèmes civiques sont placardés sur les
murs, lus à la radio, imprimés dans la* Pravda.

Ces années d'épreuve ont coïncidé pour Anna Akhma-

tova avec une période de grande fécondité poétique. *Elle porte à terme son* Requiem, *le grand poème de la Russie martyre du stalinisme qui restera longtemps tenu au secret. Elle jette les bases d'un autre chef-d'œuvre,* Le Poème sans héros. *Dans un texte autobiographique, elle a déclaré que Tachkent fut pour sa poésie un berceau féerique. Dans cette «Constantinople des pauvres», disait-elle, ses vers affluaient sans discontinuer, se talonnant, se bousculant, hors d'haleine.*

De retour à Leningrad en mai 1944, elle découvre une ville dévastée. Elle parlera plus tard de «l'horrible fantôme qui faisait semblant d'être ma ville». Et c'est là qu'à partir de l'été 1946, elle va de nouveau être soumise à l'ostracisme, suite à une infâme attaque de Jdanov qui la qualifie de «nonne fornicatrice mélangeant la prière et la débauche». Ce n'est qu'en 1958, c'est-à-dire cinq ans après la mort de Staline, qu'elle pourra de nouveau publier, réintégrer l'Union des écrivains d'où elle avait été exclue au lendemain de la guerre. Elle écrivit alors: «Pro domo mea, *je dirai que je n'ai jamais déserté la poésie, ni à tire-d'aile, ni en rampant, quoique à plusieurs reprises, à grands coups de rames sur mes mains devenues de bois, cramponnées au bord du canot, on ait tenté de me faire lâcher prise.»*

Anna Akhmatova était née Anna Gorenko. Dans sa jeunesse, lorsque son père apprit qu'elle s'apprêtait à publier ses premiers poèmes, il lui demanda de prendre un pseudonyme «pour ne pas souiller un nom honorable et respecté». Anna forgea son nom de poète sur celui d'un ancêtre maternel, le dernier khan de la Horde d'or, descendant de Gengis Khan. Comme l'a observé Joseph Brodsky, «les cinq a *d'Anna Akhmatova eurent un effet*

ALEXANDRE BLOK

1880-1921

Un homme malade se traînait sur la berge.
Une file de chariots rampait à ses côtés.

Les Tziganes roulaient vers la ville fumante ;
Des belles filles et des gars éméchés.

Et les blagues et les cris fusaient des chariots.
Et l'homme clopinait avec son baluchon.

Il suppliait de l'emmener jusqu'au village.
Une petite Tzigane lui a tendu sa main brune.

Il a couru vers elle clopinant tant et plus,
Et jeté dans le chariot son lourd baluchon.

Mais l'écume à la bouche, son cœur a lâché.
La Tzigane a hissé un mort dans son chariot.

La Tzigane a assis le mort à ses côtés,
Et il se balançait et tombait en avant.

Chantant la liberté, elle allait au village
Pour rendre à la femme son époux trépassé.

28 décembre 1903

*

Marais — orbite profonde
De l'œil géant de la terre.
Il a pleuré tant et tant
Qu'il s'est épuisé en larmes
Et l'herbe maigre a sur lui repoussé.
Mais sous les herbes, les graminées,
Sous le blanc duvet de ses cils,
Surgit une étincelle verte,
Et s'abîme aussitôt.
Et, venus de pays inconnus,
Des sorciers et des sorcières hirsutes
Racontent par les villages :
— Le marais se moque de vous.
Des forces obscures vous guettent.
Et pendant qu'ils parlent ainsi,
Les plus vieux font le signe de la croix,
Les moins vieux — s'amusent,
Tandis qu'aux épaules des jeunes filles
Poussent des ailes blanches.

3 juin 1905

La Baraque de foire

Et voici que s'ouvre la baraque de foire
Pour les enfants gais, pour les enfants gentils,
La petite fille et le petit garçon
Regardent les dames, les rois et les diables.
Et l'on entend jouer la musique infernale
Et du lugubre archet les gémissements.
Le terrible diable saisit le crapoussin,
Et ruisselle le jus de canneberge.

LE PETIT GARÇON

Il écarte le noir courroux
D'un geste de sa main blanche.
Regarde : des feux
Par la gauche surgissent...
Vois-tu les flambeaux ? Vois-tu la fumée ?
C'est sûrement la reine en personne...

LA PETITE FILLE

Ah non ! pourquoi te moquer de moi ?
C'est la suite infernale...
Une reine ne craint pas le plein jour,
Elle avance, de roses enguirlandée,
Tandis qu'une suite de soupirants-chevaliers
Portent sa traîne et font tinter leurs glaives.

Soudain le bouffon s'est penché sur la rampe
Et crie : « Au secours !

Je me vide de mon jus de canneberge !
Mon pansement — un chiffon !
Sur ma tête — un heaume de carton !
Dans ma main — un glaive de bois ! »

Fille et garçon sont en larmes,
Et l'on ferme la joyeuse baraque.

Juillet 1905

*

Dans le chœur de l'église, une fille chantait
Tous les harassés en des terres lointaines,
Tous les navires en allés sur la mer,
Et tous ceux qui ont oublié leur joie.

Ainsi s'envolait sa voix sous la voûte,
Un rayon scintillait sur son épaule blanche,
Et chacun, dans le noir, écoutait, regardait
La robe blanche dans le rayon qui chantait.

Et l'on crut alors que la joie s'annonçait,
Que tous les navires dans les anses paisibles,
Que tous les harassés des terres lointaines
Retrouveraient enfin une vie de lumière.

Et sa voix était douce, et le rayon si fin,
Et seul, tout là-haut, près de la Sainte Porte,
Aux Mystères Initié — un enfant pleurait,
Parce que personne jamais ne revient.

Août 1905

ANNA AKHMATOVA

1888-1966

En lisant Hamlet

1

Près du cimetière, à droite,
      un désert de poussière.
Au-delà, toute bleue,
      la rivière.
Tu m'as dit : « Tant pis !
      Entre au couvent
Ou bien épouse un imbécile... »
Les princes ne disent
      jamais autre chose.
Mais je me suis rappelé ces paroles.
Qu'elles coulent pendant
      une centaine de siècles.
Comme un manteau d'hermine
      qui glisse sur l'épaule.

2

Je me suis trompée.
J'ai dit : « tu ».
Une ombre de sourire
Illumine le cher visage.
Des erreurs comme celle-là
Font briller le regard.
Je t'aime,
Comme quarante sœurs
Qui seraient toute caresse.

1909

*

Le cœur perd lentement mémoire du soleil.
L'herbe jaunit.
Le vent fait voler une neige tôt venue.
Juste un peu.

Dans les canaux étroits déjà l'eau se fige,
Ne coule plus.
Il ne se passe jamais rien ici,
Oh ! jamais.

Le saule a déployé sur le ciel vide
Sa dentelle en éventail.
Peut-être il valait mieux que je ne sois jamais
Votre femme.

Le cœur perd lentement mémoire du soleil.
Qu'est-ce qu'il y a ? Du noir ?
Peut-être ! Une nuit va suffire pour que vienne
L'hiver.

1911

L'amour

C'est parfois un serpent magicien,
Lové près de ton cœur.
C'est parfois un pigeon qui roucoule,
Sur la fenêtre blanche.

C'est parfois sous le givre qui brille
La vision d'une fleur.
Mais il mène, en secret, à coup sûr,
Loin de la joie tranquille.

Il sait pleurer si doucement
Dans la prière du violon,
Il fait peur quand on le devine
Sur des lèvres que jamais on n'avait vues.

1911

Chanson de la dernière fois

J'avais froid sans recours à la poitrine.
Et pourtant je marchais légèrement.
J'ai mis à la main droite
Le gant de la main gauche.

J'ai pensé : il y a beaucoup de marches.
Il y en a trois. Je le savais.
Entre les érables une voix d'automne
Me chuchotait : « Meurs avec moi ! »

Il m'a trompée, il est lugubre,
Il est changeant, méchant, mon destin.
J'ai répondu : « Mon amour ! mon amour !
Moi aussi ! je vais mourir ! Avec toi ! »

C'est la chanson de la dernière fois !
J'ai jeté un coup d'œil dans la maison obscure.
Rien, sinon, près du lit, dans la chambre
Les bougies, leur lumière jaune, indifférente.

1911

*

Cette lettre, ami, ne la froisse pas ;
Tâche de la lire, amour, jusqu'au bout
J'en ai assez d'être une inconnue,
D'être sur ta route une étrangère.

Non, pas ces yeux-là, pas cette colère !
Je suis à toi, je suis celle que tu aimes.
Je ne suis ni bergère, ni reine,
Et, à coup sûr, tout sauf une nonne...

Dans cette robe grise de tous les jours,
Sur ces talons usés...
Comme avant mon étreinte brûle,
Et mes grands yeux disent la peur.

Cette lettre, ami, ne la froisse pas,
Le mensonge est de toujours ; ne pleure pas.
Mets-la dans ta pauvre musette,
Mets-la, s'il te plaît, tout au fond.

1912

*

Faible est ma voix, mais mon vouloir ne cède pas.
Et même, sans amour, je me sens plus légère.
Dans les hauteurs du ciel un vent souffle ample et pur
Et mes pensées ignorent la souillure.

La servante Insomnie a quitté mon chevet,
Je ne me morfonds plus près de la cendre grise,
Et sur la tour l'aiguille courbe de l'horloge
Ne me fait plus l'effet d'une aiguille qui tue.

Donc le passé sur moi perd son pouvoir.
La délivrance est proche. Je pardonne

OSSIP MANDELSTAM

1892-1938

Tristia

On m'enseigna la science de l'adieu
Dans les plaintes échevelées, nocturnes.
Mâchent les bœufs, l'attente se prolonge.
Déjà la dernière heure des vigiles.
De cette nuit des coqs je vénère le rite —
Levant le fardeau de l'errante peine
Les yeux éplorés regardaient au loin,
Mêlant un pleur de femme au chant des muses.

L'adieu — qui peut disant ce mot savoir
Ce qu'il porte de séparation,
Ce que prophétise le cri du coq
Quand la flamme brûle sur l'Acropole,
Et à l'aube d'une vie nouvelle,
Quand dans l'enclos le bœuf lentement mâche,
Pourquoi le coq, clamant la vie nouvelle,
Bat des ailes sur les murs de la ville.

Et j'aime la coutume des fileuses :
La navette va, le fuseau gémit.
Vois-tu : déjà, comme un duvet de cygne,

Délie, pieds nus, vole à notre rencontre.
Hélas ! De notre vie la maigre trame !
Comme est pauvre la langue de la joie !
Tout ce qui fut sera encore et seul
Est doux l'instant de la reconnaissance.

Ainsi sera : la silhouette transparente
Gît sur la plaque immaculée d'argile
Comme la peau tendue d'un écureuil.
Sur la cire, penchée, une femme regarde.
L'Érèbe grec nous est impénétrable.
Aux hommes le bronze, aux femmes la cire...
C'est au combat que nous échoit le sort.
Elles meurent en disant l'avenir.

1918

*

Ô cet air soûlé de révolte
Sur la place noire du Kremlin !
Les mutins secouent la branlante assemblée,
Les peupliers embaument d'inquiétude.

Le visage de cire des cathédrales,
L'épaisse forêt des clochers.
On dirait que se cache dans les chevrons de pierre
Un brigand à la langue coupée.

Et dans les cathédrales scellées
Où il fait sombre et frais
Comme dans les tendres amphores d'argile
Pétille le vin de Russie.

La Dormition, courbe parfaite,
Tout entière allégresse de cintres divins,
Et l'Annonciation, tellement verte,
On dirait, soudain, qu'elle roucoule !

Les Archanges et la Résurrection
Sont transparents comme une paume,
C'est la passion, partout cachée,
Dans les jarres, dissimulée, la flamme...

Parce que je n'ai su garder dans les miennes tes mains,
Parce que j'ai trahi les lèvres tendres et salées,
J'irai dans l'Acropole somnolente attendre l'aube.
Comme je déteste l'antique et plaintive charpente !

Les Achéens dans la ténèbre apprêtent le cheval.
Solidement, les scies dentées s'enfoncent dans les murs
Et rien ne peut apaiser la sèche rumeur du sang.
Il n'y a pas de nom pour toi, ni de bruit, ni d'empreinte.

Comment pouvais-je croire que tu reviendrais, comment ?
Pourquoi t'avoir quittée avant que l'heure soit venue,
Avant que pâlisse la nuit et que chante le coq,
Que la hache se plante incandescente dans le bois ?

La poix sourd des remparts comme une larme trans-
      parente,
La ville a pressenti le bois de ses côtes ligneuses.
Le sang s'élance vers l'échelle et se rue à l'attaque.
Et trois fois les hommes ont rêvé l'image trompeuse.

Où est, douce Troie, la maison des filles et du roi ?
Hélas ! On va détruire de Priam le haut perchoir,
Et les flèches tombent comme une sèche pluie de bois,
Et d'autres flèches comme un coudrier sur la terre
　　vont croître.

De l'ultime étoile s'éteint sans douleur la piqûre,
Le matin, grise hirondelle, se cogne à la croisée,
Et le jour lent, bœuf de son lit de paille s'éveillant,
Secoue le long sommeil parmi les places hérissées.

Décembre 1920

Le siècle

Siècle mien, brute mienne, qui saura
Plonger les yeux dans tes prunelles
Et ressouder avec son sang
Les vertèbres des deux siècles ?
Torrentiel des choses terrestres
Le sang bâtisseur ruisselle,
Et sur le seuil des jours nouveaux
Le parasite en a tremblé.

Tant qu'elle vit, la créature
Doit porter jusqu'au bout l'échine.
L'épine dorsale invisible
Ondule au rythme de la vague.
Le siècle, terre-nouveau-né,

Baiser au front — c'est effacer la mémoire.
Je baise au front.

5 juin 1917

*

Je suis une page sous ta plume.
J'accepte tout. Je suis une page blanche.
Je garde tout ton bien précieux,
Je le cultive pour te le rendre au centuple.

Je suis le village, je suis la terre noire.
Tu m'es pluie et soleil.
Tu es Maître et Dieu et moi —
Tchernoziom et papier blanc !

10 juillet 1918

(*Traduit par Pierre Léon*,
extrait de *Le ciel brûle*, de
Marina Tsvétaïéva,
Poésie/Gallimard, 1999)

*

De pierre sont les uns, d'argile d'autres sont, —
Moi je scintille, toute argentine !
Trahir est mon affaire et Marina — mon nom,
Je suis fragile écume marine.

D'argile sont les uns, les autres sont de chair —
À eux : tombes et dalles tombales !
— Baptisée dans la coupe marine — et en l'air
Sans fin brisée, je vole et m'affale.

À travers tous les cœurs, à travers tout filet
Mon caprice s'infiltre, pénètre.
De moi — ces boucles vagabondes : vise-les ! —
On ne fera pas du sel terrestre.

Contre vos genoux de granit je suis broyée
Et chaque vague me — réanime !
Vive l'écume, gloire à l'écume joyeuse,
Vive la haute écume marine !

23 mai 1920

Tentative de jalousie

Comment ça va la vie avec une autre,
Plus simple, n'est-ce pas ? — Rames, claquez ! —
S'est-il vite, le profil de la côte,
Le souvenir, s'est-il vite masqué.

De moi, de moi, île désamarrée ?
(Voguant de par le ciel, non sur les flots !)
Âmes ! Jamais amantes ne serez !
Sœurs vous serez ! Sœurs : vous ! C'est votre lot !

Comment ça va la vie près d'une femme
Simple ? C'est comment *sans* divinités ?
Votre souveraine, prince profane,
Détrônâtes (ledit trône quitté),

Comment ça va la vie, les froissis d'ailes,
Les tracas ? Le lever, comment se passe ?
Pauvre créditaire de l'immortelle
Médiocrité, comment faites-vous face ?

« Tressauts et syncopes, stop ! Je suis quitte !
Un toit me louerai ! Suffit, le déluge ! »
Comment ça va avec n'importe qui,
Dites, comment, quand on est mon élu ?

Pour sûr plus comestible, domestique,
La table ? Qu'on s'en lasse, faute à qui ?
Comment ça va la vie près d'un pastiche
Pour vous qui trahîtes le Sinaï ?

Comment ça va près d'une d'ici-bas,
D'une si peu vôtre ? Son flanc vous plaît ?
À toute bride Zeus ne fouette pas
Votre front ? La honte vous laisse en paix ?

Comment ça va « vivre », comme va-t-elle
La force d'être ? Et de chanter, la force ?
Pauvret, la blessure de l'immortelle
Conscience, comment y faites-vous face ?

Comment ça va la vie près d'un produit
De pacotille ? Un peu abrupt, le prix ?
Les marbres de Carrare reconduits,
Comment ça va la vie près d'un débris

De plâtre. (Taillé dans la masse même,
— Dieu, sa tête : presque aussitôt détruite !)

Comment ça va avec la cent millième,
Dites, pour vous qui connûtes Lilith !

L'or de pacotille vous intéresse
Encore ? Las des grâces magiciennes,
Comment ça va auprès d'une terrestre,
C'est comment une femme *sans* sixième

Sens ?
　　　Bon, la tête entre deux mains : heureux ?
Non ? Des fonds sans profondeur étant l'hôte,
Comment ça va, l'ami ? Plus douloureux,
Moins douloureux que pour moi près d'un autre ?

19 novembre 1924

(*Traduit par Ève Malleret,*
extrait de *Le ciel brûle* de
Marina Tsvétaïéva,
Poésie/Gallimard, 1999)

À Maïakovski

Plus haut que les croix, les cheminées,
Baptisé de fumée et de feu,
Archange poids lourd au pas pesant,
Salut dans les siècles, Vladimir !

Il est le cocher et le pur-sang,
Il est la lubie, il est le droit.

Il soupire et crache dans ses paumes :
« À nous deux, la gloire charretière ! »

Chantre des miracles de trottoir,
Bonjour, orgueilleux salopard,
Qui préfère le poids du caillou
Aux séductions du diamant.

Bonjour, tonnerre de pavés !
Il baille, il te salue, et, voilà
Qu'il rame à nouveau du brancard, de
L'aile d'un archange-charretier.

18 septembre 1921

(*Traduit par Elsa Triolet*, extrait
de *Marina Tsvétaïéva*, Poètes
russes contemporains/
Gallimard, 1968)

Deux poèmes pour Ossip Mandelstam

1

Personne ne nous a rien ôté —
Elle m'est douce, notre séparation !
Je vous embrasse, sans compter
Les kilomètres qui nous espacent.

Je sais : notre art est différent.
Comme jamais ma voix rend un son doux.

7

Préparant une surprise
par la somme de ses angles,
la chose échappe à
l'ordonnance des mots.

La chose n'est pas là, debout. Pas plus
qu'elle ne bouge. Incohérence.
La chose est espace, hors duquel
la chose elle-même n'est pas.

On peut la fracasser, la brûler,
l'éventrer, la briser.
La jeter. La chose pour autant
ne criera pas : « Putain ! »

8

Arbre. Ombre. Terre
sous l'arbre pour les racines.
Monogrammes enlacés.
Argile. Rangée de pierres.

Racines. Leur entrelacs.
Pierre dont le propre poids
arrive à libérer de
tout ce système de nœuds.

Elle ne bouge pas. Impossible
de la déplacer, de l'emporter.
Ombre. Homme dans l'ombre,
comme un poisson dans la nasse.

9

Chose. Couleur brune
de la chose. Au contour effacé.
Crépuscule. Plus rien.
Rien. Nature morte.

La mort viendra et trouvera
le corps, eau dormante,
qui reflétera la visite de la mort
comme la venue d'une femme.

Absurdité, mensonge,
le crâne, le squelette et la faux.
« La mort viendra, et elle
aura tes yeux. »

10

La mère dit au Christ :
« Tu es mon fils ou bien mon
Dieu ? Tu es cloué à la croix.
Comment rentrer chez moi ?

Comment franchir le seuil,
sans avoir compris ni choisi :
tu es mon fils ou bien Dieu ?
Es-tu mort ? Es-tu vivant ? »

Et lui dit en réponse :
« Mort ou vivant,
femme, quelle différence ?
Fils ou Dieu, je suis tien. »

1971

(*Traduit par Véronique Schiltz,*
extrait de *Poèmes 1961-1987,*
op. cit.)

Pour le centenaire d'Anna Akhmatova

Et la page et le feu, et la meule et le grain,
et le cheveu tranché et le fil de la hache,
Dieu conservera tout ; et plus que tout les mots
de pardon et d'amour qui sont sa voix profonde.

Le craquement des os, le pouls brisé, le choc
de la pioche : c'est là leur scansion souterraine ;
car si la vie est une, ils résonnent plus haut
aux lèvres des mortels que dans l'ouate du ciel.

Grande âme, à toi de par-delà les mers, Salut,
Toi qui trouvas les mots, toi, ta mortelle forme

dormante au sol natal, qui grâce à toi reçut
en ce monde emmuré le don de la parole.

Juillet 1989

(*Traduit par Hélène Henry*,
extrait de *Vertumne et autres
poèmes* de Joseph Brodsky, Du
Monde entier/Gallimard, 1993)